OFFICIAL BLUE BOOK OF UNI

2003 HANDBOOK OF UNITED STATES COINS

With Premium List

By R. S. YEOMAN

★

SIXTIETH EDITION

Edited by Kenneth Bressett

Containing mint records and prices paid by dealers for all U.S. coins from 1616 to the present time, including Colonials, Regular Issues, Commemoratives, Territorials, Gold, Proof Sets, and Mint Sets. Information on collecting coins—how coins are produced—mints and mint marks—grading of coins—location of mint marks—preserving and cleaning coins—starting a collection—history of mints and interesting descriptions of all U.S. copper, nickel, silver and gold coins. Fully illustrated.

Pricing analysis by Philip Bressett

Whitman® Coin Products

175 Fifth Avenue,
New York, N.Y. 10010

www.stmartins.com

A St. Martin's Griffin Edition

ISBN: 1-58238-189-5

Printed in U.S.A.

Important Notice

THIS BOOK IS *NOT A RETAIL PRICE LIST*

Premium prices are the average amount dealers will pay for coins (according to condition) if required for their stock.

IF YOU HAVE COINS TO SELL

The publisher of this book is not in the rare coin business; however, the chances are that the dealer from whom you purchased this book is engaged in the buying and selling of rare coins—contact him first. In the event that you purchased this book from a source other than a numismatic establishment, consult your local telephone directory for the names of coin dealers (they will be found sometimes under the heading of "Stamp and Coin Dealers"). If you live in a city or town that does not have any coin dealers, it is suggested that you obtain a copy of one of the trade publications in order to obtain the names and addresses of many of the country's leading dealers.

The following numismatic magazines are obtainable by subscription. They are published monthly or as indicated below. Information or sample copies may be obtained by writing to the individual publisher.

COINage Magazine
2660 E. Main St.
Ventura, California 93003

Coins Magazine
700 E. State Street
Iola, Wisconsin 54990

Numismatic News (weekly)
700 E. State Street
Iola, Wisconsin 54990

Coin World (weekly)
P.O. Box 150
Sidney, Ohio 45365

The Numismatist
818 North Cascade Ave.
Colorado Springs, Colorado 80903
(Published monthly by American Numismatic Assn.)

Current average *retail* valuations of all U.S. coins are listed in Whitman's A GUIDE BOOK OF UNITED STATES COINS by R. S. Yeoman, St. Martin's Press, New York, NY ($15.95 Hardcover; $11.95 Coil Bound).

Brief guides to grading are placed before each major coin type in this book. For those readers who desire more detailed descriptions of all coin grades, we recommend OFFICIAL A.N.A. GRADING STANDARDS FOR UNITED STATES COINS, St. Martin's Press, New York, NY.

Foreword

Since 1941, annually revised editions of this *Handbook* have aided thousands of people who have coins to sell or are actively engaged in collecting United States coins. The popular coin-folder method of collecting by date has created ever-changing premium values, based on the supply and demand of each date and mint. Through its panel of contributors, the *Handbook* has, over the years, reported these changing values. It also serves as a source of general numismatic information to all levels of interest in the hobby.

The values shown are representative prices paid by dealers for various United States coins. These are averages of prices assembled from many widely separated sources. On some issues slight differences in price among dealers may result from proximity to the various mints or heavily populated centers. Other factors, such as local supply and demand or dealers' stock conditions, may also tend to cause deviations from the prices listed. While many coins bring no premium when circulated, they usually bring premium prices in Uncirculated and Proof condition.

The publisher of this book does not deal in coins; therefore, the values shown here are not offers to purchase (or sell) but are included only as general information. Descriptions of coins are based on the most accurate data available, but could contain beliefs that may change with further research or discoveries.

COMPILERS

Lee F. Hewitt, the former editor and publisher of the NUMISMATIC SCRAPBOOK MAGAZINE, was an early contributor, having supplied many of the historical references and explanations which appear throughout this book. Charles E. Green gave valuable counsel when the first edition of the HANDBOOK was undertaken. He supplied most of the original mint data and was a regular contributor to each revised edition until his death in 1955. Richard S. Yeoman, the originator of this book, died in 1988.

CONTRIBUTORS TO THE SIXTIETH EDITION

Jeremy Poreca — Project Coordinator

Philip E. Bressett, Thomas Hallenbeck and Robert Rhue — Special Consultants

Gary Adkins
Tony Adkins
Numismatic Services, Inc.
Edina, MN 55439

Michael Aron
Michael Aron Rare Coin Auctions
P.O. Box 4388
San Clemente, CA 92674-4388

Philip E. Benedetti

George H. Blenker
Dacota Coin
P.O. Box 362
Rice Lake, WI 54868

Mark Borckardt

Q. David Bowers

Donald Brigandi
Brigandi Coin Co.
60 West 44th Street
New York, NY 10036

H. Robert Campbell
1123 East 2100 South
Salt Lake City, UT 84106

Alan & Gary Cohen
Colonial Coin & Stamp
530 Euclid Ave., Suite #7
Cleveland, OH 44115

J. H. Cline
P.O. Box 68
Palm Harbor, FL 34682

Elizabeth W. Coggan
J.J. Teaparty
49 Bromfield Street
Boston, MA 02108

John W. Dannreuther
Box 1840
Cordova, TN 38088-1840

Tom DeLorey

Kurt E. Eckstein

Col. Steven Ellsworth

Bob Entlich

Harry J. Forman
518 Ryers Avenue
Cheltenham, PA 19012

Henry G. Garrett
P.O. Box 4334
North Hollywood, CA 91617-0334

William G. Gay
Delaware Valley Rare Coin Co., Inc.
2835 West Chester Pike
Broomall, PA 19008

Dennis Gillio
Gabrelow & Albarian Rare Coins
10113 Riverside Drive
Toluca Lake, CA 91602
gilliocoin@aol.com

Ira M. Goldberg
350 S. Beverly Drive Suite #350
Beverly Hills, CA 90212

Lawrence S. Goldberg
Ira & Larry Goldberg Coins & Collectibles
350 S. Beverly Drive Suite #350
Beverly Hills, CA 90212

Kenneth M. Goldman
P.O. Box 920404
Needham, MA 02492

J.R. Grellman, Jr.
Lake Mary, FL

James L. Halperin
Heritage Plaza, 2nd Floor
100 Highland Park Village
Dallas, TX 75205-2788

Gene L. Henry
1521 Third Avenue
Seattle, WA 98101

John W. Highfill
Oklahoma Coin Exchange, Inc.
P.O. Box 25
Broken Arrow, OK 74013-0025

Karl D. Hirtzinger

Ed Hipps
6835 West Lake Ave
Dallas, TX 75214

Jesse Iskowitz
N.I. Collectibles
P.O. Box 71417
Marietta, GA 30007

Robert H. Jacobs
www.jakesmp.net

Floyd O. Janney

A.M. Kagin

Donald H. Kagin

Bradley S. Karoleff
Coins +
2092 Mall Road
Florence, KY 41042

Jerry Kimmell
P.O. Box 45
Avon Lake, OH 44012

Mike Kliman
Numismatic Enterprises
P.O. Box 9365
South Laguna, CA 92652

Denis W. Loring

Virg Marshall III
116 West D
Wymore, NE 68466

Robert T. McIntire
27 Crestview Plaza
P.O. Box 546
Jacksonville, AR 72078-0546

Glenn E. Miller
40 Dolphin Ave.
Wintrop, MA 02152

Donald A. Mituzas
Colonial Coins
P.O. Box 867
Croton Falls, NY 10519

Michael C. Moline
Advance Coin
Encino, CA 91436

Sid Nusbaum
Arch City Supply Co.
St. Louis, MO

Robert M. Paul
P.O. Box 1417
Newtown, PA 18940

William P. Paul
American Heritage Minting
The Pavillion, Suite 510
Box 1008
Jenkintown, PA 19046

John C. Porter
Clayton Jewelers
2 N. Meramec Ave.
St. Louis, MO 63105

Joel D. Rettew
Coin & Jewelry Exchange
225 S. Tustin Ave.
Orange, CA 92866

Joel D. Rettew, Jr.

Maurice Rosen
Numismatic Counseling, Inc.
P.O. Box 38
Plainview, NY 11803

Leonard R. Saunders
P.O. Box 231
Kansasville, WI 53139
lrsaunders@att.net

J.S. Schreiber

Gerald R. Scherer, Jr.
c/o Silvertowne L.P.
P.O. Box 424
Winchester, IN 47394
www.silvertowne.com

Hugh J. Sconyers

Robert R. Shaw

James Simek

Richard Snow
www.indiancent.com

William J. Spencer
American Coin & Stamp Supply, Inc.
4625 Washington Ave.
Racine, WI 53405

Maurice A. Storck, Sr.
775 W. Rogers Rd. #214
Tucson, AZ 85705

David M. Sundman

Charles Surasky

Anthony J. Swiatek
P.O. Box 218
Manhasset, NY 11030

Fred Weinberg
1611 Ventura Blvd, Suite 1288
Encino, CA 91436-2152

Mark S.Yaffe

COLLECTING COINS

Numismatics or coin collecting is one of the world's oldest hobbies, dating back several centuries. Coin collecting in America did not develop to any extent until about 1840, as our pioneer forefathers were too busy carving a country out of wilderness to afford the luxury of a hobby. The discontinuance of the large-sized cent in 1857 caused many persons to attempt to accumulate a complete set of the pieces while they were still in circulation. One of the first groups of collectors to band together for the study of numismatics was the Numismatic and Antiquarian Society of Philadelphia, organized on January 1, 1858. Lack of an economical method to house a collection held the number of devotees of coin collecting to a few thousand until the Whitman Publishing Company and other manufacturers placed the low-priced coin boards and folders on the market some years ago. Since that time the number of Americans collecting coins has increased many-fold.

The Production of Coins

To collect coins intelligently it is necessary to have some knowledge of the manner in which our coins are produced. They are made in factories called "mints." The Mint of the United States was established at Philadelphia by a resolution of Congress dated April 2, 1792. The Act also provided for the coinage of gold eagles ($10), half-eagles and quarter-eagles, the silver dollar, half-dollar, quarter-dollar, dime (originally spelled "disme") and the half-disme or half-dime; the copper cent and half cent. According to the Treasury Department, the first coins struck were one-cent and half-cent pieces, in March of 1793 on a hand-operated press. Most numismatic authorities consider the half-disme of 1792 as the first United States coinage, quoting the words of George Washington as their authority. Washington, in his annual address, November 6, 1792, having said, "There has been a small beginning in the coining of the Half-Dimes, the want of small coins in circulation calling the first attention to them." In the new Philadelphia Mint are exhibited a number of implements, etc., from the original mint, and some coins discovered when the old building was wrecked. These coins included half-dismes, and the placard identifying them states that Washington furnished the silver and gave the coined pieces to his friends as souvenirs.

Prior to the adoption of the Constitution, the Continental Congress arranged for the issuance of copper coins under private contract. These are known as the "Fugio cents" from the design of the piece, which shows a sundial and the Latin word "fugio"—"I Fly" or, in connection with the sundial, "Time Flies." The ever appropriate motto, "Mind Your Business," is also on the coin.

In the manufacture of a given coin the first step is the cutting of the "die." Prior to the latter part of the nineteenth century dies for United States coins were "cut by hand." Briefly this method is as follows: The design having been determined, a drawing the exact size of the coin is made. A tracing is made from this drawing. A piece of steel is smoothed and coated with transfer wax, and the tracing impressed into the wax. The engraver then tools out the steel where the relief or raised effect is required. If the design is such that it can all be produced by cutting away steel, the die is hardened and ready for use. Some dies are not brought to a finished state, as some part of the design can perhaps be done better in relief. In that case, when all that can be accomplished to advantage in the die is completed, it is hardened, a soft-steel impression is taken from it, and the unfinished parts are then completed. This piece of steel is in turn hardened and, by a press, driven into another piece of soft-steel, thus making a die which, when hardened, is ready for the making of coins.

This hand method of cutting dies accounts for the many die varieties of early United States coins. Where the amount of coinage of a given year was large enough to wear out several dies, each new die placed in the coining press created another die variety of that year. The dies being cut by hand, no two were exactly alike in every detail, even though some of the major elements (head, wreath, etc.) were sunk into the die by individual master punches. Of the cents dated 1794, over sixty different die varieties have been discovered.

Hundreds of dies are now used by the mints of the United States each year, but they are all made from one master die, which is produced in the following manner:

After the design is settled upon, the plaster of paris or wax model is prepared several times the actual size of the coin. When this model is finished an electrotype (an exact duplicate in metal) is made and prepared for the reducing lathe. The reducing lathe is a machine, working on the principle of the pantograph, only in this case the one point traces or follows the form of the model while another and much smaller point in the form of a drill cuts away the steel and produces a reduced size die of the model. The die is finished and details are sharpened or worked over by an engraver with chisel and graver. The master die is used to make duplicates in soft-steel which are then hardened and ready for the coining press. To harden dies, they are placed in cast-iron boxes packed with carbon to exclude the air, and when heated to a bright red are cooled suddenly with water.

In the coinage operations the first step is to prepare the metal. Alloys that have been used are: silver coins, 90% silver and 10% copper; five-cent pieces, 75% copper and 25% nickel; one-cent pieces, 95% copper and 5% zinc. (The 1943 cent consists of steel coated with zinc; and the five-cent piece 1942-1945 contains 35% silver, 56% copper and 9% manganese.) Under the Coinage Act of 1965, the composition of dimes, quarters and half dollars was changed to eliminate or reduce the silver content of these coins. The copper-nickel "clad" dimes, quarters, halves and dollars are composed of an outer layer of copper-nickel (75% copper and 25% nickel) bonded to an inner core of pure copper. The silver clad half dollar and dollar have an outer layer of 80% silver bonded to an inner core of 21% silver, with a total content of 40% silver. Current cents are made from a core of 99.2% zinc, 0.8% copper, with a plating of pure copper.

Alloys are melted in crucibles and poured into molds to form ingots. The ingots are in the form of thin bars and vary in size according to the denomination of the coin. The width is sufficient to allow three or more coins to be cut from the strips.

The ingots are next put through rolling mills to reduce the thickness to required limits. The strips are then fed into cutting presses which cut circular blanks (planchets) of the approximate size of the finished coin. The blanks are run through annealing furnaces to soften them; next through tumbling barrels, rotating cyclinders containing cleaning solutions which clean and burnish the metal, and finally into centrifugal drying machines.

The blanks are next fed into a milling machine which produces the raised or upset rim. The blank is now ready for the coining press.

The blank is held firmly by a collar, as it is struck under heavy pressure varying from 40 tons for the one-cent pieces and dimes to 170 tons for silver dollars. Upper and lower dies impress the design on both sides of the coin. The pressure is sufficient to produce a raised surface level with that of the milled rim. The collar holding the blank for silver or clad coins is grooved. The pressure forces the metal into the grooves of the collar, producing the "reeding" on the finished coin.

How a Proof Coin Is Made

Selected dies are inspected for perfection and are highly polished and cleaned. They are again wiped clean or polished after every 15 to 25 impressions and are replaced frequently to avoid imperfections from worn dies. Coinage blanks are polished and cleaned to assure high quality in striking. They are then hand fed into the coinage press one at a time, each blank receiving two blows from the dies to bring up sharp, high relief details. The coinage operation is done at slow speed with extra pressure. Finished proofs are individually inspected and are handled by gloves or tongs. They also receive a final inspection by packers before being sonically sealed in special plastic cases.

Certain coins, including Lincoln cents, Buffalo nickels, Quarter Eagles, Half Eagles, Eagles, and Double Eagles, between the years 1908 and 1916, were made with a matte or sandblast surface. Matte proofs have a dull frosted surface which was either applied to the dies, or produced by special treatment after striking.

Mints and Mint Marks

In addition to the Philadelphia Mint, the U.S. Government has from time to time established branch mints in various parts of the country. At the present time a branch mint operates in Denver. Starting in 1968, proof sets and some of the regular coins are produced at the San Francisco Assay Office. The Denver Mint has operated since 1906. A mint was operated at New Orleans from 1838 to 1861 and again from 1879 to 1909. Mints were also in service at Carson City, Nevada, from 1870 to 1893; at Charlotte, North Carolina, from 1838 to 1861; at Dahlonega, Georgia, from 1838 to 1861; and at San Francisco since 1854.

Coins struck at Philadelphia before 1979 (except 1942 to 1945 five-cent pieces) do not carry a mint mark. The mint mark is found only on coins struck at the branch mints. It is a small letter, usually found on the reverse side. The Lincoln cent is one exception to the rule. All coins minted after 1967 have the mint mark on the obverse. The letters to signify the various mints are as follows:

"C" for Charlotte, North Carolina (on gold coins only).
"CC" for Carson City, Nevada.
"D" for Dahlonega, Georgia (gold coins only, 1838 to 1861).
"D" For Denver, Colorado (from 1906 to date).
"O" for New Orleans, Louisiana.
"P" for Philadelphia, Pennsylvania.
"S" for San Francisco, California.
"W" for West Point, New York.

The mint mark is of utmost importance to collectors due to the fact that the coinage at the branch mints has usually been much smaller than at Philadelphia and many of the early branch mint pieces are very scarce.

DISTINGUISHING MARKS

The illustrations and explanations in this section will help the collector to identify certain well-known varieties.

HALF CENTS OF 1795–1796 SHOWING LOCATION OF POLE TO CAP

The end of the staff or pole lies parallel with the line of the bust, which is pointed. The die-maker, probably through error, omitted the pole on some of the dies of 1795 and 1796.

Pole to Cap

No Pole to Cap

Stemless Wreath

Stems to Wreath

STEMLESS WREATH VARIETY OF HALF CENTS AND LARGE CENTS

Observe the reverse side for this variety. Illustrations at left show both stemless and stems to wreath types for each comparison—stemless wreath found on 1804, 1805, 1806 Half cents. 1797, 1802, 1803 Large cents.

1804 HALF CENT PROTRUDING TONGUE OR SPIKED CHIN VARIETY

DISTINGUISHING MARKS

Details showing differences in 1804 plain 4 and crosslet 4. Note serif on horizontal bar of figure 4 as shown at right.

Plain 4

Crosslet 4

THE 1856 FLYING EAGLE CENT

Collectors are advised to inspect any 1856 Flying Eagle cent carefully.

A few tests will aid in establishing genuineness of this cent, as follows:

THE DATE

The 6 in the date should be as illustrated. If the lower half is thick, it is probably an altered 1858. A magnifying glass will often reveal poor workmanship.

The figure 5 slants slightly to the right on a genuine 1856. The vertical bar points to the center of the ball just beneath. On the 1858, this bar points *outside* the ball. (Compare the two illustrations.)

THE LEGEND

The center of the O in OF is crude and almost squared on the genuine 1856, but on the large letter 1858 it is rounded.

The letters A and M in America are joined in both the 1856 and large letter 1858, but they join at a slight angle on the 1856, while the bottom of the letters form a smooth curve on the 1858 large letter cent.

Large Letters

1858 FLYING EAGLE CENT

Letters A and M in the word AMERICA are joined on the LARGE LETTER variety. They are separated on the SMALL LETTER variety.

Small Letters

1864 BRONZE INDIAN HEAD CENT WITH "L" ON RIBBON

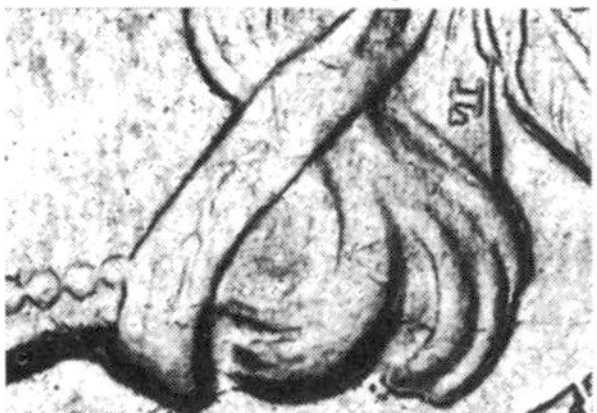

A small "L," the initial of the designer Longacre, was added to the Indian design late in 1864 and was continued through 1909. For coins in less than fine condition, this small letter will often be worn away. The point of the bust is rounded on the 1864 variety without "L"; pointed on the variety with "L." The initial must be visible, however, for the 1864 variety to bring the higher premium. If the coin is turned slightly so that the Indian faces the observer, the highlighted details will usually appear to better advantage.

DISTINGUISHING MARKS

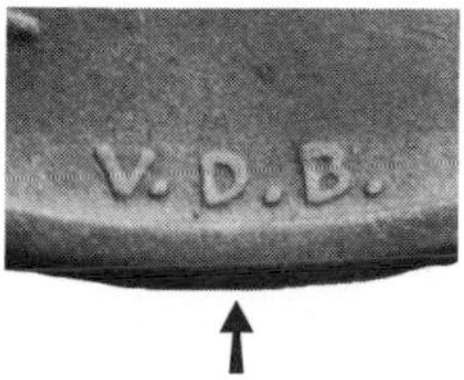

During 1909 initials appeared on the reverse. Starting in 1918 they appear below the shoulder.

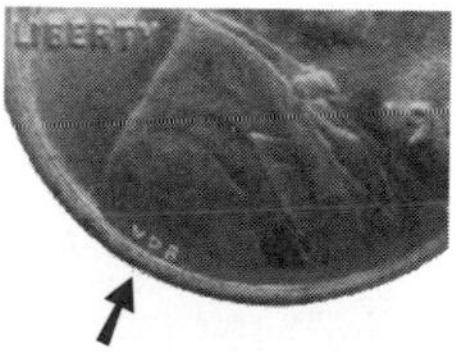

1918-S Quarter
8 Over 7
A variety of this kind is rarely found in coinage of the twentieth century.

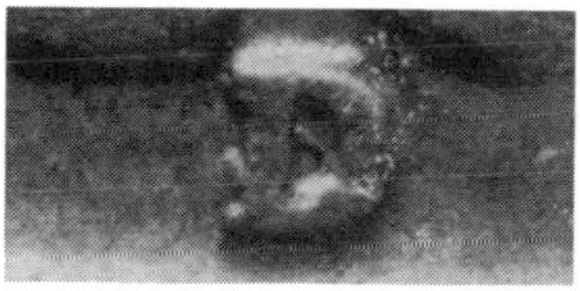

1938D over S Nickel Variety

1942 Dime with 2 over 1

1955 Cent Error
"Doubled Die" Obverse

Large Date Cent
1960

Small Date Cent
1960

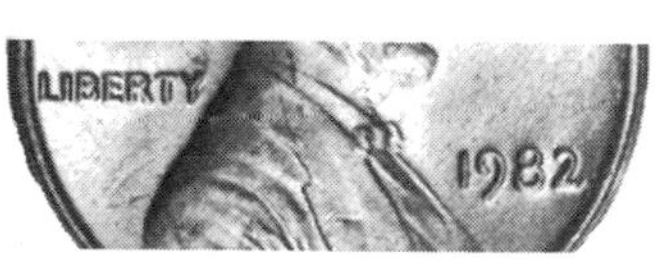

Large Date Cent
1982

Small Date Cent
1982

CONDITION OF COINS

Essential elements of the A.N.A. grading system

PROOF — A specially made coin distinguished by sharpness of detail and usually with a brilliant mirrorlike surface. Proof refers to the method of manufacture and is not a condition, but normally the term implies perfect mint state unless otherwise noted and graded as below. See page 40 for details.

MINT STATE — The terms Mint State (MS) and Uncirculated (Unc.) are interchangeably used to describe coins showing no trace of wear. Such coins may vary to some degree because of blemishes, toning or slight imperfections as described in the following subdivisions.

UNCIRCULATED (MS-70) — Perfect new condition, showing no trace of wear. The finest quality possible, with no evidence of scratches, handling or contact with other coins. Very few regular issue coins are ever found in this condition.

UNCIRCULATED (MS-65) — An above average Uncirculated coin that may be brilliant or lightly toned and has very few contact marks on the surface or rim. MS-67 or MS-63 indicates a slightly higher or lower grade of preservation.

UNCIRCULATED (MS-60) — Has no trace of wear but may show a number of contact marks, and surface may be spotted or lack some luster.

CHOICE ABOUT UNCIRCULATED (AU-55) — Barest evidence of light wear on only the highest points of the design. Most of the mint luster remains.

ABOUT UNCIRCULATED (AU-50) — Has traces of light wear on many of the high points. At least half of the mint luster is still present.

CHOICE EXTREMELY FINE (EF-45) — Light overall wear shows on highest points. All design details are very sharp. Some of the mint luster is evident.

EXTREMELY FINE (EF-40) — Design is lightly worn throughout, but all features are sharp and well-defined. Traces of luster may show.

CHOICE VERY FINE (VF-30) — Light even wear on the surface and highest parts of the design. All lettering and major features are sharp.

VERY FINE (VF-20) — Shows moderate wear on high points of design. All major details are clear.

FINE (F-12) — Moderate to considerable even wear. Entire design is bold with overall pleasing appearance.

VERY GOOD (VG-8) — Well worn with main features clear and bold although rather flat.

GOOD (G-4) — Heavily worn with design visible but faint in areas. Many details are flat.

ABOUT GOOD (AG-3) — Very heavily worn with portions of lettering, date and legends worn smooth. The date may be barely readable.

IMPORTANT: Damaged coins, such as those which are bent, corroded, scratched, holed, nicked, stained or mutilated, are worth less than those without defects. *Flawless uncirculated coins are generally worth more than values quoted in this book.* Slightly worn coins ("sliders") which have been cleaned and conditioned ("whizzed") to simulate uncirculated luster are worth considerably less than perfect pieces.

Unlike damage inflicted after striking, manufacturing defects do not always lessen values. Examples are: Colonial coins with planchet flaws and weakly struck designs; early silver and gold with weight adjustment "file marks" (parallel cuts made prior to striking); and pieces with "lint marks" (dust or other foreign matter which may mar the surface during striking).

Brief guides to grading are placed before each major coin type in this book. For those readers who desire more detailed descriptions of all coin grades, we recommend OFFICIAL A.N.A. GRADING STANDARDS FOR UNITED STATES COINS, by the American Numismatic Association.

Preserving and Cleaning Coins

Most numismatists will tell you to "never clean a coin" and it is good advice! Cleaning coins will almost always reduce their value. Collectors prefer coins in their original condition.

Some effort should be made to protect uncirculated and proof coins so they won't need cleaning. Tarnish on a coin is purely a chemical process caused by oxygen in the air acting on the metal or by chemicals with which the coin comes in contact. One of the commonest chemicals causing tarnish is sulphur; most paper, with the exception of specially manufactured "sulphur-free" kinds, contains sulphur due to the sulphuric acid that is used in paper manufacture. Therefore do not wrap coins in ordinary paper; also keep uncirculated and proof coins away from rubber bands (a rubber band placed on a silver coin for a few days will produce a black stripe on the coin where the band touched). The utmost in protection is obtained by storing the coin in an airtight box, away from moisture and humidity, and by using holders made of inert materials.

Many coins become marred by careless handling. Always hold the coin by the edge. The accompanying illustration shows the right and wrong way to handle numismatic specimens. It is a breach of numismatic etiquette to handle another collector's coin except by the edge, even if it is not an uncirculated or proof piece.

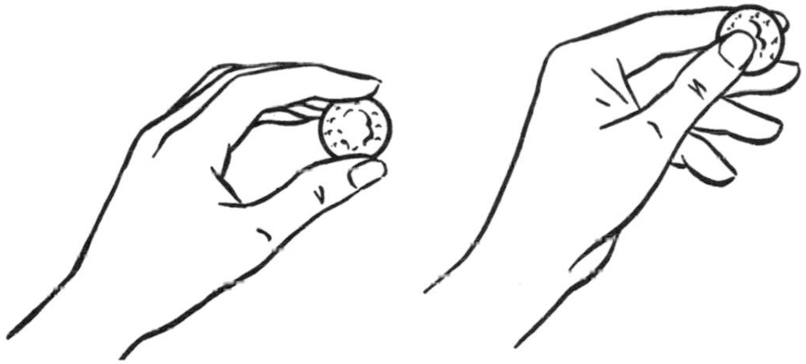

RIGHT WRONG

Starting a Collection

One may start a collection of United States coins with very little expense by systematically assembling the various dates and mint marks of all the types and denominations that are now in general circulation. Whitman's coin folders make this possible.

With the exception of the price paid for the coin folder, collecting coins received in everyday business transactions entails no expense whatever; a Jefferson nickel taken out of circulation, for example, can always be spent for 5 cents if the occasion arises. Filling an album or two out of circulation is probably the best method of determining whether coin collecting appeals to you. Not everyone can be a successful coin collector. It requires patience, intelligence of a high order, and a certain desire to know the meaning behind a lot of things that at first glance and to the ordinary person appear meaningless. You may not be cut out to be a collector but you'll never know until you look further into the subject, and if by the time an album or two of coins are collected you have no burning desire to acquire many more different coins, you will probably never be a collector. However, the chances are that you will be, because if you have read this far in this book it shows that you are interested in the subject.

Perfection is the goal of every endeavor and coin collecting is no exception. After an album has been filled with circulated specimens, the next step will be to replace them with coins in uncirculated condition, or perhaps to start collecting an obsolete series; in either case, it will be necessary to purchase some coins from dealers or other collectors. The most logical way to keep abreast with the market, or obtain the addresses of the country's leading dealers, is to subscribe to one or more of the trade publications (see page 2 for list of the coin publications). These magazines carry advertisements of various dealers listing coins for sale. Moreover, through this source the beginner may obtain price lists and catalogs from the dealers.

There are several good reference books available at reasonable prices which will be helpful to the collector who wishes to know more about U. S. coins and paper money. R. S. Yeoman's A GUIDE BOOK OF UNITED STATES COINS (Red Book) is an expanded version of THE HANDBOOK. It lists retail values of all regular U. S. coins and also lists all coins of the U.S. Colonial period and private and territorial gold coins.

Most coin, book and hobby dealers can supply the following titles:

A Guide Book of U.S. Coins — Yeoman
The Whitman Guide to Coin Collecting — Bressett
Official Grading Standards for U.S. Coins — A.N.A.
Coins, Questions and Answers — Mishler
Guide Book of United States Currency — Bressett
The Official Whitman Statehood Quarters Collector's Handbook — Bressett

Join a Coin Club

A beginner should join a "coin club" if he is fortunate enough to live in a city which has one. The association with more experienced collectors will be of great benefit. Practically all the larger cities have one or more clubs and they are being rapidly organized in the smaller towns. The publications mentioned on page 2 carry information about coin clubs and special events such as coin shows and conventions.

UNITED STATES PAPER MONEY

Paper money issued by the United States government is collected widely in this country. The first issue of "greenbacks" was made in 1861; paper money was not issued by our government for circulation prior to that date. Collectors of U.S. notes prefer them in crisp, new condition; but the old style large-sized notes even in worn condition are usually worth more than face value.

Before the issuance of the first U.S. government paper money, many banks throughout the country issued their own currency. These issues are commonly referred to as "broken bank notes" although that is somewhat of a misnomer as many of the banks did not "go broke" (a few are still in existence) and redeemed their paper money issues. There are thousands of varieties of these notes in existence, most of which are very common and worth from $2.50 to $10.00 each. Before and during the American Revolution the various individual states and the Continental Congress issued paper money. The common varieties of these Colonial notes are worth from $5.00 to $25.00; a few are quite rare.

"Broken Bank" note of 1863

I. THE BRITISH COLONIES IN AMERICA

SOMMER ISLANDS (Bermuda)

This coinage, the first struck for the English colonies in America, was issued about 1616. The coins were known as "Hogge Money" or "Hoggies."

The pieces were made of copper lightly silvered, in four denominations: shilling, sixpence, threepence and twopence, indicated by Roman numerals. The hog is the main device and appears on the obverse side of each. SOMMER ISLANDS is inscribed within beaded circles. The reverse shows a full-rigged galleon with the flag of St. George on each of four masts.

Shilling

	Good	V. Good	Fine	V. Fine
Twopence	$1,500	$2,500	$3,500	$6,000
Threepence (V. Rare)	—	—	—	—
Sixpence	1,200	2,000	3,000	6,000
Shilling	1,800	2,700	4,000	7,500

MASSACHUSETTS

"NEW ENGLAND" COINAGE (1652)

In 1652 the General Court of Massachusetts ordered the first metallic currency to be struck in the English Americas, the New England silver threepence, sixpence, and shilling. These coins were made from silver bullion procured principally from the West Indies. Joseph Jenks made the punches for the first coins at his Iron Works in Saugus, Massachusetts, close to Boston where the mint was located. John Hull was appointed mintmaster; his assistant was Robert Sanderson.

Note: Early American coins are rare in conditions better than listed and valued much higher.

NE Shilling (1652)

	V. Good	Fine	V. Fine
NE Threepence *(unique)*	—	—	—
NE Sixpence *(8 known)*	—	—	$40,000
NE Shilling	$11,000	$20,000	40,000

MASSACHUSETTS

WILLOW TREE COINAGE (1653-1660)

The simplicity of the design on the N.E. coins invited counterfeiting and clipping of the edges. Therefore, they were soon replaced by the Willow, Oak and Pine Tree series. The Willow Tree coins were struck from 1653 to 1660, the Oak Trees 1660 to 1667, and the Pine Trees 1667 to 1682. All of them (with the exception of the Oak Tree twopence) bore the date 1652.

Many varieties of all of these coins exist. Values shown are for the most common types.

Sixpence

	Fair	*Good*	*V. Good*	*Fine*
Willow Tree Threepence 1652 (*3 known*)	—	—	—	—
Willow Tree Sixpence 1652	—	$5,000	$8,000	$16,000
Willow Tree Shilling 1652	$2,200	5,000	7,500	15,000

OAK TREE COINAGE (1660-1667)

Twopence

Threepence

	Good	*V. Good*	*Fine*	*V. Fine*
Oak Tree Twopence 1662	$200.00	$350.00	$750.00	$1,500
Oak Tree Threepence 1652	235.00	475.00	900.00	2,100
Oak Tree Sixpence 1652	225.00	435.00	875.00	2,400
Oak Tree Shilling 1652	250.00	475.00	950.00	2,400

PINE TREE COINAGE (1667-1682)

The first pine tree coins were minted on the same size planchets as the Oak Tree pieces. Subsequent issues of the shilling were narrower and thicker to conform to the size of English coins.

Shilling, Large Planchet (1667-1674)

MASSACHUSETTS
PINE TREE COINAGE (1667-1682)

Shilling, Small Planchet (1675-1682)

	Good	*V. Good*	*Fine*	*V. Fine*
Pine Tree Threepence 1652	$175.00	$325.00	$550.00	$1,300
Pine Tree Sixpence 1652	200.00	350.00	600.00	1,400
Pine Tree Shilling, large planchet 1652	300.00	500.00	900.00	2,200
Pine Tree Shilling, small planchet 1652	225.00	400.00	750.00	1,750

MARYLAND

In 1659 Cecil Calvert, the "Lord Proprietor of Maryland," had coinage struck in England for use in Maryland.

There were four denominations: shillings, sixpence, and fourpence (groat) in silver, and a copper penny (denarium). The silver coins have the bust of Lord Baltimore on the obverse, and the Baltimore family arms with the denomination in Roman numerals on the reverse.

Lord Baltimore Shilling

Fourpence (groat)

	Good	*V. Good*	*Fine*	*V. Fine*
Penny (Copper) (Ex. Rare)	—	—	—	—
Fourpence	$500.00	$1,000	$2,500	$5,000
Sixpence	475.00	850.00	1,900	3,300
Shilling	700.00	1,275	2,600	4,800

NEW JERSEY
ST. PATRICK OR MARK NEWBY COINAGE

Mark Newby, who came to America from Dublin, Ireland, in November 1681, brought copper pieces believed by numismatists to have been struck in England c. 1670-1675. These are called St. Patrick coppers.

The coin received wide circulation in the New Jersey Province, having been authorized to pass as legal tender by the General Assembly in May 1682.

The smaller piece, known as a farthing, was never specifically authorized for circulation in the Colonies.

NEW JERSEY

St. Patrick Farthing

	V. Good	Fine	V. Fine
St. Patrick "Farthing"	$60.00	$175.00	$500.00
St. Patrick "Halfpenny"	125.00	350.00	800.00

II. COINAGE AUTHORIZED BY ROYAL PATENT

AMERICAN PLANTATIONS TOKEN

These tokens struck in nearly pure tin were the first authorized coinage for the British colonies in America. They were made under a franchise granted in 1688 to Richard Holt. Restrikes were made c. 1828 from original dies.

	Fine	E. Fine	Unc.
(1688) James II Plantation Token farthing,			
1/24 PART REAL — Tin Original	$175.00	$450.00	$1,250
1/24 PART REAL — Tin Restrike	100.00	250.00	600.00

COINAGE OF WILLIAM WOOD

ROSA AMERICANA COINS

William Wood, an Englishman, obtained a patent from George I to make tokens for Ireland and the American Colonies.

The Rosa Americana pieces were issued in three denominations: halfpenny, penny and twopence, and were intended for use in America.

Penny

ROSA AMERICANA

	V. Good	Fine	V. Fine	E. Fine
Twopence (no date)	$50.00	$100.00	$215.00	$450.00
1722 Halfpenny DEI GRATIS REX UTILE DULCI	30.00	80.00	150.00	300.00
1722 Penny	30.00	80.00	150.00	300.00
1722 Twopence	50.00	100.00	180.00	400.00

Halfpenny

1723 Halfpenny	25.00	70.00	125.00	300.00

Twopence

1723 Penny	30.00	70.00	125.00	245.00
1723 Twopence (illustrated)	45.00	90.00	180.00	375.00

WOOD'S HIBERNIA COINAGE

The type intended for Ireland had a seated figure with a harp on the reverse side and the word HIBERNIA. Denominations struck were halfpenny and farthing with dates 1722, 1723 and 1724. Hibernia coins were unpopular in Ireland, so many of them were sent to the American colonies.

1722 Hibernia Halfpenny **First Type** **Second Type**

	V. Good	Fine	V. Fine	E. Fine
1722 Farthing (2nd type)		$100.00	$175.00	$375.00
1722 Halfpenny (1st or 2nd type)	$18.00	25.00	50.00	145.00

WOOD'S HIBERNIA COINAGE

1723 Hibernia Farthing

1724 Hibernia Halfpenny

	V. Good	*Fine*	*V. Fine*	*E. Fine*
1723 Farthing	$15.00	$25.00	$50.00	$110.00
1723 Halfpenny	15.00	30.00	40.00	100.00
1724 Farthing	22.00	55.00	125.00	250.00
1724 Halfpenny	22.00	45.00	120.00	200.00

VIRGINIA HALFPENNY

In 1773 coinage of a copper halfpenny was authorized for Virginia by the English Crown. The style is similar to the regular English coinage. These pieces were never popular, but did circulate by necessity.

	V. Good	*Fine*	*V. Fine*	*E. Fine*	*Unc.*
1773 Halfpenny	$25.00	$35.00	$80.00	$140.00	$375.00

III. EARLY AMERICAN TOKENS

Struck in America or England for use by American Merchants

LONDON ELEPHANT TOKENS

Struck c. 1672-1684 during the reign of Charles II, the London Token, an early historian states, was produced during the great plague raging in London. The legend on this piece relates directly to that crisis. It has also been stated that the London

Token was to have been current in Tangier, Africa, but was never used in that locality. No date appears on this token.

It is unlikely that many ever circulated in America. They are associated with the 1694 pieces through use of a common obverse die.

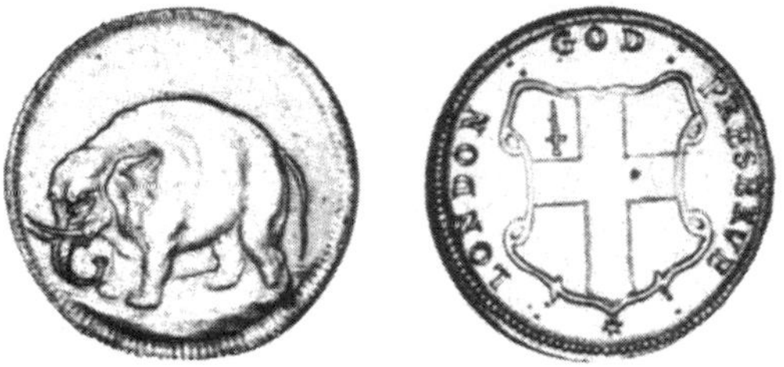

	V. Good	Fine	V. Fine	E. Fine
(1694) Halfpenny GOD PRESERVE LONDON (Thick or thin planchet)	$100.00	$175.00	$325.00	$700.00

CAROLINA AND NEW ENGLAND ELEPHANT TOKENS

Although no law is known authorizing coinage for Carolina, very interesting pieces known as Elephant Tokens were made with the date 1694. These copper tokens were of halfpenny denomination. The reverse reads GOD PRESERVE CAROLINA AND THE LORDS PROPRIETERS. 1694.

The Carolina pieces were probably struck in England and perhaps intended only as tokens, or possibly as advertising to heighten interest in the Carolina Plantation.

Like the Carolina Tokens, the New England Elephant Tokens were believed to have been struck in England as a promotional piece to increase interest in the American Colonies.

	V. Good	Fine
1694 CAROLINA	$1,500	$2,800

NEW ENGLAND ELEPHANT TOKEN

	V. Good	Fine
1694 NEW ENGLAND	11,000	

THE NEW YORKE TOKEN

Little is known about the origin of this token. The design of displayed eagle on a regulated staff with oak leaf finials is identical to the crest found on the arms of William Lovelace, governor of New York 1663-1673. It seems likely that this piece is a token farthing struck by Lovelace for use in New York.

UNDATED

	V. Good	*Fine*
Brass	$1,750	$3,500

GLOUCESTER TOKEN

This token appears to have been a private coinage by a merchant of Gloucester (county), Virginia. The only specimens known are struck in brass. The exact origin and use of these pieces are unknown.

1714 Shilling Brass	15,000

HIGLEY OR GRANBY COPPERS

The Higley coppers were never officially authorized. All the tokens were made of pure copper. There were seven obverse and four reverse dies. The first issue, in 1737, bore the legend THE VALUE OF THREEPENCE. After a time the quantity exceeded the local demand, and a protest arose against the value of the piece. The inscription was changed to VALUE ME AS YOU PLEASE.

	Good	*V. Good*
1737 THE • VALUE • OF • THREE • PENCE. — 3 Hammers — CONNECTICVT	$3,250	$4,750
1737 THE • VALUE • OF • THREE • PENCE. — 3 Hammers — I • AM • GOOD • COPPER	3,250	5,000
1737 VALUE • ME • AS • YOU • PLEASE — 3 Hammers — I • AM • GOOD • COPPER	3,250	5,000
(1737) VALUE • ME • AS • YOU • PLEASE — Broad Axe — J • CUT • MY • WAY• THROUGH	3,250	5,000
1739 VALUE • ME • AS • YOU • PLEASE — Broad Axe — J • CUT • MY • WAY • THROUGH	4,000	6,000

HIBERNIA-VOCE POPULI

These coins, struck in the year 1760, were made in Dublin. Like other Irish tokens, some of these pieces found their way to Colonial America.

Farthing 1760

Halfpenny 1760

	Good	*Fine*	*V. Fine*	*E. Fine*
1760 Farthing	$90.00	$200.00	$400.00	$900.00
1760 Halfpenny	35.00	75.00	135.00	225.00

PITT TOKENS

William Pitt is the subject of these pieces, probably intended as commemorative medalets. The halfpenny served as currency during a shortage of regular coinage.

	V. Fine
1766 Farthing	$4,000

1766 Halfpenny (illustrated)

V. Good	*Fine*	*E. Fine*
$130.00	$250.00	$800.00

RHODE ISLAND SHIP MEDAL

Although this medal has a Dutch inscription, the spelling and design indicate an English or Anglo-American origin. It is believed that this token was struck in England c. 1779-1780 as propaganda to pursuade the Dutch to sign the Treaty of Armed Neutrality. Specimens are known in brass, copper, tin and pewter. Modern copies exist.

1778-1779 Rhode Island Ship Medal

V. Fine	*E. Fine*
$350.00	$650.00

J. CHALMERS — Annapolis, Maryland

John Chalmers, a silversmith, struck a series of silver tokens at Annapolis in 1783. The shortage of change and the refusal of the people to use underweight coins prompted the issuance of these pieces.

	V. Good	*Fine*	*V. Fine*
1783 Threepence	$400.00	$800.00	$1,600
1783 Sixpence	700.00	1,300	2,500
1783 Shilling (Rev. illustrated)	400.00	750.00	1,600

IV. THE FRENCH COLONIES

None of the coins of the French regime is strictly American. They were all general issues for the French colonies of the New World. The copper of 1717 to 1722 was authorized by edicts of 1716 and 1721 for use in New France, Louisiana, and the French West Indies.

COPPER SOU OR NINE DENIERS

	V. Good	*Fine*
1721-B (Rouen)	$35.00	$75.00
1721-H (La Rochelle)	30.00	60.00
1722-H	20.00	40.00

FRENCH COLONIES IN GENERAL

Coined for use in the French colonies and only unofficially circulated in Louisiana along with other foreign coins and tokens. Most were counterstamped RF (République Française) for use in the West Indies.

	V. Good	*V. Fine*	*E. Fine*
1767 French Colonies, Sou	$22.00	$80.00	$200.00
1767 French Colonies, Sou. Counterstamped RF	20.00	55.00	125.00

V. SPECULATIVE ISSUES, TOKENS AND PATTERNS

THE CONTINENTAL CURRENCY

The Continental Currency was probably a pattern issue only and never reached general circulation. It was the first silver dollar size coin ever proposed for the United States. The coins were probably struck in Philadelphia. Many modern copies and replicas exist.

	Good	Fine	E. Fine	Unc.
1776 CURENCY — Pewter	$850.00	$1,900	$4,500	$11,000
1776 CURENCY — Silver		40,000		
1776 CURRENCY — Pewter	900.00	2,200	4,750	12,000
1776 CURRENCY — Pewter, EG FECIT above date.	875.00	2,100	4,500	11,000

NOVA CONSTELLATIO COPPERS

The Nova Constellatio pieces were struck supposedly by order of Gouverneur Morris. Evidence indicates that they were all struck in Birmingham and imported for American circulation as a private business venture.

1783
"CONSTELLATIO"
Pointed Rays

V. Good	$30.00
Fine	85.00
V. Fine	150.00
E. Fine	300.00

1783
"CONSTELATIO"
Blunt Rays

V. Good	$35.00
Fine	90.00
V. Fine	190.00
E. Fine	350.00

NOVA CONSTELLATIO COPPERS

1785
"CONSTELATIO"
Blunt Rays

V. Good	$40.00
Fine	100.00
V. Fine	225.00
E. Fine	400.00

1785
"CONSTELLATIO"
Pointed Rays

V. Good	$35.00
Fine	90.00
V. Fine	160.00
E. Fine	375.00

IMMUNE COLUMBIA PIECES

These are considered experimental or pattern pieces. No laws describing them are known.

1785 Copper, Star reverse... $6,000

1785
George III Obverse

Good	$1,100
Fine	2,000

1785
Vermon Auctori Obverse

Good	$1,200
Fine	2,200

1787
IMMUNIS COLUMBIA
Eagle Reverse

V. Good	$175.00
Fine	400.00
V. Fine	1,000
E. Fine	2,000

CONFEDERATIO COPPERS

The Confederatio Coppers are experimental or pattern pieces. This will explain why the die with the CONFEDERATIO legend was combined with other designs such as a bust of George Washington, Libertas et Justitia of 1785, Immunis Columbia of 1786, the New York "Excelsiors," Inimica Tyrannis Americana and others. There were in all thirteen dies struck in fourteen combinations.

There are two types of the Confederatio reverse. In one instance the stars are contained in a small circle; in the other larger stars are in a larger circle.

Typical Obverse

Small Circle Reverse

Large Circle Reverse

	V.Fine
1785 Stars in small circle — various obverses	$6,500
1785 Stars in large circle — various obverses	6,000

SPECULATIVE PATTERNS

1786 IMMUNIS COLUMBIA

Eagle Reverse

Shield Reverse

1786 IMMUNIS COLUMBIA, eagle reverse	$13,000
1786 IMMUNIS COLUMBIA, shield reverse	9,000
1786 (No date) Washington obverse	22,000
1786 Eagle obverse	15,000
1786 Washington obverse, eagle reverse (Unique)	—

VI. COINAGE OF THE STATES

NEW HAMPSHIRE

New Hampshire was the first of the states to consider the subject of coinage following the Declaration of Independence.

NEW HAMPSHIRE

William Moulton was empowered to make a limited quantity of coins of pure copper authorized by the State House of Representatives in 1776.

	V. Good
1776 New Hampshire copper	$7,000

MASSACHUSETTS

The coinage of Massachusetts copper cents and half cents in 1787 and 1788 was under the direction of Joshua Witherle. These were the first coins bearing the denomination "Cent" as established by Congress. Many varieties exist, the most valuable being that with arrows in the eagle's right talon.

1787 Half Cent	
Good	$30.00
Fine	60.00
V. Fine	200.00
E. Fine	425.00

	Good	*Fine*	*V. Fine*	*E. Fine*
1787 Cent, arrows in left talon (illustrated)	$27.50	$60.00	$200.00	$425.00
1787 Cent, arrows in right talon	—	4,000	—	—

1788 Half Cent	
Good	$30.00
Fine	60.00
Very Fine	200.00
E. Fine	425.00

MASSACHUSETTS

1788 Cent

Good	$30.00
Fine	60.00
V. Fine	200.00
E. Fine	425.00

CONNECTICUT

Authority for establishing a mint near New Haven was granted by the State to Samuel Bishop, Joseph Hopkins, James Hillhouse and John Goodrich in 1785.

1785 Copper
Bust Facing Right

Good	$20.00
V. Good	30.00
Fine	65.00
V. Fine	175.00

1785 Copper
Bust Facing Left

Good	$65.00
V. Good	120.00
Fine	215.00
V. Fine	350.00

	Good	*V. Good*	*Fine*	*V. Fine*
1786 Bust facing right	$25.00	$35.00	$65.00	$150.00
1787 Mailed bust facing right	35.00	55.00	125.00	350.00

CONNECTICUT

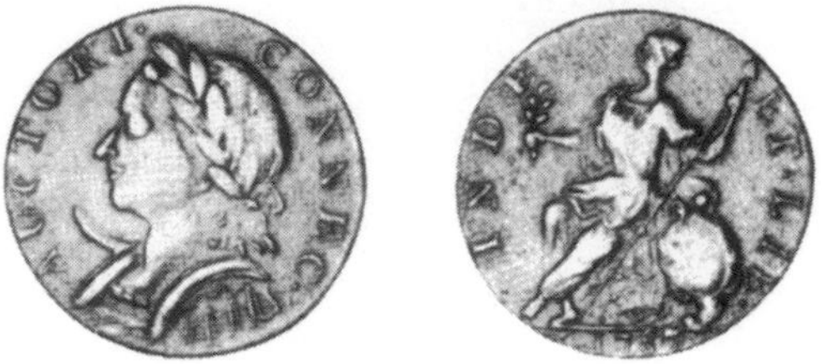

	Good	V. Good	Fine	V. Fine
1786 Mailed bust facing left	$18.00	$25.00	$50.00	$125.00
1787 Mailed bust facing left	15.00	22.00	40.00	120.00

1787 Draped bust facing left	17.00	25.00	40.00	110.00

1788 Mailed bust facing right	16.00	27.00	65.00	150.00

1788 Mailed bust facing left	15.00	24.00	57.50	120.00

CONNECTICUT

	Good	V. Good	Fine	V. Fine
1788 Draped bust facing left	$15.00	$24.00	$75.00	$150.00

NEW YORK

THE BRASHER DOUBLOON

Perhaps the most famous pieces coined before the establishment of the U.S. Mint at Philadelphia were those produced by a well-known goldsmith and jeweler, Ephraim Brasher.

Brasher produced a gold piece weighing about 408 grains, approximately equal in value to a Spanish doubloon (about $15.00).

The punch-mark EB appears in either of two positions as illustrated. This mark is found on some foreign gold coins as well, and probably was so used by Brasher as evidence of his testing of their value.

1787 Doubloon, punch on breast. Gold (Unique)	—
1787 Doubloon, punch on wing. Gold	—

COPPER COINAGE

No coinage was authorized for New York following the Revolutionary War although several propositions were considered. The only coinage laws passed were those regulating coins already in use.

1786
NON VI VIRTUTE VICI

Good	$1,500
Fine	3,000
V. Fine	6,000

NEW YORK

	Good	*Fine*	*V. Fine*
1787 EXCELSIOR copper, eagle on globe facing right	$500.00	$1,800	$3,500
1787 EXCELSIOR copper, eagle on globe facing left	450.00	1,700	3,000

1787 George Clinton

Good	$2,000
Fine	5,000
V. Fine	10,500

1787
Indian and N.Y. Arms

Good	$1,750
Fine	3,750
V. Fine	7,000

1787
Indian and Eagle
on Globe

Good	$2,000
Fine	5,500
V. Fine	10,000

NEW YORK
THE NOVA EBORACS

1787
NOVA EBORAC
Reverse Seated
Figure Facing Right

Fair	$15.00
Good	35.00
Fine	130.00
V. Fine	350.00

1787
NOVA EBORAC
Reverse Seated
Figure Facing Left

Fair	$14.00
Good	30.00
Fine	100.00
V. Fine	325.00

NEW JERSEY

On June 1, 1786, the New Jersey Colonial legislature granted to Thomas Goadsby, Albion Cox and Walter Mould authority to coin some three million coppers, no later than June 1788, on condition that they delivered to the Treasurer of the State, "one-tenth part of the full sum they shall strike and coin," in quarterly installments. These coppers were to pass current at 15 to the shilling.

Narrow Shield

Wide Shield

	Good	Fine	V. Fine
1786 Narrow shield	$16.00	$65.00	$175.00
1786 Wide shield	17.00	75.00	200.00

NEW JERSEY

Small Planchet

	Good	*Fine*	*V. Fine*
1787 Small planchet	$16.00	$70.00	$175.00
1787 Large planchet	17.00	75.00	200.00

1788 Horse's head facing right	16.00	65.00	160.00
1788 Horse's head facing left	80.00	275.00	800.00

VERMONT

Reuben Harmon, Jr., of Rupert, Vermont, was granted permission to coin copper pieces for a period of two years beginning July 1, 1785. The well-known Vermont plow coppers were first produced in that year. The franchise was extended for eight years in 1786.

	Good	*Fine*
1785 IMMUNE COLUMBIA	$1,200	$2,200

	Good	*Fine*
1785 Plow type	$100.00	$350.00
1786 Plow type	90.00	300.00

	Good	*Fine*
1786 Baby head	$110.00	$500.00

VERMONT

	Good	*Fine*
1786 Bust left	$50.00	$250.00
1787 Bust left	1,400	4,000

	Good	*Fine*
1787 BRITANNIA...........	$30.00	$100.00

1787 Bust right.........	$40.00	$135.00

1788 Bust right..........	$40.00	$150.00

1788 GEORGIVS III REX*.....................	$135.00	$425.00

*This piece should not be confused with the common English halfpence with similar design and reverse legend BRITANNIA.

VII. PRIVATE TOKENS AFTER CONFEDERATION

NORTH AMERICAN TOKEN

This piece was struck in Dublin, Ireland. The obverse shows the seated figure of Hibernia facing left.

Copper or Brass

	V. Good	*Fine*	*V. Fine*
1781	$17.00	$35.00	$90.00

BAR "COPPER"

The Bar "Copper" is undated and of uncertain origin. It has thirteen parallel and unconnected bars on one side. On the other side is the large roman letter USA monogram. The design was supposedly copied from a Continental button.

	V. Good	*Fine*	*V. Fine*	*E. Fine*
Undated (about 1785) Bar "Copper"	$300.00	$450.00	$1,000	$1,500

AUCTORI PLEBIS TOKEN

This token is sometimes included with the coins of Connecticut as it greatly resembles issues of that state. It was struck in England by an unknown maker, possibly for use in America.

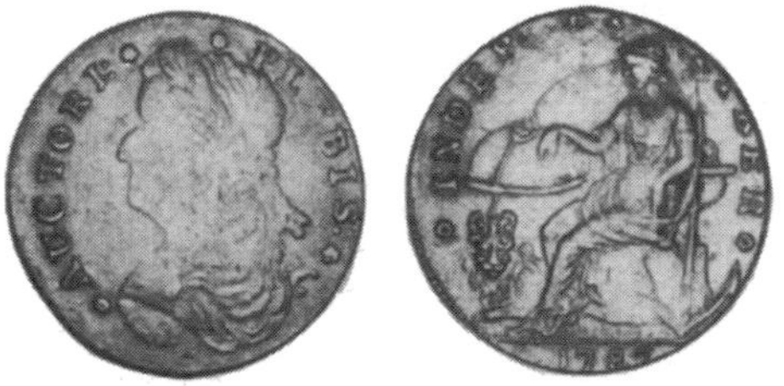

1787 AUCTORI PLEBIS	
Good	$25.00
V. Good	40.00
Fine	80.00
V. Fine	185.00

MOTT TOKEN

This was one of the first tradesman's tokens issued in America. Its exact date of manufacture and origin are unknown. They were distributed by Messrs. Mott of New York probably as a commemorative.

	V. Good	*Fine*	*V. Fine*	*E. Fine*
1789 Mott Token	$40.00	$85.00	$160.00	$300.00

STANDISH BARRY, BALTIMORE, MARYLAND

Standish Barry, a Baltimore silversmith, circulated a silver threepence in 1790. The tokens were believed to have been an advertising venture at a time when small change was scarce.

	V. Good	*Fine*	*V. Fine*
1790 Threepence	$750.00	$2,100	$5,000

KENTUCKY TOKEN

These tokens were struck in England about 1792-94. Each star in the triangle represents a state, identified by its initial letter. These pieces are usually called Kentucky Cents because the letter K (for Kentucky) happens to be at the top.

	V. Good	*V. Fine*	*E. Fine*	*Unc.*
Cent (1792-94)	$35.00	$85.00	$150.00	$450.00

FRANKLIN PRESS

This piece is an English tradesmans' token but, being associated with Benjamin Franklin, has accordingly been included in American collections.

	V. Good	*V. Fine*	*E. Fine*	*Unc.*
1794 Franklin Press Token	$35.00	$85.00	$150.00	$450.00

TALBOT, ALLUM & LEE CENTS

Talbot, Allum & Lee, engaged in the India trade and located in New York, placed a large quantity of English-made coppers in circulation during 1794 and 1795. ONE CENT appears on the 1794 issue.

1794 Cent with NEW YORK

V. Good	$27.50
V. Fine	75.00
E. Fine	125.00
Unc.	400.00

1794 Cent Without NEW YORK

Good	$70.00
V. Fine	275.00
Unc.	1,750

1795 Cent

V. Good	$22.00
V. Fine	50.00
E. Fine	140.00
Unc.	425.00

VIII. WASHINGTON PIECES

An interesting series of coins and tokens dated from 1783 to 1795 bear the portrait of George Washington. The likenesses in most instances were faithfully reproduced and were designed to honor Washington. Many of these pieces were of English origin and made later than the dates indicate.

	Fine	*V. Fine*	*E. Fine*
1783 Large military bust	$27.00	$50.00	$150.00

1783 Draped bust	30.00	60.00	175.00

WASHINGTON PIECES

UNITY STATES

V. Good	$25.00
V. Fine	90.00
E. Fine	150.00

Undated
Double Head
Cent

Fine	$30.00
V. Fine	80.00
E. Fine	160.00

Large Eagle **Small Eagle**

	Fine	*E. Fine*	*Unc.*
1791 Cent, large eagle	$150.00	$375.00	$950.00
1791 Cent, small eagle	150.00	375.00	950.00

1791 Liverpool
Halfpenny
Lettered Edge

Fine	$325.00
E. Fine	850.00
A. Unc.	2,000

1792 Eagle with Stars

Copper	—
Silver	—
Gold	—

WASHINGTON PIECES

(1792) Undated Cent
"WASHINGTON BORN VIRGINIA"

	Fine
Copper	$1,100

1792 Cent
"WASHINGTON PRESIDENT"

	Fine
Plain edge	$2,000

	V. Good	*Fine*
1792 Small eagle. Copper	$1,500	$3,000

1793 Ship
Halfpenny

Fine	$85.00
V. Fine	140.00
E. Fine	275.00

1795 Halfpenny
Grate Token

	V. Fine	*E. Fine*	*Unc.*
1795 lettered edge	$130.00	$275.00	$600.00
1795 reeded edge	70.00	140.00	315.00

WASHINGTON PIECES

Liberty and Security Tokens

	Fine	V. Fine	E. Fine
1795 Halfpenny, plain edge	$60.00	$120.00	$240.00
1795 Halfpenny, lettered edge	50.00	100.00	200.00

Liberty and
Security Penny

Fine	$100.00
V. Fine	175.00
E. Fine	350.00
Unc.	1,000

SUCCESS MEDALS

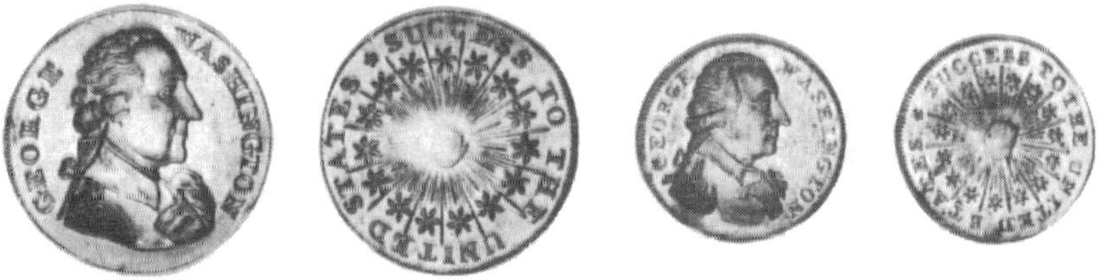

	Fine	V. Fine	E. Fine
Medal, large. Plain or reeded edge	$75.00	$165.00	$300.00
Medal, small. Plain or reeded edge	85.00	185.00	325.00

NORTH WALES HALFPENNY

	Good	Fine
1795 Halfpenny	$40.00	$125.00

IX. THE FUGIO CENTS

The first coins issued by authority of the United States were the "Fugio" cents.

The legends have been credited to Benjamin Franklin by many, and the coin, as a consequence, has been referred to as the Franklin Cent.

1787 With pointed rays

1787 With club rays

	V. Good	*Fine*	*V. Fine*	*E. Fine*	*Unc.*
STATES UNITED at sides of circle (illustrated)	$75.00	$135.00	$225.00	$375.00	$875.00
UNITED STATES at sides of circle	75.00	135.00	225.00	375.00	875.00
Club Rays. Rounded end	110.00	200.00	500.00		

MODERN PROOF COINS

Proof coins can usually be distinguished by their sharpness of detail, high wire edge, and extremely brilliant, mirrorlike surface. All proofs are originally sold by the mint at a premium.

Proof coins were not struck during 1943-1949 or 1965-67. Sets from 1936 through 1972 include the cent, nickel, dime, quarter and half; from 1973 through 1981 the dollar was also included. Proof sets may be ordered during the year of issue from the United States Mint, Customer Service Center, 10003 Derekwood Lane, Lanham, MD 20706. *Values shown are for original unblemished sets.*

Figures in parentheses represent the total number of full sets minted.

1936 (3,837)	$3,200
1937 (5,542)	1,500
1938 (8,045)	600.00
1939 (8,795)	600.00
1940 (11,246)	500.00
1941 (15,287)	450.00
1942 both nickels } (21,120)	500.00
1942 one nickel } (21,120)	450.00
1950 (51,386)	300.00
1951 (57,500)	300.00
1952 (81,980)	125.00
1953 (128,800)	125.00
1954 (233,300)	70.00
1955 Box } (378,200)	45.00
1955 Flat pack } (378,200)	50.00
1956 (669,384)	21.00
1957 (1,247,952)	8.00
1958 (875,652)	15.00
1959 (1,149,291)	11.00
1960 (1,691,602 both kinds) with lg. date 1¢	7.00
1960 with sm. date 1¢	16.00
1961 (3,028,244)	5.00
1962 (3,218,019)	$5.00
1963 (3,075,645)	6.00
1964 (3,950,762)	5.50
1968S (3,041,506)	3.25
1969S (2,934,631)	3.25
1970S (2,632,810)	5.50
1970S small date 1¢	30.00
1971S (3,220,733)	2.75
1972S (3,260,996)	2.50
1973S (2,760,339)	6.00
1974S (2,612,568)	7.00
1975S (2,845,450)	7.50
1976S (4,149,730)	5.00
1976S 3-pc. set (3,998,621)	10.00
1977S (3,251,152)	4.00
1978S (3,127,781)	5.00
1979S filled S } (3,677,175)	5.00
1979S clear S } (3,677,175)	45.00
1980S (3,554,806)	5.00
1981S (4,063,083)	4.00
1982S (3,857,479)	3.00
1983S (3,138,765)	3.00
1983S Prestige Set (140,361)	40.00

MODERN PROOF COINS

1984S (2,748,430)	$4.00
1984S Prestige Set (316,680)	11.00
1985S (3,362,821)	3.00
1986S (2,411,180)	11.00
1986S Prestige Set (599,317)	16.00
1987S (3,792,233)	3.00
1987S Prestige Set (435,495)	10.00
1988S (3,031,287)	6.00
1988S Prestige Set (231,661)	15.00
1989S (3,009,107)	5.00
1989S Prestige Set (211,087)	17.00
1990S (2,793,433)	8.00
1990S Prestige Set (506,126)	12.50
1991S (2,610,833)	14.00
1991S Prestige Set (256,954)	33.00
1992S (2,675,618)	6.00
1992S Prestige Set (183,293)	20.00
1992S Silver (1,009,586)	8.00
1992S Silver Premier Set (308,055)	8.00
1993S (2,409,394)	8.00
1993S Prestige Set (224,045)	25.00
1993S Silver (570,213)	18.00
1993S Silver Premier Set (191,140)	18.00
1994S (2,308,701)	6.50
1994S Prestige Set (175,893)	30.00
1994S Silver (636,009)	18.00

1994S Silver Premier Set (149,320)	$19.00
1995S (2,010,384)	20.00
1995S Prestige Set (107,112)	60.00
1995S Silver (549,878)	40.00
1995S Silver Premier Set (130,107)	42.00
1996S (1,695,244)	6.00
1996S Prestige Set (55,000)	110.00
1996S Silver (623,655)	25.00
1996S Silver Premier Set (151,366)	25.00
1997S (1,975,000)	25.00
1997S Prestige Set (Botenical)(80,000)	90.00
1997S Silver (605,473)	35.00
1997S Silver Premier Set (136,205)	35.00
1998S	13.00
1998S Silver (638,134)	16.00
1998S Silver Premier Set (240,658)	17.00
1999S 9-Piece Set	24.00
1999S Silver 9-Piece Set (800,000)	60.00
1999S 5-Piece 25¢ Set	24.00
2000S 10-Piece Set (2,968,900)	14.00
2000S Silver 10-Piece Set (856,400)	18.00
2000S 5-Piece 25¢ Set (937,600)	9.00
2001S 10-Piece Set	14.00
2001S Silver 10-Piece Set	18.00
2001S 5-Piece 25¢ Set	9.00

Original issue prices: 1936 thru 1942, $1.89; 1950 thru 1964, $2.10; 1968 thru 1972S, $5.00; 1973S thru 1976S, $7.00; 1977S thru 1979S, $9.00; 1980S, $10.00; 1981S to 1991S, $11.00; 1992S to 1998S, $12.50.

UNCIRCULATED MINT SETS

Official Mint Sets are specially packaged by the government for sale to collectors. They contain uncirculated specimens of each year's coins for every denomination issued from each mint. Sets from 1947 through 1958 contain two examples of each regular issue coin. No official sets were produced in 1950, 1982 or 1983. Privately assembled sets are valued according to individual coin prices. Only official sets are included in the following list. Unlike the proof sets, these are normal coins intended for circulation and are not minted with any special consideration for quality. Current year sets may be ordered by telephoning 1-800-USAMINT.

1947 P-D-S	*5,000*	$575.00
1948 P-D-S	*6,000*	250.00
1949 P-D-S	*5,000*	400.00
1951 P-D-S	8,654	350.00
1952 P-D-S	11,499	300.00
1953 P-D-S	15,538	250.00
1954 P-D-S	25,599	150.00
1955 P-D-S	49,656	75.00
1956 P-D	45,475	60.00
1957 P-D	34,324	100.00
1958 P-D	50,314	75.00
1959 P-D	187,000	18.00
1960 P-D	260,485	9.00
1961 P-D	223,704	18.00
1962 P-D	385,285	9.00
1963 P-D	606,612	5.00
1964 P-D	1,008,108	5.00
1965	*2,360,000	5.00
1966	*2,261,583	4.50
1967	*1,863,344	5.00
1968 P-D-S	2,105,128	2.00
1969 P-D-S	1,817,392	3.00
1970 P-D-S	2,038,134	10.00
1971 P-D-S	2,193,396	2.00
1972 P-D-S	2,750,000	2.00
1973 P-D-S	1,767,691	10.00
1974 P-D-S	1,975,981	3.50
1975 P-D-S	1,921,488	$5.00
1976 3 pieces	4,908,319	8.00
1976 P-D	1,892,513	6.00
1977 P-D	2,006,869	4.00
1978 P-D	2,162,609	4.00
1979 P-D	2,526,000	4.00
1980 P-D-S	2,815,066	5.00
1981 P-D-S	2,908,145	8.00
1984 P-D	1,832,857	4.00
1985 P-D	1,710,571	3.50
1986 P-D	1,153,536	10.00
1987 P-D	2,890,758	3.50
1988 P-D	1,646,204	4.50
1989 P-D	1,987,915	4.00
1990 P-D	1,809,184	3.50
1991 P-D	1,352,101	6.00
1992 P-D	1,500,098	3.50
1993 P-D	1,297,431	4.25
1994 P-D	1,234,813	5.00
1995 P-D	1,038,787	9.00
1996 P-D plus W dime	1,457,949	9.00
1997 P-D	950,473	8.00
1998 P-D	1,187,325	9.00
1999 P-D (18 pieces)	1,243,867	12.00
2000 P-D (20 pieces)	1,416,000	10.00
2001 P-D (20 pieces)		10.00

*Special Mint Sets

UNITED STATES REGULAR ISSUES
HALF CENTS — 1793-1857

The half cent was authorized to be coined April 2, 1792. Originally the weight was to have been 132 grains, but this was changed to 104 grains by the Act of January 14, 1793, before coinage commenced. The weight was again changed to 84 grains January 26, 1796 by presidential proclamation in conformity with the Act of March 3, 1795. Coinage was discontinued by the Act of February 21, 1857. All were coined at the Philadelphia Mint.

LIBERTY CAP TYPE — 1793-1797

AG-3 ABOUT GOOD—*Clear enough to identify.*
G-4 GOOD—*Outline of bust clear, no details. Date readable. Reverse lettering incomplete.*
VG-8 VERY GOOD—*Some hair details. Reverse lettering complete.*
F-12 FINE—*Most of hair detail shows. Leaves worn but all visible.*
VF-20 VERY FINE—*Hair near ear and forehead worn, other areas distinct. Some details in leaves show.*
EF-40 EXTREMELY FINE—*Light wear on highest parts of head and wreath.*

Head Facing Left 1793

	Quan. Minted	*AG-3*	*G-4*	*VG-8*	*F-12*	*VF-20*	*EF-40*
1793	35,334	$350.00	$850.00	$1,350	$1,900	$3,000	$5,500

Head Facing Right 1794-1797

	Quan. Minted	*AG-3*	*G-4*	*VG-8*	*F-12*	*VF-20*	*EF-40*
1794	81,600	60.00	135.00	210.00	375.00	700.00	1,500

Pole to Cap

Punctuated Date

No Pole to Cap

	Quan. Minted	*AG-3*	*G-4*	*VG-8*	*F-12*	*VF-20*	*EF-40*
1795 All kinds	139,690						
1795 Lettered edge, with pole		$40.00	$110.00	$170.00	$300.00	$575.00	$1,350
1795 Lettered edge, punctuated date		40.00	110.00	170.00	300.00	575.00	1,350

HALF CENTS

	Quan. Minted	*AG-3*	*G-4*	*VG-8*	*F-12*	*VF-20*	*EF-40*
1795 Plain edge, punctuated date		$37.50	$100.00	$160.00	$275.00	$550.00	$1,200
1795 Pl. edge, no pole		37.50	100.00	160.00	275.00	550.00	1,200
1796 With pole	} 1,390	1,500	3,000	4,500	7,000	10,500	—
1796 No pole		3,500	8,000	11,000	16,000	26,500	

1797 Plain Edge

1797, 1 above 1, Plain Edge

	Quan. Minted	*AG-3*	*G-4*	*VG-8*	*F-12*	*VF-20*	*EF-40*
1797 All kinds	127,840						
1797 Lettered edge		120.00	350.00	650.00	1,200	2,400	—
1797 Plain edge		50.00	110.00	175.00	325.00	650.00	1,300
1797 Gripped edge		1,500	3,000	7,500	—	—	
1797, 1 above 1, plain edge		35.00	100.00	125.00	250.00	475.00	1,100

DRAPED BUST TYPE 1800-1808

AG-3 ABOUT GOOD—*Clear enough to identify.*
G-4 GOOD—*Bust outline clear, few details, date readable. Reverse lettering worn and incomplete.*
VG-8 VERY GOOD—*Some drapery shows. Date and legends complete.*
F-12 FINE—*Shoulder drapery and hair over brow worn smooth.*
VF-20 VERY FINE—*Only slight wear in above areas. Slight wear on reverse.*
EF-40 EXTREMELY FINE—*Light wear on highest parts of head and wreath.*

1st Reverse

2nd Reverse

	Quan. Minted	*AG-3*	*G-4*	*VG-8*	*F-12*	*VF-20*	*EF-40*
1800	202,908	$9.00	$18.00	$24.00	$35.00	$60.00	$140.00
1802, 2 over 0	20,266	65.00	175.00	385.00	950.00	2,500	6,000
1803	92,000	7.50	18.00	24.00	40.00	75.00	250.00

Plain 4

Crosslet 4

Stemless Wreath

Stems to Wreath

	Quan. Minted	*AG-3*	*G-4*	*VG-8*	*F-12*	*VF-20*	*EF-40*
1804 All Kinds	1,055,312						
1804 Plain 4, stems		6.50	19.00	30.00	50.00	85.00	250.00
1804 Pl. 4, stemless		6.50	16.00	24.00	35.00	40.00	95.00
1804 Cr. 4, stems		6.50	16.00	24.00	35.00	40.00	95.00
1804 Cr. 4, stemless		6.50	16.00	24.00	35.00	40.00	95.00

HALF CENTS

1804 "Spiked Chin"

Small 5

Large 5

	Quan. Minted	*AG-3*	*G-4*	*VG-8*	*F-12*	*VF-20*	*EF-40*
1804 "Spiked chin"	Inc. above	$8.00	$18.00	$26.00	$40.00	$55.00	$125.00
1805 All Kinds	814,464						
1805 Medium 5, stemless		7.00	16.00	24.00	27.00	40.00	90.00
1805 Small 5, stems		50.00	150.00	350.00	800.00	1,500	—
1805 Large 5, stems		6.50	16.00	24.00	27.00	40.00	90.00

Small 6

Large 6

1808, 8 over 7

Normal Date

1806 All Kinds	356,000						
1806 Small 6, stems		16.00	60.00	125.00	200.00	360.00	800.00
1806 Small 6, stemless		7.00	16.00	24.00	27.00	37.50	90.00
1806 Large 6, stems		7.00	16.00	24.00	27.00	37.50	90.00
1807	476,000	7.00	16.00	24.00	27.00	40.00	110.00
1808, 8 over 7 }	400,000	18.00	35.00	75.00	150.00	350.00	900.00
1808 Normal date }		7.00	16.00	24.00	30.00	45.00	120.00

CLASSIC HEAD TYPE 1809-1836

G-4 GOOD—*LIBERTY only partly visible on hair band. Lettering, date, stars, worn but visible.*
VG-8 VERY GOOD—*LIBERTY entirely visible on hair band. Lower curls worn.*
F-12 FINE—*Only part wear on LIBERTY and hair at top worn in spots.*
VF-20 VERY FINE—*Lettering clear-cut. Hair only slightly worn.*
EF-40 EXTREMELY FINE—*Light wear on highest points of hair and leaves.*
MS-60 UNCIRCULATED—*Typical brown to red surface. No trace of wear.*

Brilliant or red uncirculated coins are worth more than prices shown. Spotted, cleaned or discolored pieces are worth less.

	Quan. Minted	*G-4*	*VG-8*	*F-12*	*VF-20*	*EF-40*	*MS-60*
1809	1,154,572	$13.00	$16.00	$21.00	$32.50	$45.00	$190.00
1810	215,000	14.00	20.00	35.00	60.00	125.00	600.00
1811	63,140	45.00	80.00	175.00	475.00	1,000	2,200
1825	63,000	14.00	18.00	25.00	30.00	55.00	250.00
1826	234,000	13.00	17.00	20.00	28.00	40.00	180.00

HALF CENTS

13 Stars

12 Stars

	Quan. Minted	G-4	VG-8	F-12	VF-20	EF-40	MS-60	Proof-63
1828, 13 Stars	606,000	$12.00	$14.00	$17.00	$25.00	$37.50	$115.00	
1828, 12 Stars		13.00	16.00	20.00	35.00	65.00	325.00	
1829	487,000	12.00	14.00	17.00	25.00	40.00	125.00	
1831 (Beware of altered date)	2,200						—	$4,200
1832	51,000	12.00	15.00	18.00	26.00	35.00	110.00	1,700
1833	103,000	12.00	15.00	18.00	26.00	35.00	110.00	1,700
1834	141,000	12.00	15.00	18.00	26.00	35.00	110.00	1,700
1835	398,000	12.00	15.00	18.00	26.00	35.00	110.00	1,700
1836								2,800

CORONET TYPE 1840-1857

	Proof-63		Proof-63
1840 Original	$2,000	1845 Original	$2,850
1840 Restrike	1,900	1845 Restrike	2,600
1841 Original	2,100	1846 Original	2,600
1841 Restrike	2,000	1846 Restrike	2,100
1842 Original	2,300	1847 Original	2,100
1842 Restrike	2,000	1847 Restrike	2,100
1843 Original	2,100	1848 Original	2,100
1843 Restrike	2,100	1848 Restrike	2,100
1844 Original	2,850	1849 Original. Small date	2,400
1844 Restrike	2,100	1849 Restrike. Small date	2,400

Brilliant or red uncirculated coins are worth more than prices shown. Spotted, cleaned or discolored pieces are worth less.

G-4 GOOD—*Hair and bun show few details, parts of LIBERTY show.*
VG-8 VERY GOOD—*Beads uniformly distinct. Hairlines show in spots.*
F-12 FINE—*Hairlines above ear worn. Beads sharp.*
VF-20 VERY FINE—*Lowest curl shows wear, hair otherwise distinct.*
EF-40 EXTREMELY FINE—*Light wear on highest points of hair and leaves.*
MS-60 UNCIRCULATED—*No trace of wear, light blemishes.*

Small Date

Large Date

	Quan. Minted	G-4	VG-8	F-12	VF-20	EF-40	MS-60	Proof-63
1849 Large date	39,864	$16.00	$20.00	$22.00	$30.00	$50.00	$130.00	—
1850	39,812	16.00	20.00	22.00	30.00	50.00	130.00	—
1851	147,672	13.00	18.00	19.00	25.00	40.00	100.00	—
1852								$2,500
1853	129,694	13.00	18.00	19.00	25.00	40.00	100.00	
1854	55,358	13.00	18.00	19.00	25.00	40.00	100.00	2,500
1855	56,500	13.00	18.00	19.00	25.00	40.00	100.00	2,500
1856	40,430	15.00	18.00	21.00	30.00	45.00	110.00	2,500
1857	35,180	16.00	21.00	23.00	34.00	57.00	140.00	2,500

LARGE CENTS — 1793-1857

Cents and half cents were the first coins struck under the authority of the United States Government. Coinage began in 1793 with laws specifying that the cent should weigh exactly twice as much as the half cent. Large cents were coined every year from 1793 to 1857 with the exception of 1815, when a lack of copper prevented production. All were coined at the Philadelphia Mint. Varieties listed are those most significant to collectors. Numerous other die varieties may be found because each of the early dies was individually made.

FLOWING HAIR, CHAIN TYPE REVERSE 1793

AG-3 ABOUT GOOD—*Date and devices clear enough to identify.*
G-4 GOOD—*Lettering worn but readable. Bust has no detail.*
VG-8 VERY GOOD—*Date and lettering distinct, some details of head visible.*
F-12 FINE—*About half of hair, etc. details show.*
VF-20 VERY FINE—*Ear visible. Most of details can be seen.*
EF-40 EXTREMELY FINE—*Highest points of hair and back of temple show wear.*

Obverse

AMERI. Reverse

AMERICA Reverse

	Quan. Minted	*AG-3*	*G-4*	*VG-8*	*F-12*	*VF-20*	*EF-40*
1793 Chain	36,103						
1793 AMERI. in legend		$600.00	$1,400	$2,200	$3,700	$6,800	$13,500
1793 AMERICA		500.00	1,000	1,800	3,250	5,750	11,000

FLOWING HAIR, WREATH TYPE REVERSE 1793

Wreath Type

Strawberry Leaf Var.

	Quan. Minted	*AG-3*	*G-4*	*VG-8*	*F-12*	*VF-20*	*EF-40*
1793 Wreath	63,353						
1793 Vine/bars edge		$160.00	$400.00	$650.00	$1,200	$2,000	$4,000
1793 Lettered Edge		185.00	475.00	800.00	1,300	2,150	4,125
1793 Strawberry leaf (*4 known*)							

LARGE CENTS
LIBERTY CAP TYPE 1793-1796

1793 Vine and Bar edge
Chain and Wreath Type Only

Lettered edge 1793-1795
ONE HUNDRED FOR A DOLLAR

Beaded Border, 1793 Only

1793-1794

"Head of 1793"
Head is in high
rounded relief

1794 Only

"Head of 1794"
Well defined hair,
hook on lowest curl

1794-1796

"Head of 1795"
Head in low relief,
no hook on lowest curl

	Quan. Minted	*AG-3*	*G-4*	*VG-8*	*F-12*	*VF-20*	*EF-40*
1793 Lib. Cap	11,056	$400.00	$900.00	$1,600	$2,700	$6,000	$15,000
1794 All kinds	918,521						
1794 "Head of 1793"		120.00	250.00	500.00	1,100	2,500	5,500
1794 "Head of 1794"		23.00	65.00	110.00	200.00	385.00	1,100
1794 "Head of 1795"		23.00	65.00	110.00	200.00	375.00	1,000
1795 Ltd. ed.	37,000	23.00	65.00	110.00	200.00	425.00	1,200
1795 Plain ed.	501,500	22.00	60.00	95.00	150.00	350.00	825.00
1796 Lib. Cap	109,825	23.00	65.00	110.00	220.00	500.00	1,400

DRAPED BUST TYPE 1796-1807

AG-3 ABOUT GOOD—*Clear enough to identify.*
G-4 GOOD—*Lettering worn, but clear; date clear. Bust lacks details.*
VG-8 VERY GOOD—*Drapery partly visible. Less wear in date and lettering.*
F-12 FINE—*Hair over brow is smooth, some details showing in other parts of hair.*
VF-20 VERY FINE—*Hairlines slightly worn. Hair over brow better defined.*
EF-40 EXTREMELY FINE—*Hair above forehead and left of eye outlined and detailed. Only slight wear on olive leaves.*

LARGE CENTS

LIHERTY error

Gripped Edge

Stems

Stemless

	Quan. Minted	*AG-3*	*G-4*	*VG-8*	*F-12*	*VF-20*	*EF-40*
1796 Draped Bust	363,375	$22.00	$42.00	$80.00	$175.00	$425.00	$1,000
1796 LIHERTY error		35.00	75.00	175.00	350.00	1,300	3,500
1797 All kinds	897,510						
1797 Gr. edge, '96 rev		11.00	25.00	60.00	120.00	250.00	750.00
1797 Pl. edge, '96 rev		12.00	27.00	65.00	125.00	275.00	900.00
1797, '97 rev., Stems		10.00	20.00	45.00	75.00	170.00	425.00
1797, '97 rev., Stemless		15.00	30.00	70.00	130.00	325.00	1,100

1798, 8 over 7

1799, 9 over 8

1800 over 1798

1800, 80 over 79

	Quan. Minted	*AG-3*	*G-4*	*VG-8*	*F-12*	*VF-20*	*EF-40*
1798 All kinds	1,841,745						
1798, 8 over 7		15.00	30.00	65.00	140.00	450.00	1,500
1798		8.00	16.00	25.00	65.00	135.00	450.00
1799, 9 over 8	*	250.00	650.00	1,200	3,000	8,000	—
1799 Nor. date	(Incl. above)	225.00	550.00	1,000	2,500	6,500	—
1800 All kds.	2,822,175						
1800 over 1798		6.00	14.00	22.00	50.00	175.00	600.00
1800, 80 over 79		5.00	12.00	20.00	40.00	130.00	350.00
1800 Normal date		5.00	12.00	20.00	40.00	130.00	350.00

*Mintage for 1799, 9 over 8 variety is included with the 1798 figure.

Fraction 1/000

Corrected Fraction

1801 Reverse, 3 Errors

	Quan. Minted	*AG-3*	*G-4*	*VG-8*	*F-12*	*VF-20*	*EF-40*
1801 All kds.	1,362,837						
1801 Normal rev.		4.50	12.00	20.00	40.00	120.00	300.00
1801, 3 errors: 1/000, one stem & IINITED		15.00	30.00	50.00	175.00	450.00	1,700
1801 Fraction 1/000		6.00	15.00	25.00	65.00	135.00	450.00
1801, 1/100 over 1/000		6.00	17.00	30.00	80.00	175.00	475.00
1802 All kds.	3,435,100						
1802 Normal rev.		4.50	12.00	20.00	40.00	90.00	275.00
1802 Fraction 1/000		6.00	15.00	24.00	45.00	120.00	350.00
1802 Stemless wreath		4.50	12.00	20.00	40.00	100.00	300.00

1803 Sm. Date, Blunt 1

1803 Large Date, Pointed 1

Small Fraction

Large Fraction

	Quan. Minted	*AG-3*	*G-4*	*VG-8*	*F-12*	*VF-20*	*EF-40*
1803 All kds.	3,131,691						
1803 Sm. dt., sm. fract.		$4.50	$12.00	$18.00	$37.00	$100.00	$250.00
1803 Sm. dt., lg. fract.		4.50	12.00	18.00	37.00	100.00	250.00
1803 Lg. dt., sm. fract.		450.00	1,400	3,000	5,500	8,000	
1803 Lg. dt., lg. fract.		13.00	22.00	45.00	90.00	200.00	800.00
1803 1/100 over 1/000		5.00	14.00	27.50	55.00	135.00	375.00
1803 Stemless wreath		5.00	12.00	25.00	55.00	135.00	375.00

1804 With Normal or Broken Dies (broken dies illustrated)

All genuine 1804 Cents have a crosslet 4 in the date and a large fraction. The 0 in the date is in line with the O in OF on the reverse of the coin.

	Quan. Minted	*AG-3*	*G-4*	*VG-8*	*F-12*	*VF-20*	*EF-40*
1804	96,500	140.00	300.00	500.00	1,000	1,600	3,250
1805	941,116	4.50	12.00	18.00	45.00	130.00	250.00
1806	348,000	6.00	15.00	27.50	60.00	150.00	450.00

Sm. 1807, 7 over 6, blunt 1

Lg. 1807, 7 over 6, pointed 1

	Quan. Minted	*AG-3*	*G-4*	*VG-8*	*F-12*	*VF-20*	*EF-40*
1807 All kinds	829,221						
1807 Small 7 over 6, Blunt 1		200.00	750.00	1,500	2,700	5,500	—
1807 Large 7 over 6		4.50	12.00	18.00	40.00	125.00	300.00
1807 Small fraction		5.00	13.00	22.00	43.00	125.00	375.00
1807 Large fraction		5.00	13.00	22.00	43.00	125.00	375.00

CLASSIC HEAD TYPE 1808-1814

AG-3 ABOUT GOOD—*Details clear enough to identify.*
G-4 GOOD—*Legends, stars, date worn, but plain.*
VG-8 VERY GOOD—*LIBERTY all readable. Ear shows. Details worn but plain.*
F-12 FINE—*Hair on forehead and before ear nearly smooth. Ear and hair under ear sharp.*
VF-20 VERY FINE—*All hairlines show some detail. Leaves on rev. show slight wear.*
EF-40 EXTREMELY FINE—*All hairlines sharp. Very slight wear on high points.*

LARGE CENTS

	Quan. Minted	AG-3	G-4	VG-8	F-12	VF-20	EF-40
1808	1,007,000	$6.25	$18.00	$35.00	$75.00	$175.00	$475.00
1809	222,867	17.00	35.00	70.00	125.00	375.00	950.00

1810, 10 over 09

1810 Normal Date

1811, Last 1 over 0

1811 Normal Date

	Quan. Minted	AG-3	G-4	VG-8	F-12	VF-20	EF-40
1810 All kinds	1,458,500						
1810, 10 over 09		5.00	16.00	30.00	75.00	200.00	425.00
1810 Normal date		5.00	16.00	30.00	45.00	160.00	385.00
1811 All kinds	218,025						
1811 Last 1 over 0		12.00	24.00	50.00	125.00	350.00	1,200
1811 Normal date		12.00	24.00	40.00	100.00	250.00	600.00
1812	1,075,500	5.00	15.00	25.00	60.00	180.00	400.00
1813	418,000	7.50	17.00	32.00	75.00	200.00	450.00
1814	357,830	5.00	15.00	25.00	60.00	180.00	420.00

CORONET TYPE 1816-1857

G 4 GOOD—*Head details partly visible. Even wear in date and legends.*
VG-8 VERY GOOD—*LIBERTY, date, stars, legends clear. Part of hair cord visible.*
F-12 FINE—*All hairlines show. Hair cords show uniformly.*
VF-20 VERY FINE—*Hair cords only slightly worn. Hairlines only partly worn, all well defined.*
EF-40 EXTREMELY FINE—*Both hair cords stand out sharply. All hairlines sharp.*
MS-60 UNCIRCULATED—*Typical brown to red surface. No trace of wear.*

13 Stars

15 Stars

Brilliant or red uncirculated coins are worth more than prices shown. Spotted, cleaned or discolored pieces are worth less.

	Quan. Minted	G-4	VG-8	F-12	VF-20	EF-40	MS-60
1816	2,820,982	$5.00	$6.00	$10.00	$20.00	$40.00	$160.00
1817, 13 stars	} 3,948,400	5.00	6.00	8.00	18.00	35.00	125.00
1817, 15 stars		6.00	8.00	11.00	30.00	100.00	500.00
1818	3,167,000	5.00	6.00	8.00	18.00	40.00	125.00

LARGE CENTS

1819, 9 over 8

1820, 20 over 19

	Quan. Minted	*G-4*	*VG-8*	*F-12*	*VF-20*	*EF-40*	*MS-60*
1819, 9 over 8	} 2,671,000	$5.00	$6.00	$10.00	$25.00	$75.00	$210.00
1819		4.50	5.00	8.00	18.00	40.00	125.00
1820, 20 over 19		5.00	6.00	10.00	25.00	80.00	225.00
1820	4,407,550	4.50	5.00	8.00	18.00	40.00	125.00
1821	389,000	8.00	14.00	30.00	100.00	250.00	2,000
1822	2,072,339	4.50	6.00	12.00	30.00	65.00	275.00

1823, 3 over 2

1824, 4 over 2

1826, 6 over 5

	Quan. Minted	*G-4*	*VG-8*	*F-12*	*VF-20*	*EF-40*	*MS-60*
1823, 3 over 2	} Included with 1824	15.00	25.00	85.00	175.00	650.00	—
1823 Normal date		15.00	30.00	100.00	200.00	700.00	—
1824, 4 over 2	} 1,262,000	5.25	7.00	14.00	75.00	250.00	—
1824 Normal date		5.00	6.00	10.00	45.00	125.00	600.00
1825	1,461,100	4.50	5.00	9.00	20.00	100.00	400.00
1826, 6 over 5	} 1,517,425	6.00	10.00	15.00	60.00	250.00	700.00
1826 Normal date		4.50	5.00	8.00	20.00	60.00	200.00
1827	2,357,732	4.50	5.00	8.00	20.00	50.00	160.00

This date size appears on cents before 1828.

This date size appears on cents after 1828.

	Quan. Minted	*G-4*	*VG-8*	*F-12*	*VF-20*	*EF-40*	*MS-60*
1828 Lg. narrow date	} 2,260,624	4.50	5.00	8.00	18.00	45.00	200.00
1828 Sm. wide date		4.75	5.50	12.00	30.00	55.00	300.00
1829	1,414,500	4.50	5.00	8.00	18.00	40.00	150.00
1830	1,711,500	4.50	5.00	8.00	18.00	40.00	150.00
1831	3,359,260	4.50	5.00	7.00	14.00	32.00	125.00
1832	2,362,000	4.50	5.00	7.00	14.00	32.00	125.00
1833	2,739,000	4.50	5.00	7.00	14.00	32.00	125.00
1834	1,855,100	4.50	5.00	7.00	14.00	32.00	200.00
1835	3,878,400	4.50	5.00	7.00	14.00	32.00	175.00
1836	2,111,000	4.50	5.00	7.00	14.00	32.00	150.00

LARGE CENTS

Young Head 1835-1857

G-4 GOOD—*Considerably worn. LIBERTY readable.*
VG-8 VERY GOOD—*Hairlines smooth but visible, outline of ear clearly defined.*
F-12 FINE—*Hairlines at top of head and behind ear worn but visible. Braid over brow plain, ear clear.*
VF-20 VERY FINE—*All details more sharp. Hair over brow shows only slight wear.*
EF-40 EXTREMELY FINE—*Hair above ear detailed, but slightly worn.*
MS-60 UNCIRCULATED—*Typical brown to red surface. No trace of wear.*

1839 over 1836

Brilliant or red uncirculated coins are worth more than prices shown. Spotted, cleaned or discolored pieces are worth less.

	Quan. Minted	*G-4*	*VG-8*	*F-12*	*VF-20*	*EF-40*	*MS-60*
1837	5,558,300	$4.50	$5.00	$7.00	$13.00	$32.00	$150.00
1838	6,370,200	4.50	5.00	7.00	11.00	30.00	125.00
1839	3,128,661	4.50	5.25	8.00	14.00	36.00	150.00
1839, 9 over 6		70.00	150.00	325.00	750.00	2,000	—
1840	2,462,700	4.00	5.00	7.00	10.00	30.00	125.00
1841	1,597,367	4.00	5.00	7.00	10.00	27.00	125.00
1842	2,383,390	4.00	5.00	7.00	10.00	27.00	110.00

"Head of 1840"
Petite Head
1839-1843

"Head of 1844"
Mature Head
1843-1857

Small Letters

Large Letters

1843 Petite, sm. let.	2,425,342	4.00	5.00	7.00	10.00	27.00	100.00
1843 Petite, lg. let.		6.00	8.50	14.00	25.00	45.00	250.00
1843 Mature, lg. let.		5.00	6.00	9.00	13.00	32.00	100.00
1844 Normal date	2,398,752	4.00	5.00	7.00	10.00	26.00	100.00
1844 over 81 (error, photo page 54)		5.00	6.00	10.00	17.00	60.00	325.00
1845	3,894,804	3.75	4.50	6.50	9.00	25.00	90.00
1846	4,120,800	4.00	5.00	7.00	10.00	27.00	100.00
1847	6,183,669	4.00	5.00	7.00	9.00	25.00	90.00
1847, 7 over "sm." 7		5.00	6.00	10.00	15.00	35.00	150.00

LARGE CENTS

	Quan. Minted	G-4	VG-8	F-12	VF-20	EF-40	MS-60
1848	6,415,799	$3.75	$4.50	$7.00	$9.00	$25.00	$85.00
1849	4,178,500	3.75	4.50	7.00	9.00	25.00	85.00
1850	4,426,844	3.75	4.50	7.00	9.00	25.00	85.00

1844, 44 over 81

1851, 51 over 81

1847, 7 over "Small" 7

Brilliant or red uncirculated coins are worth more than prices shown. Spotted, cleaned or discolored pieces are worth less.

1851 Normal date	} 9,889,707	3.750	4.50	7.00	9.00	25.00	80.00
1851 over 81 (error)		4.50	6.00	8.00	17.00	30.00	175.00
1852	5,063,094	3.75	4.50	7.00	9.00	25.00	75.00
1853	6,641,131	3.75	4.50	7.00	9.00	25.00	75.00
1854	4,236,156	3.75	4.50	7.00	9.00	25.00	80.00

1855 Upright 5's

1855 Slanting 5's

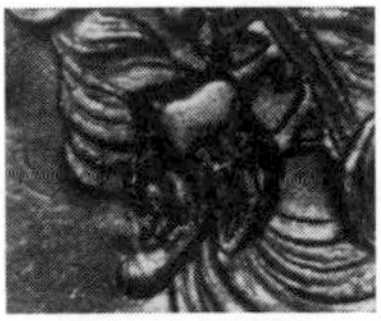

1855 Knob on ear

1855 All kinds	1,574,829						
1855 Upright 5's		3.75	4.50	7.00	9.00	25.00	75.00
1855 Slanting 5's		3.75	4.50	7.00	9.00	25.00	100.00
1855 Slanting 5's, knob on ear		4.00	5.00	8.00	12.00	30.00	110.00
1856 Upright 5	} 2,690,463	3.75	4.50	7.00	9.00	25.00	75.00
1856 Slanting 5		3.75	4.50	7.00	9.00	25.00	75.00

1857 Large Date

1857 Small Date

1857 Large date	} 333,456	10.00	16.00	22.00	25.00	30.00	150.00
1857 Small date		12.00	18.00	25.00	28.00	35.00	175.00

SMALL CENTS — 1856 to Date
FLYING EAGLE TYPE 1856-1858

The Act of February 21, 1857 provided for the coinage of the small cent. The 1856 Eagle cent was not an authorized mint issue, as the law governing the new size coin was enacted after the date of issue. It is believed that about 1,500 to 2,500 of these pieces were struck. They are properly referred to as patterns.

G-4 GOOD—*All details worn, but readable.*
VG-8 VERY GOOD—*Feather details and eye of eagle are evident but worn.*
F-12 FINE—*Eagle head details and feather tips sharp.*
VF-20 VERY FINE—*Feathers in right wing and tail show considerable detail.*
EF-40 EXTREMELY FINE—*Slight wear, all details sharp.*
MS-60 UNCIRCULATED—*No trace of wear. Light blemishes.*

1858, 8 over 7

1856-1858 Large Letters

1858 Small Letters

Brilliant uncirculated and proof coins are worth more than prices shown. Spotted, cleaned or discolored pieces are worth less.

		Quan. Minted
1856		est. 2,000
1857	(485)	17,450,000
1858 Lg. letters	(80)	24,600,000
1858 Sm. letters	(200)	

	G-4	VG-8	F-12	VF-20	EF-40	MS-60	Proof-63
1856	$2,100	$2,500	$2,900	$3,300	$3,600	$4,800	$5,250
1857	7.50	8.50	12.00	18.00	50.00	125.00	2,500
1858 Lg. let.	7.50	8.50	12.00	18.00	50.00	125.00	2,500
1858, 8 over 7		25.00	60.00	130.00	275.00	750.00	
1858 Sm let.	7.50	8.50	12.00	18.00	50.00	125.00	2,500

SMALL CENTS
INDIAN HEAD TYPE 1859-1909

The small cent was redesigned in 1859, and a representation of an Indian princess was adopted as the obverse device. The 1859 reverse was also changed to represent a laurel wreath. In 1860 the reverse was modified to display an oak wreath with a small shield at the top. From 1859 to 1863 cents were struck in copper-nickel. In 1864 the composition was changed to bronze, although copper-nickel cents were also struck during that year.

SMALL CENTS

G-4 GOOD—*No LIBERTY visible.*
VG-8 VERY GOOD—*At least three letters of LIBERTY readable on head band.*
F-12 FINE—*LIBERTY completely visible.*
VF-20 VERY FINE—*Slight but even wear on LIBERTY.*
EF-40 EXTREMELY FINE—*LIBERTY sharp. All other details sharp. Only slight wear on ribbon end.*
MS-60 UNCIRCULATED—*No trace of wear. Light blemishes.*

Without Shield at Top of Wreath
1859 Only

With Shield on Reverse
1860 to 1909

Brilliant uncirculated and proof coins are worth more than prices shown. Spotted, cleaned or discolored pieces are worth less.

Copper-nickel, Laurel Wreath Reverse 1859

	Quan. Minted	*G-4*	*VG-8*	*F-12*	*VF-20*	*EF-40*	*MS-60*	*Proof-63*
1859 ....*(800)*	36,400,000	$4.00	$4.50	$5.50	$15.00	$37.00	$100.00	$550.00

Copper-nickel, Oak Wreath with Shield Reverse 1860-1864

1860 ....*(1,000)*	20,566,000	2.50	3.00	4.50	7.50	20.00	65.00	375.00
1861 ....*(1,000)*	10,100,000	7.00	8.00	12.00	19.00	35.00	85.00	425.00
1862 ....*(550)*	28,075,000	2.00	3.00	3.50	6.00	11.00	40.00	375.00
1863 ....*(460)*	49,840,000	2.00	3.00	3.50	6.00	11.00	40.00	375.00
1864 ....*(370)*	13,740,000	5.00	6.00	9.00	14.00	22.00	60.00	400.00

Bronze 1864-1909

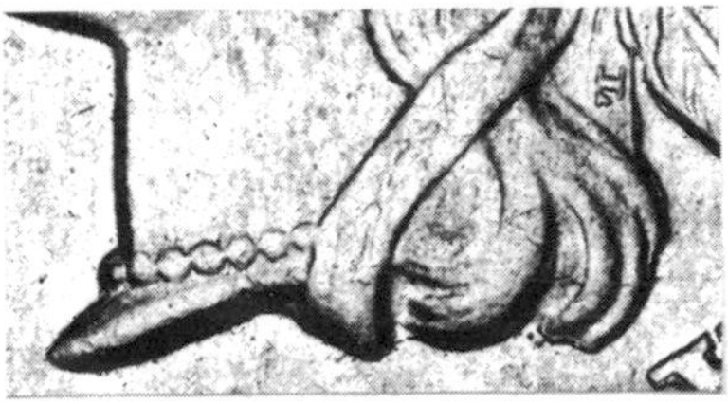

1864 Indian Head Cent with "L"

	Quan. Minted	*G-4*	*VG-8*	*F-12*	*VF-20*	*EF-40*	*MS-60*	*Proof-63*
1864 All kinds.........	39,233,714							
1864 No L............................*(150)*		$2.00	$3.00	$5.00	$10.00	$15.00	$35.00	$375.00
1864 L must show.................*(20)*		15.00	25.00	40.00	60.00	80.00	160.00	—
1865 ....*(500)*	35,429,286	1.75	2.50	4.50	8.00	14.00	35.00	200.00
1866 ....*(725)*	9,826,500	12.00	14.00	21.00	35.00	60.00	110.00	200.00
1867 ....*(625)*	9,821,000	12.00	14.00	21.00	35.00	60.00	110.00	200.00
1868 ....*(600)*	10,266,500	12.00	14.00	21.00	35.00	60.00	110.00	200.00
1869 ....*(600)*	6,420,000	18.00	23.00	60.00	100.00	135.00	190.00	235.00
1870 ....*(1,000)*	5,275,000	17.00	20.00	55.00	90.00	125.00	200.00	235.00
1871 ....*(960)*	3,929,500	19.00	25.00	85.00	110.00	135.00	200.00	250.00
1872 ....*(950)*	4,042,000	25.00	35.00	100.00	135.00	180.00	240.00	275.00
1873 ....*(1,100)*	11,676,500	6.00	8.00	15.00	18.00	50.00	70.00	150.00
1874 ....*(700)*	14,187,500	5.00	6.00	9.00	16.00	35.00	70.00	150.00
1875 ....*(700)*	13,528,000	5.00	7.00	12.00	17.00	35.00	70.00	150.00
1876 ....*(1,150)*	7,944,000	8.00	12.00	15.00	25.00	50.00	85.00	150.00
1877 ....*(510)*	852,500	190.00	250.00	350.00	450.00	700.00	1,250	1,300

SMALL CENTS

Brilliant or red uncirculated coins are worth more than prices shown. Spotted, cleaned or discolored pieces are worth less.

	Quan. Minted	*G-4*	*VG-8*	*F-12*	*VF-20*	*EF-40*	*MS-60*	*Proof-63*
1878 ....(2,350)	5,799,850	$9.00	$12.00	$18.00	$30.00	$55.00	$85.00	$140.00
1879 ....(3,200)	16,231,200	2.00	2.50	4.50	8.00	18.00	35.00	100.00
1880 ....(3,955)	38,964,955	1.00	1.25	2.00	3.00	9.00	22.00	90.00
1881 ....(3,575)	39,211,575	1.00	1.25	1.75	3.00	8.00	21.00	90.00
1882 ....(3,100)	38,581,100	1.00	1.25	1.75	3.00	8.00	21.00	90.00
1883 ....(6,609)	45,598,109	1.00	1.25	1.75	3.00	8.00	21.00	90.00
1884 ....(3,942)	23,261,742	1.25	1.50	2.25	4.00	9.00	23.00	100.00
1885 ....(3,790)	11,765,384	2.00	2.25	4.00	8.00	17.00	45.00	100.00
1886 ....(4,290)	17,654,290	1.00	1.50	5.00	10.00	24.00	50.00	100.00
1887 ....(2,960)	45,226,483	.45	.60	.85	1.50	5.00	18.00	90.00
1888 ....(4,582)	37,494,414	.45	.60	.85	1.50	5.00	18.00	90.00
1889 ....(3,336)	48,869,361	.45	.60	.85	1.50	5.00	18.00	90.00
1890 ....(2,740)	57,182,854	.45	.60	.85	1.50	5.00	18.00	90.00
1891 ....(2,350)	47,072,350	.45	.60	.85	1.50	5.00	18.00	90.00
1892 ....(2,745)	37,649,832	.45	.60	.85	1.50	5.00	18.00	90.00
1893 ....(2,195)	46,642,195	.45	.60	.85	1.50	5.00	18.00	90.00
1894 ....(2,632)	16,752,132	.60	1.00	2.50	4.00	8.00	22.00	100.00
1895 ....(2,062)	38,343,636	.40	.50	.75	1.00	4.00	14.00	90.00
1896 ....(1,862)	39,057,293	.40	.50	.75	1.00	4.00	14.00	90.00
1897 ....(1,938)	50,466,330	.40	.50	.75	1.00	4.00	14.00	90.00
1898 ....(1,795)	49,823,079	.40	.50	.75	1.00	4.00	14.00	90.00
1899 ....(2,031)	53,600,031	.40	.50	.75	1.00	4.00	14.00	90.00
1900 ....(2,262)	66,833,764	.35	.40	.60	.85	3.00	11.00	75.00
1901 ....(1,985)	79,611,143	.35	.40	.60	.85	3.00	11.00	75.00
1902 ....(2,018)	87,376,722	.35	.40	.60	.85	3.00	11.00	75.00
1903 ....(1,790)	85,094,493	.35	.40	.60	.85	3.00	11.00	75.00
1904 ....(1,817)	61,328,015	.35	.40	.60	.85	3.00	11.00	75.00
1905 ....(2,152)	80,719,163	.35	.40	.60	.85	3.00	11.00	75.00
1906 ....(1,725)	96,022,255	.35	.40	.60	.85	3.00	11.00	75.00
1907 ....(1,475)	108,138,618	.35	.40	.60	.85	3.00	11.00	75.00

Location of mint mark S on reverse of Indian cent (1908 and 1909 only).

1908 ....(1,620)	32,327,987	.35	.40	.60	.85	3.00	12.00	80.00
1908S	1,115,000	17.00	20.00	23.00	27.00	42.00	110.00	
1909 ....(2,175)	14,370,645	.50	.65	1.00	1.50	6.00	15.00	100.00
1909S	309,000	120.00	140.00	155.00	180.00	240.00	275.00	

LINCOLN TYPE, WHEAT EARS REVERSE 1909-1958

Victor D. Brenner designed this cent which was issued to commemorate the hundredth anniversary of Lincoln's birth. The designer's initials V.D.B. appear on the reverse of a limited quantity of cents of 1909. Later in the year they were removed from the dies but restored in 1918 as very small incuse letters beneath the shoulder. The Lincoln type was the first cent to have the motto IN GOD WE TRUST.

G-4 GOOD—*Date worn but apparent. Lines in wheat heads missing. Full rims.*
VG-8 VERY GOOD—*Half of lines show in upper wheat heads.*
F-12 FINE—*Wheat lines worn but visible.*
VF-20 VERY FINE—*Cheek and jaw bones worn but separated. No worn spots on wheat heads.*
EF-40 EXTREMELY FINE—*Slight wear. All details sharp.*
MS-60 UNCIRCULATED—*No trace of wear. Light blemishes or discoloration.*
MS-63 SELECT UNCIRCULATED—*No trace of wear. Slight blemishes.*

SMALL CENTS

Location of mint mark S or D on obverse of Lincoln cent.

Location of designer's initials V.D.B. on 1909 only.

No V.D.B. on reverse 1909-1958.

Bronze 1909-1942

Brilliant uncirculated coins are worth more than prices shown. Spotted, cleaned or discolored pieces are worth less.

	Quan. Minted	*G-4*	*VG-8*	*F-12*	*VF-20*	*EF-40*	*MS-60*
1909 V.D.B.	27,995,000	$1.00	$1.25	$1.50	$1.75	$2.00	$4.00
1909 V.D.B. Matte proof-63	(1,194)						650.00
1909S, V.D.B.	484,000	200.00	220.00	250.00	300.00	350.00	400.00
1909	72,702,618	.25	.40	.55	1.00	1.25	6.00
1909 Matte proof-63	(2,352)						110.00
1909S	1,825,000	20.00	23.00	27.50	35.00	45.00	65.00
1910	146,801,218	.05	.08	.15	.25	.75	6.50
1910 Matte proof-63	(4,083)						100.00
1910S	6,045,000	3.00	3.50	4.00	5.00	9.00	30.00
1911	101,177,787	.05	.08	.20	.40	.75	8.00
1911 Matte proof-63	(2,411)						110.00
1911D	12,672,000	1.50	2.00	2.75	5.00	15.00	35.00
1911S	4,026,000	6.00	7.00	8.00	11.00	16.00	60.00
1912	68,153,060	.06	.15	.45	1.00	1.75	13.00
1912 Matte proof-63	(2,145)						110.00
1912D	10,411,000	1.50	2.00	3.00	6.00	18.00	55.00
1912S	4,431,000	4.50	6.00	7.00	8.50	16.00	45.00
1913	76,532,352	.05	.10	.30	.75	1.35	10.00
1913 Matte proof-63	(2,848)						110.00
1913D	15,804,000	.50	1.00	1.50	3.00	10.00	42.00
1913S	6,101,000	2.50	3.00	3.50	5.00	12.00	55.00
1914	75,238,432	.05	.20	.50	1.00	3.50	18.00
1914 Matte proof-63	(1,365)						120.00
1914D*	1,193,000	45.00	55.00	75.00	110.00	250.00	500.00
1914S	4,137,000	4.50	5.00	6.00	9.00	18.00	100.00
1915	29,092,120	.30	.50	1.35	3.00	15.00	40.00
1915 Matte proof-63	(1,150)						190.00
1915D	22,050,000	.35	.50	.65	1.50	4.00	25.00
1915S	4,833,000	3.00	3.50	4.00	5.00	13.00	60.00
1916	131,833,677	.03	.05	.10	.30	.80	5.00
1916 Matte proof-63	(1,050)						275.00
1916D	35,956,000	.08	.13	.40	1.00	3.00	24.00
1916S	22,510,000	.30	.40	.75	1.25	3.50	28.00
1917	196,429,785	.03	.05	.10	.25	.60	5.00
1917D	55,120,000	.08	.13	.35	.80	2.50	25.00
1917S	32,620,000	.08	.13	.35	.80	2.50	27.50

*Beware of altered date or mint mark. No V.D.B. on shoulder of genuine 1914D cent.

SMALL CENTS

Brilliant uncirculated coins before 1934 are worth more than prices shown. Spotted, cleaned or discolored pieces are worth less

Designer's initials restored starting 1918.

	Quan. Minted	*G-4*	*VG-8*	*F-12*	*VF-20*	*EF-40*	*MS-60*	*MS-63*
1918	288,104,634	$.03	$.05	$.10	$.20	$.75	$5.50	
1918D	47,830,000	.08	.13	.35	.80	2.50	25.00	
1918S	34,680,000	.08	.13	.35	.80	2.50	27.50	
1919	392,021,000	.03	.04	.05	.15	.50	4.00	
1919D	57,154,000	.04	.06	.10	.40	1.50	20.00	
1919S	139,760,000	.04	.06	.10	.30	.80	15.00	
1920	310,165,000	.03	.04	.05	.15	.50	3.50	
1920D	49,280,000	.04	.06	.10	.30	1.50	24.00	
1920S	46,220,000	.04	.06	.10	.30	1.50	32.00	
1921	39,157,000	.05	.08	.15	.35	1.50	18.00	
1921S	15,274,000	.35	.45	.70	1.25	6.50	55.00	
1922D	} 7,160,000	2.50	3.00	4.00	5.00	9.00	35.00	
1922 Plain†		110.00	150.00	210.00	325.00	850.00	3,000	
1923	74,723,000	.03	.04	.05	.15	.85	4.50	
1923S	8,700,000	.50	.60	.75	2.00	8.00	85.00	
1924	75,178,000	.03	.04	.06	.15	1.00	10.00	
1924D	2,520,000	4.00	4.50	5.00	11.00	24.00	120.00	
1924S	11,696,000	.35	.45	.70	1.10	5.00	55.00	
1925	139,949,000	.03	.04	.05	.15	.50	3.50	
1925D	22,580,000	.04	.06	.10	.30	2.00	24.00	
1925S	26,380,000	.04	.06	.10	.25	2.00	30.00	
1926	157,088,000	.03	.04	.05	.15	.50	3.50	
1926D	28,020,000	.04	.06	.10	.30	2.00	23.00	
1926S	4,550,000	.85	1.25	1.75	2.50	4.50	50.00	
1927	144,440,000	.03	.04	.05	.20	.50	3.50	
1927D	27,170,000	.04	.06	.10	.25	1.00	14.00	
1927S	14,276,000	.25	.30	.50	.90	2.50	30.00	
1928	134,116,000	.03	.04	.05	.15	.50	3.50	
1928D	31,170,000	.04	.06	.10	.25	.85	10.00	
1928S	17,266,000	.06	.10	.25	.50	1.75	22.00	
1929	185,262,000	.03	.04	.05	.15	.35	3.00	
1929D	41,730,000	.04	.06	.10	.25	.60	7.00	
1929S	50,148,000	.03	.05	.10	.15	.50	4.25	
1930	157,415,000	.03	.04	.05	.15	.25	1.50	$3.50
1930D	40,100,000	.04	.06	.10	.25	.60	5.00	11.00
1930S	24,286,000	.03	.05	.10	.15	.40	3.00	7.00
1931	19,396,000	.15	.20	.30	.40	.60	7.00	16.00
1931D	4,480,000	1.00	1.25	1.50	2.00	3.00	22.00	35.00
1931S	866,000	18.00	20.00	22.00	24.00	29.00	33.00	38.00
1932	9,062,000	.40	.50	.60	1.00	1.25	8.50	11.00
1932D	10,500,000	.25	.35	.40	.50	.85	7.00	12.00
1933	14,360,000	.25	.35	.45	.60	1.10	8.00	12.00
1933D	6,200,000	.60	.75	1.00	1.25	1.75	9.00	11.00
1934	219,080,000	.03	.03	.03	.03	.10	1.50	2.00
1934D	28,446,000	.04	.06	.08	.10	.25	5.50	9.00
1935	245,388,000	.03	.03	.03	.04	.06	.50	1.00
1935D	47,000,000	.03	.03	.03	.04	.10	1.00	2.00
1935S	38,702,000	.03	.04	.04	.04	.12	3.00	5.00
1936	309,637,569	.03	.03	.03	.04	.06	.30	.50
1936 Proof-63	(5,569)							55.00
1936D	40,620,000	.03	.03	.03	.04	.08	.60	1.00
1936S	29,130,000	.03	.03	.03	.04	.10	.65	1.10

†The 1922 without D was caused by a defective die. Beware of removed mint mark. Those with weak D are worth considerably less.

SMALL CENTS

	Quan. Minted	G-4	VG-8	F-12	VF-20	EF-40	MS-60	MS-63
1937	309,179,320	$.02	$.02	$.02	$.03	$.05	$.20	$.30
1937 Proof-63	(9,320)							22.00
1937D	50,430,000	.02	.02	.02	.03	.06	.30	.60
1937S	34,500,000	.03	.03	.03	.04	.06	.30	.60
1938	156,696,734	.02	.02	.02	.03	.05	.30	.60
1938 Proof-63	(14,734)							20.00
1938D	20,010,000	.02	.03	.04	.06	.15	.40	.75
1938S	15,180,000	.06	.08	.10	.12	.15	.30	.75
1939	316,479,520	.02	.02	.02	.03	.05	.20	.30
1939 Proof-63	(13,520)							16.00
1939D	15,160,000	.06	.08	.10	.12	.15	.35	1.00
1939S	52,070,000	.03	.03	.03	.04	.10	.30	.70
1940	586,825,872	.02	.02	.02	.03	.03	.20	.30
1940 Proof-63	(15,872)							13.00
1940D	81,390,000	.02	.02	.02	.03	.03	.20	.40
1940S	112,940,000	.02	.02	.02	.03	.04	.20	.40
1941	887,039,100	.02	.02	.02	.03	.03	.20	.30
1941 Proof-63	(21,100)							12.00
1941D	128,700,000	.02	.02	.02	.03	.03	.40	.80
1941S	92,360,000	.02	.02	.02	.03	.04	.35	.80
1942	657,828,600	.02	.02	.02	.03	.03	.10	.15
1942 Proof-63	(32,600)							12.00
1942D	206,698,000	.02	.02	.02	.03	.03	.10	.15
1942S	85,590,000	.02	.02	.02	.03	.10	1.00	2.00

Zinc-coated Steel 1943 Only

		F-12	VF-20	EF-40	MS-60	MS-63
1943	684,628,670	.05	.10	.15	.30	.75
1943D	217,660,000	.05	.10	.15	.35	.75
1943S	191,550,000	.05	.12	.20	.60	1.25

Bronze Resumed 1944-1958

	Quan. Minted	VF-20	EF-40	MS-63
1944	1,435,400,000	$.02	$.03	$.15
1944D	} 430,578,000	.02	.03	.20
1944D, D over S		50.00	65.00	*180.00
1944S	282,760,000	.02	.03	.15
1945	1,040,515,000	.02	.03	.20
1945D	226,268,000	.02	.03	.15
1945S	181,770,000	.02	.03	.10
1946	991,655,000	.02	.03	.10
1946D	315,690,000	.02	.03	.15
1946S	198,100,000	.02	.03	.25
1947	190,555,000	.02	.03	.25

*Value for MS-60 uncirculated is $125.00.

1944D, D over S

1955 Doubled Die Error

	Quan. Minted	VF-20	EF-40	MS-63	Proof-63
1947D	194,750,000	$.02	$.02	$.12	
1947S	99,000,000	.02	.03	.15	
1948	317,570,000	.02	.02	.15	
1948D	172,637,500	.02	.02	.12	
1948S	81,735,000	.02	.03	.20	
1949	217,775,000	.02	.02	.30	
1949D	153,132,500	.02	.02	.20	

SMALL CENTS

		Quan. Minted	VF-20	EF-40	MS-63	Proof-63
1949S		64,290,000	$.03	$.05	$.50	
1950	(51,386)	272,686,386	.02	.02	.25	$10.00
1950D		334,950,000	.02	.02	.10	
1950S		118,505,000	.02	.03	.25	
1951	(57,500)	284,633,500	.02	.02	.25	9.00
1951D		625,355,000	.02	.02	.10	
1951S		136,010,000	.02	.03	.30	
1952	(81,980)	186,856,980	.02	.02	.15	5.00
1952D		746,130,000	.02	.02	.15	
1952S		137,800,004	.02	.03	.50	
1953	(128,800)	256,883,800	.02	.03	.10	3.00
1953D		700,515,000	.02	.02	.10	
1953S		181,835,000	.02	.03	.12	
1954	(233,300)	71,873,350	.03	.05	.10	1.75
1954D		251,552,500	.02	.02	.05	
1954S		96,190,000	.02	.03	.05	
1955 Doubled die obv. (see illus. pg.60)			260.00	320.00	*700.00	
1955	(378,200)	330,958,200	.02	.02	.06	1.00
1955D		563,257,500	.02	.02	.05	
1955S		44,610,000	.10	.15	.15	
1956	(669,384)	421,414,384	.02	.02	.05	.25
1956D		1,098,201,100	.02	.02	.05	
1957	(1,247,952)	283,787,952	.02	.02	.05	.25
1957D		1,051,342,000	.02	.02	.03	
1958	(875,652)	253,400,652	.02	.02	.03	.50
1958D		800,953,300	.02	.02	.03	

*Value for MS-60 Uncirculated is $475.00.

LINCOLN TYPE, MEMORIAL REVERSE 1959 TO DATE

Small Date

Large Date

		Quan. Minted	MS-63	Proof-63
1959	(1,149,291)	610,864,291	$.01	$.25
1959D		1,279,760,000	.01	
1960 Large date	(1,691,602)	588,096,602	.01	.25
1960 Small date			.60	2.00
1960D Large date		1,580,884,000	.01	
1960D Small date			.02	
1961	(3,028,244)	756,373,244	.01	.15
1961D		1,753,266,700	.01	
1962	(3,218,019)	609,263,019	.01	.15
1962D		1,793,148,400	.01	
1963	(3,075,645)	757,185,645	.01	.15
1963D		1,774,020,400	.01	
1964	(3,950,762)	2,652,525,762	.01	.15
1964D		3,799,071,500	.01	
1965		1,497,224,900	.02	
1966		2,188,147,783	.04	
1967		3,048,667,100	.03	
1968		1,707,880,970	.02	
1968D		2,886,269,600	.01	
1968S	(3,041,506)	261,311,507	02	.15
1969		1,136,910,000	.05	
1969D		4,002,832,200	.03	
1969S	(2,934,631)	547,309,631	03	.15
1969S Doubled die obv			—	

SMALL CENTS

Small Date Numbers aligned at top

Large Date Low 7 in date

Enlarged Detail of 1972 Doubled Die Error

1969S Doubled Die Error

	Quan. Minted	MS-63	Proof-63
1970	1,898,315,000	$.05	
1970D	2,891,438,900	.02	
1970S (2,632,810)			
	693,192,814		
1970S Sm. date (high 7)		10.00	$25.00
1970S Lg. date (low 7)		.03	.15
1971	1,919,490,000	.05	
1971D	2,911,045,600	.03	
1971S (3,220,733)			
	528,354,192	.03	.15
1972 Doubled die obv.		120.00	
1972	2,933,255,000	.01	
1972D	2,665,071,400	.02	
1972S (3,260,996)			
	380,200,104	.02	.15
1973	3,728,245,000	.01	
1973D	3,549,576,588	.01	
1973S (2,760,339)			
	319,937,634	.02	.15
1974	4,232,140,523	.01	
1974D	4,235,098,000	.01	
1974S (2,612,568)			
	412,039,228	.03	.15
1975	5,451,476,142	.01	
1975D	4,505,275,300	.01	
1975S Proof	(2,845,450)		.75
1976	4,674,292,426	$.01	
1976D	4,221,592,455	.02	
1976S Proof	(4,149,730)		$.50
1977	4,469,930,000	.01	
1977D	4,194,062,300	.01	
1977S Proof	(3,251,152)		.35
1978	5,558,605,000	.01	
1978D	4,280,233,400	.01	
1978S Proof	(3,127,781)		.35
1979	6,018,515,000	.01	
1979D	4,139,357,254	.01	
1979S Proof	(3,677,175)		
Filled S			.35
Clear S			.80
1980	7,414,705,000	.01	
1980D	5,140,098,660	.01	
1980S Proof	(3,554,806)		.25
1981	7,491,750,000	.01	
1981D	5,373,235,677	.01	
1981S Proof	(4,063,083)		.35
1982	10,712,525,000		
Lg. Date		.01	
Sm. Date		.02	
1982D	6,012,979,368		
Lg. Date		.01	
1982S Proof	(3,857,479)		.25

Large Date

Small Date

1995 Double Die showing strong doubling on word "LIBERTY"

Copper Plated Zinc

	Quan. Minted	MS-63	Proof-63
1982 Lg. Date	inc. above	$.01	
1982 Sm. Date	inc. above	.01	
1982D Lg. Date	inc. above	.05	
1982D Sm. Date	inc. above	.01	
1983	7,752,355,000	.01	
1983D	6,467,199,428	.01	
1983S Proof	(3,279,126)	.01	$.50
1984	8,151,079,000	.01	
1984D	5,569,238,906	.01	
1984S Proof	(3,065,110)		.50
1985	5,648,489,887	.01	
1985D	5,287,399,926	.01	
1985S Proof	(3,362,821)		$.50
1986	4,491,395,493	$.01	
1986D	4,442,866,698	.01	
1986S Proof	(3,010,497)		1.25
1987	4,682,466,931	.01	
1987D	4,879,389,511	.01	
1987S Proof	(4,227,728)		.35
1988	6,092,810,000	.01	
1988D	5,253,740,443	.01	
1988S Proof	(3,262,948)		.35
1989	7,261,535,000	.01	
1989D	5,345,467,111	.01	

SMALL CENTS

	Quan. Minted	MS-63	Proof-63
1989S Proof	(3,220,194)		$.60
1990	6,851,765,000	$.01	
1990D	4,922,894,553	.01	
1990S Proof	(3,299,559)		.90
1991	5,165,940,000	.01	
1991D	4,158,442,076	.01	
1991S Proof	(2,867,787)		2.00
1992	4,648,905,000	.01	
1992D	4,448,673,300	.01	
1992S Proof	(4,176,560)		1.00
1993	5,684,705,000	.01	
1993D	6,426,650,571	.01	
1993S Proof	(3,394,792)		1.50
1994	(6,500,850,000)	.01	
1994D	7,131,765,000	.01	
1994S Proof	(3,269,923)		1.00
1995	6,411,440,000	.01	
1995 Doubled die obv		10.00	
1995D	7,128,560,000	.01	
1995S Proof			1.50
1996	6,612,465,000	.01	
1996D	6,510,795,000	.01	
1996S Proof			1.00
1997	4,622,800,000	$.01	
1997D	4,576,555,000	.01	
1997S Proof	(1,975,000)		$1.00
1998	5,032,155,000	.01	
1998 wide AM*		6.00	
1998D	5,225,353,500	.01	
1998S Proof			1.00
1999	5,237,600,000	.01	
1999 wide AM*		10.00	
1999D	6,360,065,000	.01	
1999S Proof			1.00
2000	5,503,200,000	.01	
2000 wide AM*		3.00	
2000D	8,774,220,000	.01	
2000S Proof			1.00
2001		.01	
2001D		.01	
2001S Proof			1.00
2002		.01	
2002D		.01	
2002S Proof		.01	1.00

*Varieties were made using Proof dies that have a wide space between AM in AMERICA. The letters nearly touch on other uncirculated cents.

TWO-CENT PIECES — 1864-1873

The Act of April 22, 1864, which changed the weight and composition of the cent, included a provision for the bronze two-cent piece. The weight was specified as 96 grains, the alloy being the same as for the cent.

There are two varieties for the first year of issue, 1864: the small motto and the large motto. The differences are explained in the illustrations below.

1864 Small Motto

1864 Large Motto

On the obverse the D in GOD is narrow on the large motto. The stem to the leaf shows plainly on the small motto variety.

G-4 GOOD—*At least IN GOD visible.*
VG-8 VERY GOOD—*WE weakly visible.*
F-12 FINE—*Complete motto visible. WE weak.*
EF-40 EXTREMELY FINE—*WE is bold.*
MS-60 UNCIRCULATED—*No trace of wear. Light blemishes.*

Brilliant red choice uncirculated and proof coins are worth more than prices shown. Cleaned or discolored pieces are worth less.

	Quan. Minted	*G-4*	*VG-8*	*F-12*	*EF-40*	*MS-60*	*Proof-63*
1864 Sm. motto		$25.00	$30.00	$55.00	$150.00	$300.00	—
1864 Lg. motto......*(100+)*	19,847,500	5.00	6.00	8.00	15.00	40.00	$250.00
1865 ....*(500+)*	13,640,000	5.00	6.00	8.00	15.00	40.00	225.00
1866 ....*(725+)*	3,177,000	5.00	6.00	8.00	15.00	40.00	225.00
1867 ....*(625+)*	2,938,750	5.00	6.00	8.00	15.00	47.50	225.00
1868 ....*(600+)*	2,803,750	5.00	6.00	8.00	16.00	50.00	225.00
1869 ....*(600+)*	1,546,500	5.50	6.50	9.00	20.00	60.00	250.00
1870 ....*(1,000+)*	861,250	6.00	7.00	10.00	25.00	100.00	275.00
1871 ....*(960+)*	721,250	7.00	8.00	15.00	35.00	110.00	325.00
1872 ....*(950+)*	65,000	40.00	50.00	90.00	200.00	425.00	475.00
1873 Proofs only *(1,000+)*							725.00

SILVER THREE-CENT PIECES 1851-1873

This smallest of United States silver coins was authorized by Congress March 3, 1851. The first three-cent silver pieces had no lines bordering the six-pointed star. From 1854 through 1858 there were three lines, while issues of the last fifteen years show only two lines. Issues from 1854 through 1873 have an olive sprig over the III and a bundle of three arrows beneath.

No outline around star.

Mint Mark O ←

G-4 GOOD—*Star worn smooth. Legend and date readable.*
VG-8 VERY GOOD—*Outline of shield defined. Legend and date clear.*
F-12 FINE—*Only star points worn smooth.*
VF-20 VERY FINE—*Only partial wear on star ridges.*
EF-40 EXTREMELY FINE—*Ridges on star points show.*
MS-60 UNCIRCULATED—*No trace of wear. Light blemishes.*

Well struck specimens command higher prices.

	Quan. Minted	*G-4*	*VG-8*	*F-12*	*VF-20*	*EF-40*	*MS-60*	*Proof-63*
1851	5,447,400	$8.00	$9.00	$12.00	$14.00	$25.00	$70.00	—
1851O	720,000	10.00	12.00	16.50	27.00	55.00	165.00	
1852	18,663,500	8.00	9.00	12.00	14.00	25.00	65.00	—
1853	11,400,000	8.00	9.00	12.00	14.00	25.00	65.00	

Three outlines to star, large date.

	Quan. Minted	*G-4*	*VG-8*	*F-12*	*VF-20*	*EF-40*	*MS-60*	*Proof-63*
1854	671,000	9.00	10.00	13.00	20.00	42.00	160.00	—
1855	139,000	10.00	14.00	20.00	35.00	70.00	265.00	$1,300
1856	1,458,000	8.00	9.00	12.00	18.00	40.00	135.00	1,200
1857	1,042,000	8.00	9.00	12.00	18.00	40.00	135.00	1,200
1858 ....*(300+)*	1,604,000	8.00	9.00	12.00	18.00	40.00	135.00	1,100

Two outlines to star, small date.

1862 2 over 1

	Quan. Minted	*G-4*	*VG-8*	*F-12*	*VF-20*	*EF-40*	*MS-60*	*Proof-63*
1859 ....(800)	365,000	8.00	9.00	12.00	17.00	30.00	70.00	250.00
1860 ....(1,000)	287,000	8.00	9.00	12.00	17.00	30.00	70.00	250.00
1861 ....(1,000)	498,000	8.00	9.00	12.00	17.00	30.00	70.00	250.00
1862, 2 over 1.... }	343,550	9.00	10.00	13.00	20.00	35.00	100.00	
1862 ....(550) }		8.00	9.00	12.00	17.00	30.00	70.00	225.00
1863 ....(460)	21,460				100.00	125.00	250.00	250.00
1864 ....(470)	12,470				125.00	140.00	250.00	275.00
1865 ....(500)	8,500				125.00	140.00	250.00	275.00
1866 ....(725)	22,725				125.00	140.00	250.00	275.00
1867 ....(625)	4,625				125.00	140.00	250.00	275.00
1868 ....(600)	4,100				125.00	140.00	250.00	275.00
1869 ....(600)	5,100				125.00	140.00	250.00	275.00
1870 ....(1,000)	4,000				125.00	140.00	275.00	300.00
1871 ....(960)	4,360				125.00	140.00	275.00	300.00
1872 ....(950)	1,950				125.00	140.00	275.00	300.00
1873 ....(600)	(Proof only)							500.00

THREE-CENT PIECES (NICKEL)
ISSUED 1865-1889

The three-cent pieces struck in nickel composition were designed to replace the silver three cent coins. Composition is 75% copper and 25% nickel. All were coined at Philadelphia and have plain edges.

G-4 GOOD—*Date and legends complete though worn. III smooth.*
VG-8 VERY GOOD—*III is half worn. Rims complete.*
F-12 FINE—*Hair curls well defined.*
EF-40 EXTREMELY FINE—*Slight, even wear.*
MS-60 UNCIRCULATED—*No trace of wear. Light blemishes.*

Brilliant choice uncirculated and proof coins are worth more than prices shown. Spotted, cleaned or discolored pieces are worth less.

	Quan. Minted	*G-4*	*VG-8*	*F-12*	*VF-20*	*EF-40*	*MS-60*	*Proof-63*
1865	*(500+)* 11,382,000	$5.00	$5.50	$6.00	$7.00	$10.00	$40.00	$500.00
1866	*(725+)* 4,801,000	5.00	5.50	6.00	7.00	10.00	40.00	140.00
1867	*(625+)* 3,915,000	5.00	5.50	6.00	7.00	10.00	40.00	140.00
1868	*(600+)* 3,252,000	5.00	5.50	6.00	7.00	10.00	40.00	140.00
1869	*(600+)* 1,604,000	5.00	5.50	6.00	7.00	10.00	40.00	140.00
1870	*(1,000+)* 1,335,000	5.00	5.50	6.00	7.00	11.00	40.00	140.00
1871	*(960+)* 604,000	5.00	5.50	6.00	7.00	11.00	45.00	140.00
1872	*(950+)* 862,000	5.00	5.50	6.00	7.00	11.00	45.00	140.00
1873	*(1,100+)* 1,173,000	5.00	5.50	6.00	7.00	11.00	45.00	140.00
1874	*(700+)* 790,000	5.50	6.00	6.50	7.50	12.00	45.00	140.00
1875	*(700+)* 228,000	5.50	6.50	7.00	8.00	16.00	80.00	140.00
1876	*(1,150+)* 162,000	5.50	6.50	8.00	9.00	18.00	90.00	150.00
1877	*(510+)* (Proofs only)				425.00	525.00		700.00
1878	(2,350) (Proofs only)				275.00	300.00		325.00
1879	(3,200) 41,200	22.00	25.00	30.00	35.00	40.00	125.00	150.00
1880	(3,955) 24,955	27.00	40.00	45.00	50.00	65.00	140.00	175.00
1881	(3,575) 1,080,575	5.00	5.50	6.00	7.00	10.00	40.00	140.00
1882	(3,100) 25,300	23.00	32.00	37.50	45.00	55.00	140.00	175.00
1883	(6,609) 10,609	55.00	65.00	80.00	100.00	125.00	200.00	175.00
1884	(3,942) 5,642	90.00	100.00	125.00	150.00	175.00	300.00	200.00
1885	(3,790) 4,790	90.00	100.00	125.00	150.00	175.00	400.00	200.00
1886	(4,290) 4,290				125.00	175.00		200.00
1887 All kinds } (2,960)	7,961	90.00	100.00	125.00	150.00	175.00	250.00	200.00
1887, 7 over 6 }					150.00	175.00		200.00
1888	(4,582) 41,083	18.00	20.00	25.00	30.00	37.50	125.00	140.00
1889	(3,436) 21,561	27.00	35.00	45.00	50.00	55.00	130.00	140.00

NICKEL FIVE-CENT PIECES — 1866 to Date
SHIELD TYPE 1866-1883

The shield type nickel was made possible by the Act of May 16, 1866. Its weight was set at 77-16/100 grains with the same composition as the nickel three-cent piece which was authorized in 1865.

Rays Between Stars 1866-1867

G-4 GOOD—*All letters in motto readable.*
VG-8 VERY GOOD—*Motto stands out clearly. Rims worn slightly but even. Part of shield lines visible.*
F-12 FINE—*Half of each olive leaf is smooth.*
EF-40 EXTREMELY FINE—*Leaf tips show slight wear. Cross over shield slightly worn.*
MS-60 UNCIRCULATED—*No trace of wear. Light blemishes.*

NICKEL FIVE-CENT PIECES

Brilliant choice uncirculated and proof coins are worth more than prices shown. Spotted, cleaned or discolored pieces are worth less.

	Quan. Minted	*G-4*	*VG-8*	*F-12*	*EF-40*	*MS-60*	*Proof-63*
1866 Rays...........*(200+)*	14,742,500	$7.00	$8.00	$12.00	$45.00	$100.00	$1,000
1867 Rays.............*(25+)*	2,019,000	7.50	9.00	14.00	50.00	175.00	7,500

Without Rays 1867-1883

Typical example of 1883, 3 over 2. Other varieties exist.

1867 No rays......*(600+)*	28,890,500	5.00	6.00	7.00	15.00	50.00	140.00
1868....................*(600+)*	28,817,000	5.00	6.00	7.00	15.00	50.00	140.00
1869....................*(600+)*	16,395,000	5.00	6.00	7.00	15.00	50.00	140.00
1870.................*(1,000+)*	4,806,000	5.00	6.00	7.00	16.00	60.00	140.00
1871....................*(960+)*	561,000	13.00	18.00	22.00	50.00	120.00	175.00
1872....................*(950+)*	6,036,000	5.00	6.00	7.00	16.00	50.00	140.00
1873 Closed 3..*(1,100+)*	436,050	5.00	6.00	7.00	18.00	65.00	140.00
1873 Open 3..................	4,113,950	5.00	6.00	7.00	16.00	60.00	
1874....................*(700+)*	3,538,000	6.00	7.00	8.00	18.00	60.00	140.00
1875....................*(700+)*	2,097,000	7.00	8.00	12.00	22.00	75.00	140.00
1876.................*(1,150+)*	2,530,000	6.50	7.50	11.00	20.00	60.00	140.00
1877 Est. Issued *(510+)*				350.00	675.00		850.00
1878...................(2,350)				170.00	285.00		325.00
1879...................(3,200)	29,100	130.00	160.00	190.00	275.00	300.00	300.00
1880...................(3,955)	19,955	140.00	170.00	200.00	300.00	375.00	375.00
1881...................(3,575)	72,375	85.00	110.00	135.00	190.00	225.00	250.00
1882...................(3,100)	11,476,000	4.50	5.50	6.50	15.00	50.00	140.00
1883...................(5,419) }	1,456,919	4.50	5.50	6.50	15.00	50.00	140.00
1883, 3 over 2 .... }			30.00	50.00	85.00	190.00	

LIBERTY HEAD TYPE 1883-1913

In 1883 the design was changed to the familiar "Liberty head." This type first appeared without the word CENTS on the coin, merely a large letter "V." These "centless" coins were goldplated and passed for five dollars. Later in that year the word CENTS was added.

Without CENTS 1883 Only

G-4 GOOD—*No details in head. LIBERTY obliterated.*
VG-8 VERY GOOD—*At least 3 letters in LIBERTY readable.*
F-12 FINE—*All letters in LIBERTY show.*
VF-20 VERY FINE—*LIBERTY bold, including letter I.*
EF-40 EXTREMELY FINE—*LIBERTY sharp. Corn grains at bottom of wreath show, on reverse.*
MS-60 UNCIRCULATED—*No trace of wear. Light blemishes.*

Brilliant choice uncirculated and proof coins are worth more than prices shown. Spotted, cleaned or discolored pieces are worth less.

	Quan. Minted	*G-4*	*VG-8*	*F-12*	*VF-20*	*EF-40*	*MS-60*	*Proof-63*
1883 without cents ....(5,219)	5,479,519	$1.75	$2.00	$2.50	$3.00	$4.00	$12.00	$150.00

NICKEL FIVE-CENT PIECES
With CENTS 1883-1913

Location of mint mark

	Quan. Minted	*G-4*	*VG-8*	*F-12*	*VF-20*	*EF-40*	*MS-60*	*Proof-63*
1883 with CENTS ....(6,783)	16,032,983	$3.50	$4.00	$5.50	$9.00	$20.00	$50.00	$125.00
1884 .....(3,942)	11,273,942	4.00	6.00	7.00	10.00	21.00	60.00	135.00
1885 .....(3,790)	1,476,490	115.00	125.00	200.00	250.00	325.00	450.00	500.00
1886 .....(4,290)	3,330,290	35.00	45.00	85.00	110.00	140.00	225.00	250.00
1887 .....(2,960)	15,263,652	2.50	3.50	7.50	9.00	19.00	50.00	110.00
1888 .....(4,582)	10,720,483	6.00	7.00	9.00	16.00	22.00	75.00	110.00
1889 .....(3,336)	15,881,361	2.00	3.00	6.00	8.00	15.00	50.00	100.00
1890 .....(2,740)	16,259,272	2.00	3.00	6.00	8.00	15.00	50.00	100.00
1891 .....(2,350)	16,834,350	1.50	3.00	6.00	8.00	15.00	50.00	100.00
1892 .....(2,745)	11,699,642	1.50	3.00	6.00	8.00	15.00	50.00	100.00
1893 .....(2,195)	13,370,195	1.50	3.00	6.00	8.00	15.00	50.00	100.00
1894 .....(2,632)	5,413,132	3.00	5.00	18.00	30.00	50.00	95.00	110.00
1895 .....(2,062)	9,979,884	1.00	2.00	6.00	9.00	15.00	40.00	100.00
1896 .....(1,862)	8,842,920	1.50	3.00	6.00	9.00	15.00	40.00	100.00
1897 .....(1,938)	20,428,735	.50	.75	2.50	4.50	10.00	35.00	100.00
1898 .....(1,795)	12,532,087	.50	.75	2.50	4.50	10.00	35.00	100.00
1899 .....(2,031)	26,029,031	.50	.75	2.50	4.50	10.00	35.00	100.00
1900 .....(2,262)	27,255,995	.35	.40	1.25	2.00	9.00	30.00	90.00
1901 .....(1,985)	26,480,213	.35	.40	1.25	2.00	9.00	30.00	90.00
1902 .....(2,018)	31,489,579	.35	.40	1.25	2.00	9.00	30.00	90.00
1903 .....(1,790)	28,006,725	.35	.40	1.25	2.00	9.00	30.00	90.00
1904 .....(1,817)	21,404,984	.35	.40	1.25	2.00	9.00	30.00	90.00
1905 .....(2,152)	29,827,276	.35	.40	1.25	2.00	9.00	30.00	90.00
1906 .....(1,725)	38,613,725	.35	.40	1.25	2.00	9.00	30.00	90.00
1907 .....(1,475)	39,214,800	.35	.40	1.25	2.00	9.00	30.00	90.00
1908 .....(1,620)	22,686,177	.35	.40	1.25	2.00	9.00	30.00	90.00
1909 .....(4,763)	11,590,526	.35	.40	1.25	2.00	9.00	35.00	90.00
1910 .....(2,405)	30,169,353	.35	.40	1.25	2.00	9.00	30.00	90.00
1911 .....(1,733)	39,559,372	.35	.40	1.25	2.00	9.00	30.00	90.00
1912 .....(2,145)	26,236,714	.35	.40	1.25	2.00	9.00	30.00	90.00
1912D..............	8,474,000	.40	.60	2.00	4.00	21.00	100.00	
1912S	238,000	24.00	30.00	40.00	115.00	250.00	400.00	
1913 Liberty Head (*5 known*)								750,000

INDIAN HEAD or BUFFALO TYPE 1913-1938

The Buffalo nickel was designed by James E. Fraser, whose initial F is below the date. He modeled the bison after Black Diamond in the New York Zoological Gardens.

Variety 1 — FIVE CENTS on Raised Ground

NICKEL FIVE-CENT PIECES

G-4 GOOD—*Legends and date readable. Horn worn off.*
VG-8 VERY GOOD—*Half horn shows.*
F-12 FINE—*Three-quarters of horn shows. Obv. rim intact.*
VF-20 VERY FINE—*Full horn shows. Indian's cheekbone worn.*
EF-40 EXTREMELY FINE—*Full horn. Slight wear on Indian's hair ribbon.*
MS-60 UNCIRCULATED—*No trace of wear. Light blemishes. Attractive mint luster.*

Brilliant choice uncirculated coins are worth more than prices shown. Spotted, cleaned, weakly struck or discolored pieces are worth less.

	Quan. Minted	*G-4*	*VG-8*	*F-12*	*VF-20*	*EF-40*	*MS-60*	*Matte Proof-63*
1913 Var. 1 (1,520)	30,993,520	$1.50	$2.50	$3.00	$3.00	$6.50	$14.00	$500.00
1913D Var. 1	5,337,000	3.25	3.75	4.50	6.00	9.00	24.00	
1913S Var. 1	2,105,000	6.50	8.00	10.00	12.00	20.00	28.00	

Variety 2 — FIVE CENTS in Recess

Mint mark below FIVE CENTS

1916 Doubled Die Obverse

1918D, 8 over 7

	Quan. Minted	G-4	VG-8	F-12	VF-20	EF-40	MS-60	Matte Proof-63
1913 Var. 2..(1,514)	29,858,700	2.00	2.50	3.00	4.00	7.00	15.00	400.00
1913D Var. 2	4,156,000	20.00	22.00	28.00	32.00	40.00	85.00	
1913S Var. 2	1,209,000	47.00	65.00	85.00	100.00	120.00	200.00	
1914, 4 over 3	20,665,738				—	—		
1914............(1,275)		4.00	5.50	7.50	8.00	9.00	25.00	400.00
1914D	3,912,000	18.00	22.00	28.00	35.00	65.00	115.00	
1914S	3,470,000	4.00	6.00	8.00	12.00	20.00	60.00	
1915............(1,050)	20,987,270	1.25	1.50	2.00	3.00	7.00	25.00	425.00
1915D	7,569,000	4.00	5.00	8.00	15.00	25.00	85.00	
1915S	1,505,000	6.00	8.00	15.00	30.00	60.00	175.00	
1916...............(600)	63,498,066	.75	1.00	1.25	1.50	3.00	19.00	750.00
1916 Doubled die obv.		650.00	1,350	2,200	3,200	5,200	12,000	
1916D	13,333,000	3.00	3.50	5.00	12.00	25.00	65.00	
1916S	11,860,000	1.50	2.00	3.00	10.00	20.00	75.00	
1917	51,424,019	.35	.45	.75	2.00	4.50	20.00	—
1917D	9,910,000	2.50	3.00	8.00	22.00	45.00	120.00	
1917S	4,193,000	3.00	5.00	12.00	25.00	60.00	135.00	
1918	32,086,314	.35	.55	1.00	3.00	8.00	35.00	
1918D, 8 over 7	8,362,000	175.00	300.00	475.00	1,000	2,500	6,500	
1918D		2.50	4.00	8.00	35.00	70.00	175.00	
1918S	4,882,000	2.00	4.00	9.00	25.00	60.00	150.00	
1919	60,868,000	.30	.40	.60	1.00	4.00	22.00	
1919D†	8,006,000	2.25	3.50	10.00	35.00	70.00	220.00	
1919S†	7,521,000	1.75	4.00	9.00	30.00	70.00	225.00	
1920	63,093,000	.30	.40	.60	1.50	4.00	25.00	
1920D†	9,418,000	2.00	3.00	6.00	30.00	90.00	210.00	
1920S	9,689,000	.85	1.50	5.00	25.00	67.00	150.00	
1921	10,663,000	.50	.75	1.25	4.00	12.00	45.00	
1921S†	1,557,000	12.00	18.00	32.00	165.00	320.00	600.00	
1923	35,715,000	.25	.40	.50	1.00	3.00	20.00	
1923S†	6,142,000	1.00	1.50	3.00	32.00	100.00	125.00	
1924	21,620,000	.25	.30	.35	1.00	4.50	25.00	
1924D	5,258,000	1.25	2.00	5.00	25.00	65.00	145.00	
1924S	1,437,000	2.50	4.00	18.00	175.00	550.00	875.00	

†Uncirculated pieces with full sharp details are worth considerably more.

NICKEL FIVE-CENT PIECES

Brilliant choice uncirculated coins are worth more than prices shown. Spotted, cleaned, weakly struck or discolored pieces are worth less.

1937D "3-Legged" Variety

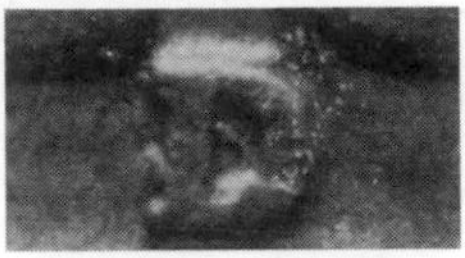

1938D, D over S

	Quan. Minted	*G-4*	*VG-8*	*F-12*	*VF-20*	*EF-40*	*MS-60*
1925	35,565,100	$.25	$.30	$.35	$ 1.00	$3.00	$15.00
1925D†	4,450,000	2.00	3.50	10.00	32.00	65.00	175.00
1925S	6,256,000	1.00	1.75	4.50	25.00	60.00	175.00
1926	44,693,000	.25	.30	.35	.60	1.75	16.00
1926D†	5,638,000	1.25	2.00	5.50	30.00	55.00	100.00
1926S	970,000	2.50	4.00	15.00	135.00	350.00	1,200
1927	37,981,000	.25	.30	.40	.60	2.00	14.00
1927D	5,730,000	.50	1.00	1.25	7.00	28.00	60.00
1927S	3,430,000	.30	.50	.90	9.00	30.00	160.00
1928	23,411,000	.25	.30	.35	.50	1.50	14.00
1928D	6,436,000	.30	.40	.75	3.00	7.00	15.00
1928S	6,936,000	.30	.35	.55	1.25	6.00	60.00
1929	36,446,000	.25	.30	.35	.50	1.50	12.00
1929D	8,370,000	.30	.40	.60	1.75	7.00	22.00
1929S	7,754,000	.25	.30	.35	.75	3.50	17.00
1930	22,849,000	.25	.30	.35	.50	1.75	12.00
1930S	5,435,000	.25	.30	.35	.50	3.50	16.00
1931S	1,200,000	1.50	2.00	3.00	4.00	5.00	20.00
1934	20,213,003	.22	.25	.30	.40	1.10	10.00
1934D	7,480,000	.22	.25	.30	.45	3.00	15.00
1935	58,264,000	.22	.25	.30	.35	.75	7.00
1935D	12,092,000	.22	.25	.30	.35	1.10	13.00
1935S	10,300,000	.22	.25	.30	.35	.90	10.00
1936	119,001,420	.22	.25	.30	.35	.50	6.00
1936 Proof-63	(4,420)						400.00
1936D	24,814,000	.22	.25	.30	.35	.60	6.00
1936S	14,930,000	.22	.25	.30	.35	.60	5.00
1937	79,485,769	.22	.25	.30	.35	.50	5.00
1937 Proof-63	(5,769)						350.00
1937D	17,826,000	.25	.25	.30	.35	.60	6.00
1937D 3-Legged*		75.00	120.00	145.00	170.00	225.00	600.00
1937S	5,635,000	.22	.25	.30	.35	.60	6.00
1938D	7,020,000	.22	.25	.30	.35	.60	5.00
1938D, D over S				2.00	3.00	5.00	15.00

†Uncirculated pieces with full sharp details are worth considerably more. *Beware of removed leg.

JEFFERSON TYPE 1938 to Date

This nickel was designed by Felix Schlag. He won an award of $1,000 in a competition with some 390 artists. It established the definite public approval of portrait and pictorial rather than symbolic devices on our coinage. On October 8, 1942, the wartime five-cent piece composed of copper (56%), silver (35%) and manganese (9%) was introduced to eliminate nickel, a critical war material. A larger mint mark was placed above the dome. Letter P (Philadelphia) was used for the first time, indicating the change of alloy. The designer's initials FS were added below the bust starting in 1966. Mint mark position was moved to the obverse starting in 1968.

VG-8 VERY GOOD—*Second porch pillar from right nearly gone, other three still visible but weak.*
F-12 FINE—*Cheekbone worn flat. Hairlines and eyebrow faint. Second pillar weak, especially at bottom.*
VF-20 VERY FINE—*Second pillar plain and complete on both sides.*
EF-40 EXTREMELY FINE—*Cheekbone, hairlines, eyebrow slightly worn but well defined. Base of triangle above pillars visible but weak.*
MS-63 SELECT UNCIRCULATED—*No trace of wear. Slight blemishes.*

NICKEL FIVE-CENT PIECES

Mint mark located at right of building

Wartime Silver

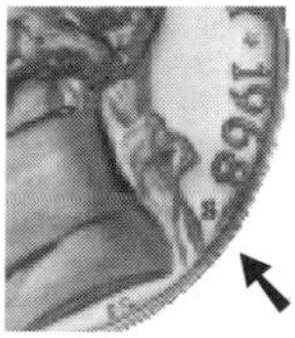

Mint mark location starting 1968

Uncirculated pieces with fully struck steps are valued higher.

	Quan. Minted	*VG-8*	*F-12*	*VF-20*	*EF-40*	*MS-63*	*Proof-63*
1938 (19,365)	19,515,365	$.06	$.08	$.10	$.20	$.75	$12.00
1938D	5,376,000	.20	.30	.40	.65	1.00	
1938S	4,105,000	.35	.50	.75	1.20	1.75	
1939 (12,535)	120,627,535	.06	.08	.10	.20	.50	10.00
1939D	3,514,000	1.00	1.50	2.00	3.00	20.00	
1939S	6,630,000	.20	.25	.30	1.00	10.00	
1940 (14,158)	176,499,158			.05	.08	.35	9.00
1940D	43,540,000			.05	.08	.50	
1940S	39,690,000			.05	.10	.50	
1941 (18,720)	203,283,720			.05	.08	.25	9.00
1941D	53,432,000			.05	.08	1.00	
1941S	43,445,000			.05	.09	1.25	
1942 (29,600)	49,818,600			.05	.08	1.00	9.00
1942D	13,938,000	.06	.08	.20	.40	8.00	
Wartime Silver Five-Cent Pieces 1942-1945							
1942P (27,600)	57,900,600	*.15*	*.15*	*.20*	.35	3.00	30.00
1942S	32,900,000	*.15*	*.15*	*.20*	.35	2.00	
1943P, 3 over 2 }	271,165,000		15.00	20.00	30.00	100.00	
1943P }		*.15*	*.15*	*.20*	.35	1.00	
1943D	15,294,000	*.15*	*.30*	*.35*	.50	1.00	
1943S	104,060,000	*.15*	*.15*	*.20*	.35	1.25	
1944P	119,150,000	*.15*	*.15*	*.20*	.35	1.25	
1944D	32,309,000	*.15*	*.15*	*.20*	.35	2.50	
1944S	21,640,000	*.15*	*.15*	*.20*	.35	2.50	
1945P	119,408,100	*.15*	*.15*	*.20*	.35	1.50	
1945D	37,158,000	*.15*	*.15*	*.20*	.35	1.25	
1945S	58,939,000	*.15*	*.15*	*.20*	.35	1.00	
Prewar composition and mint mark style resumed 1946-1967							
1946	161,116,000			.05	.05	.15	
1946D	45,292,200			.05	.05	.15	
1946S	13,560,000			.05	.06	.15	
1947	95,000,000			.05	.05	.25	
1947D	37,822,000			.05	.05	.25	
1947S	24,720,000			.05	.06	.20	
1948	89,348,000			.05	.05	.10	
1948D	44,734,000			.05	.06	.25	
1948S	11,300,000			.05	.06	.20	
1949	60,652,000			.05	.05	.25	
1949D }	36,498,000			.05	.05	.25	
1949D, D over S }				16.00	27.50	110.00	
1949S	9,716,000			.05	.10	.35	
1950 (51,386)	9,847,386			.05	.10	.50	10.00
1950D	2,630,030			2.00	2.25	3.00	
1951 (57,500)	28,609,500			.05	.05	.25	9.00
1951D	20,460,000			.05	.05	.20	
1951S	7,776,000			.05	.10	.50	
1952 (81,980)	64,069,980			.05	.05	.20	4.00

Italic prices indicate unsettled values due to fluctuating bullion market.
See Bullion Chart.

NICKEL FIVE-CENT PIECES

	Quan. Minted	VF-20	EF-40	MS-63	Proof-63
1952D	30,638,000	$.05	$.05	$.50	
1952S	20,572,000	.05	.05	.20	
1953 (128,800)	46,772,800	.05	.05	.08	$3.00
1953D	59,878,600	.05	.05	.08	
1953S	19,210,900	.05	.05	.10	
1954 (233,300)	47,917,350	.05	.05	.08	1.25
1954D	117,183,060	.05	.05	.08	
1954S	29,384,000	.05	.05	.10	
1954S, S over D		2.50	5.00	15.00	
1955 (378,200)	8,266,200	.06	.08	.15	1.00

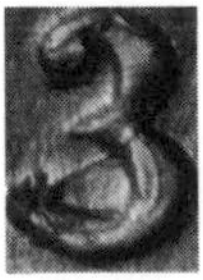

1943, 3 over 2

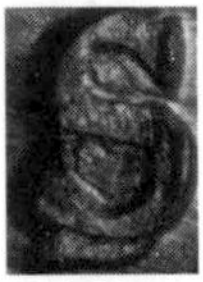

1954S, S over D

1955D, D over S*

	Quan. Minted	VF-20	EF-40	MS-63	Proof-63
1955D	74,464,100	.05	.05	.07	
1955D, D over S*		3.00	5.00	27.50	
1956 (669,384)	35,885,384		.05	.06	.30
1956D	67,222,940		.05	.06	
1957 (1,247,952)	39,655,952		.05	.07	.20
1957D	136,828,900		.05	.07	
1958 (875,652)	17,963,652		.05	.08	.25
1958D	168,249,120		.05	.06	
1959 (1,149,291)	28,397,291		.05	.06	.20
1959D	160,738,240		.05	.05	
1960 (1,691,602)	57,107,602		.05	.05	.15
1960D	192,582,180		.05	.05	
1961 (3,028,144)	76,668,244		.05	.05	.15
1961D	229,342,760		.05	.05	
1962 (3,218,019)	100,602,019		.05	.05	.15
1962D	280,195,720		.05	.07	
1963 (3,075,645)	178,851,645		.05	.05	.15
1963D	276,829,460			.05	
1964 (3,950,762)	1,028,622,762			.05	.15
1964D	1,787,297,160			.05	
1965	136,131,380			.05	
1966	156,208,283			.05	
1967	107,325,800			.05	
1968D	91,227,880			.05	
1968S	103,437,510			.05	
1968S Proof	(3,041,506)				.15
1969D	202,807,500			.05	
1969S	123,099,631			.05	
1969S Proof	(2,934,631)				.15
1970D	515,485,380			.05	
1970S	241,464,814			.05	
1970S Proof	(2,632,810)				.15
1971	106,884,000			.20	
1971D	316,144,800			.07	
1971S Proof	(3,220,733)				.30
1972	202,036,000			.05	
1972D	351,694,600			.05	
1972S Proof	(3,260,996)				.30
1973	384,396,000			.05	
1973D	261,405,000			.05	
1973S Proof	(2,760,339)				.30
1974	601,752,000			.05	
1974D	277,373,000			.06	

*Varieties exist. Value is for that illustrated.

NICKEL FIVE-CENT PIECES

	Quan. Minted	*MS-63*	*Proof-63*
1974S Proof	(2,612,568)		$.25
1975	181,772,000	$.07	
1975D	401,875,300	.06	
1975S Proof	(2,845,450)		.25
1976	367,124,000	.05	
1976D	563,964,147	.06	
1976S Proof	(4,149,730)		.25
1977	585,376,000	.05	
1977D	297,313,422	.07	
1977S Proof	(3,251,152)		.25
1978	391,308,000	.05	
1978D	313,092,780	.05	
1978S Proof	(3,127,781)		.25
1979	463,188,000	.05	
1979D	325,867,672	.05	
1979S Proof	(3,677,175)		
Filled S			.20
Clear S			.50
1980P	593,004,000	.05	
1980D	502,323,448	.05	
1980S Proof	(3,554,806)		.25
1981P	657,504,000	.05	
1981D	364,801,843	.05	
1981S Proof	(4,063,083)		.25
1982P	292,355,000	.20	
1982D	373,726,544	.35	
1982S Proof	(3,857,479)		.40
1983P	561,615,000	.50	
1983D	536,726,276	.25	
1983S Proof	(3,279,126)		.50
1984P	746,769,000	.40	
1984D	517,675,146	.05	
1984S Proof	(3,065,110)		.50
1985P	647,114,962	.05	
1985D	459,747,446	.05	
1985S Proof	(3,362,821)		.40
1986P	536,883,483	.06	
1986D	361,819,140	.25	
1986S Proof	(3,010,497)		1.00
1987P	371,499,481	.05	
1987D	410,590,604	.05	
1987S Proof	(4,227,728)		.40
1988P	771,360,000	.05	
1988D	663,771,652	.05	
1988S Proof	(3,262,948)		.60
1989P	898,812,000	$.05	
1989D	570,842,474	.05	
1989S Proof	(3,220,194)		$.40
1990P	661,636,000	.05	
1990D	663,938,503	.05	
1990S Proof	(3,299,559)		.75
1991P	614,104,000	.05	
1991D	436,496,678	.05	
1991S Proof	(2,867,787)		1.00
1992P	399,552,000	.08	
1992D	450,565,113	.05	
1992S Proof	(4,176,560)		.75
1993P	412,076,000	.05	
1993D	406,084,135	.05	
1993S Proof	(3,394,792)		.75
1994P	722,160,000	.05	
1994D	715,762,110	.05	
1994S Proof	(3,269,923)		1.00
1995P	774,156,000	.05	
1995D	888,112,000	.05	
1995S Proof	(2,797,481)		1.50
1996P	829,332,000	.05	
1996D	817,736,000	.05	
1996S Proof	(2,525,265)		.50
1997P	470,972,000	.05	
1997D	466,640,000	.05	
1997S Proof	(2,796,678)		1.00
1998P	688,272,000	.05	
1998D	635,360,000	.05	
1998S Proof			.90
1999P	1,212,000,000	.05	
1999D	1,066,720,000	.05	
1999S Proof			1.00
2000P	846,240,000	.05	
2000D	1,509,520,000	.05	
2000S Proof			1.00
2001P	675,704,000	.05	
2001D	627,680,000	.05	
2001S Proof			1.00
2002P		.05	
2002D		.05	
2002S Proof			1.00

HALF DIMES 1794-1873

The half dime types present the same general characteristics as larger United States silver coins. Authorized by the Act of April 2, 1792, they were not coined until February, 1795, although dated 1794. At first the weight was 20.8 grains, and fineness 892.4. By the Act of January 18, 1837, the weight was slightly reduced to 20 5/8 grains and the fineness changed to .900. Finally the weight was reduced to 19.2 grains by the Act of February 21, 1853.

FLOWING HAIR TYPE 1794-1795

AG-3 ABOUT GOOD—*Details clear enough to identify.*
G-4 GOOD—*Eagle, wreath, bust outlined but lack details.*
VG-8 VERY GOOD—*Some details remain on face. All lettering readable.*
F-12 FINE—*Hair ends show. Hair at top smooth.*
VF-20 VERY FINE—*Hairlines at top show. Hair about ear defined.*
EF-40 EXTREMELY FINE—*Hair above forehead and at neck well defined but shows some wear.*
MS-60 UNCIRCULATED—*No trace of wear. Light blemishes.*

Weakly struck uncirculated coins are worth less than values shown.

	Quan. Minted	*AG-3*	*G-4*	*VG-8*	*F-12*	*VF-20*	*EF-40*	*MS-60*
1794	86,416 (1794–1795)	$135.00	$350.00	$450.00	$650.00	$1,000	$1,800	$4,750
1795		125.00	300.00	350.00	500.00	750.00	1,400	3,000

HALF DIMES

DRAPED BUST TYPE, SMALL EAGLE REVERSE 1796-1797

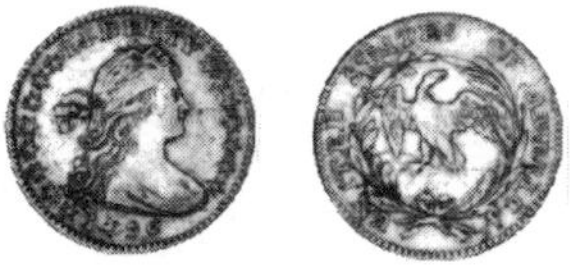

AG-3 ABOUT GOOD—*Details clear enough to identify.*
G-4 GOOD—*Date, stars, LIBERTY readable. Bust outlined but no details.*
VG-8 VERY GOOD—*Some details show.*
F-12 FINE—*Hair and drapery lines worn, but visible.*
VF-20 VERY FINE—*Only left of drapery indistinct.*
EF-40 EXTREMELY FINE—*All hairlines show details.*
MS-60 UNCIRCULATED—*No trace of wear. Light blemishes.*

	Quan. Minted	*AG-3*	*G-4*	*VG-8*	*F-12*	*VF-20*	*EF-40*	*MS-60*
1796, 6 over 5	10,230	$185.00	$425.00	$525.00	$750.00	$1,300	$2,300	$6,000
1796 Nor. dt.		175.00	400.00	475.00	650.00	1,100	1,800	4,000
1796 LIKERTY		175.00	400.00	475.00	650.00	1,100	1,800	4,300
1797, 15 stars	44,527	150.00	400.00	425.00	650.00	1,000	1,700	3,200
1797, 16 stars		150.00	400.00	425.00	650.00	1,000	1,700	3,200
1797, 13 stars		150.00	400.00	425.00	650.00	1,000	1,800	4,750

DRAPED BUST TYPE, HERALDIC EAGLE REVERSE 1800-1805

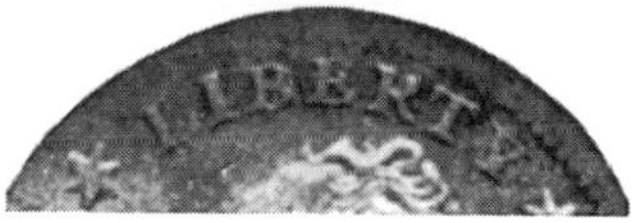

1800 LIBEKTY

1800	24,000	75.00	225.00	300.00	450.00	650.00	1,200	2,500
1800 LIBEKTY	16,000	75.00	225.00	300.00	450.00	650.00	1,200	2,500
1801	27,760	75.00	225.00	300.00	450.00	650.00	1,400	3,000
1802	3,060	2,000	4,750	6,750	12,000	22,000	33,500	—
1803	37,850	75.00	225.00	300.00	450.00	650.00	1,200	3,000
1805	15,600	75.00	300.00	400.00	525.00	750.00	1,800	—

CAPPED BUST TYPE 1829-1837

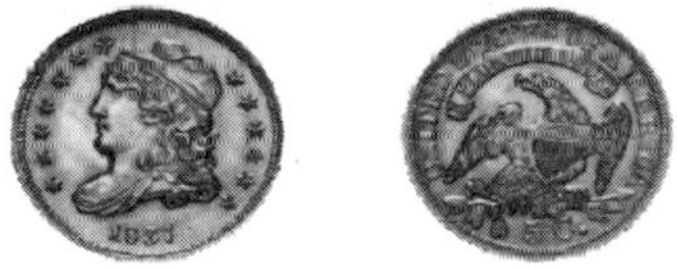

G-4 GOOD—*Bust outlined, no detail. Date and legend readable.*
VG-8 VERY GOOD—*Complete legend and date plain. At least 3 letters of LIBERTY show clearly.*
F-12 FINE—*All letters in LIBERTY show.*
VF-20 VERY FINE—*Full rims. Ear and shoulder clasp show plainly.*
EF-40 EXTREMELY FINE—*Ear very distinct, eyebrow and hair well defined.*
MS-60 UNCIRCULATED—*No trace of wear. Light blemishes.*

	Quan. Minted	*G-4*	*VG-8*	*F-12*	*VF-20*	*EF-40*	*MS-60*
1829	1,230,000	$8.00	$11.00	$15.00	$25.00	$50.00	$150.00
1830	1,240,000	8.00	11.00	15.00	25.00	50.00	150.00
1831	1,242,700	8.00	11.00	15.00	25.00	50.00	150.00
1832	965,000	8.00	11.00	15.00	25.00	50.00	150.00
1833	1,370,000	8.00	11.00	15.00	25.00	50.00	150.00
1834	1,480,000	8.00	11.00	15.00	25.00	50.00	150.00
1835	2,760,000	8.00	11.00	15.00	25.00	50.00	150.00
1836	1,900,000	8.00	11.00	15.00	25.00	50.00	150.00
1837 Small 5¢	871,000	9.00	13.00	20.00	40.00	80.00	450.00
1837 Large 5¢		8.00	11.00	15.00	25.00	50.00	150.00

HALF DIMES

LIBERTY SEATED TYPE 1837-1873
No Stars on Obverse 1837-1838

G-4 GOOD—*LIBERTY On shield smooth. Date and letters readable.*
VG-8 VERY GOOD—*At least 3 letters in LIBERTY are visible.*
F-12 FINE—*Entire LIBERTY visible, weak spots.*
VF-20 VERY FINE—*Entire LIBERTY strong and even.*
EF-40 EXTREMELY FINE—*LIBERTY and scroll edges distinct.*
MS-60 UNCIRCULATED—*No trace of wear. Light blemishes.*

	Quan. Minted	*G-4*	*VG-8*	*F-12*	*VF-20*	*EF-40*	*MS-60*
1837	1,405,000	$10.00	$15.00	$25.00	$40.00	$80.00	$300.00
1838O No stars	70,000	30.00	42.00	75.00	140.00	275.00	800.00

Stars on Obverse 1838-1853

From 1838 through 1859 the mint mark is located above bow on reverse. Large, medium or small mint mark varieties occur for several dates.

1838	2,255,000	3.50	4.50	7.00	12.00	25.00	150.00
1839	1,069,150	3.50	4.50	7.00	12.00	25.00	160.00
1839O	1,034,039	4.50	7.00	10.00	15.00	35.00	250.00
1840	1,344,085	3.25	4.50	6.00	10.00	25.00	150.00
1840O	935,000	3.50	5.50	10.00	17.00	42.00	300.00
1841	1,150,000	3.25	4.50	6.00	10.00	20.00	100.00
1841O	815,000	5.50	9.00	12.00	20.00	35.00	350.00
1842	815,000	3.25	4.50	6.00	10.00	20.00	110.00
1842O	350,000	10.00	14.00	24.00	65.00	175.00	—
1843	1,165,000	3.25	4.50	6.00	10.00	22.00	100.00
1844	430,000	3.25	4.50	6.00	10.00	22.00	100.00
1844O	220,000	22.00	27.50	50.00	135.00	350.00	—
1845	1,564,000	3.25	4.50	6.00	10.00	22.00	100.00
1846	27,000	75.00	100.00	160.00	300.00	600.00	—
1847	1,274,000	3.25	4.50	6.00	10.00	22.00	100.00
1848	668,000	3.25	4.50	6.00	10.00	22.00	100.00
1848O	600,000	6.00	10.00	13.00	25.00	35.00	200.00
1849, 9 over 6		4.50	7.00	9.00	10.00	22.00	200.00
1849, 9 over 8	1,309,000	4.50	8.00	11.00	15.00	35.00	225.00
1849 Nor. date		3.25	4.50	6.00	10.00	22.00	100.00
1849O	140,000	11.00	20.00	35.00	100.00	200.00	—
1850	955,000	3.50	4.50	6.00	10.00	22.00	100.00
1850O	690,000	6.00	8.00	10.00	20.00	35.00	325.00
1851	781,000	3.50	4.50	6.00	10.00	22.00	100.00
1851O	860,000	6.00	9.00	10.00	20.00	35.00	275.00
1852	1,000,500	3.50	4.50	6.00	10.00	22.00	100.00
1852O	260,000	12.00	16.00	25.00	60.00	110.00	—
1853 No arrows	135,000	7.00	12.00	18.00	30.00	55.00	275.00
1853O No arrows	160,000	60.00	100.00	135.00	225.00	475.00	—

Arrows at Date 1853-1855

As on the dimes, quarters and halves, arrows were placed at the sides of the date for a short period starting in 1853 to denote reduction of weight.

HALF DIMES

	Quan. Minted	G-4	VG-8	F-12	VF-20	EF-40	MS-60	Proof-63
1853	13,210,020	$4.00	$5.00	$6.00	$8.00	$21.00	$110.00	
1853O	2,200,000	5.00	5.50	8.00	12.00	30.00	130.00	
1854	5,740,000	4.00	4.50	5.50	9.00	19.00	110.00	
1854O	1,560,000	4.00	4.50	7.00	11.00	25.00	200.00	
1855	1,750,000	4.00	4.50	5.50	10.00	21.00	110.00	$2,500
1855O	600,000	5.50	8.50	11.00	17.00	40.00	275.00	

No Arrows at Date 1856-1859

	Quan. Minted	G-4	VG-8	F-12	VF-20	EF-40	MS-60	Proof-63
1856	4,880,000	4.00	4.50	5.50	10.00	15.00	80.00	900.00
1856O	1,100,000	4.00	5.00	7.00	14.00	30.00	210.00	
1857	7,280,000	4.00	4.50	5.50	10.00	15.00	80.00	900.00
1857O	1,380,000	4.00	5.00	7.00	12.00	25.00	200.00	

1858 over Inverted Date

	Quan. Minted	G-4	VG-8	F-12	VF-20	EF-40	MS-60	Proof-63
1858	3,500,000	4.00	4.50	5.50	10.00	15.00	80.00	800.00
1858 over inv. date		8.50	15.00	30.00	50.00	100.00	250.00	
1858O	1,660,000	4.00	5.00	6.50	11.00	20.00	150.00	
1859	340,000	5.00	6.50	11.00	20.00	35.00	125.00	800.00
1859O	560,000	5.00	6.50	11.00	20.00	35.00	175.00	

Legend on Obverse 1860-1873

	Quan. Minted	G-4	VG-8	F-12	VF-20	EF-40	MS-60	Proof-63
1860 (1,000)	799,000	4.00	4.50	5.50	7.50	15.00	80.00	350.00
1860O	1,060,000	4.00	4.50	6.00	8.00	18.00	135.00	
1861 (1,000)	3,361,000	4.00	4.50	5.50	7.50	14.00	80.00	325.00
1862 (550)	1,492,550	4.00	4.50	6.00	7.50	14.00	80.00	325.00
1863 (460)	18,460	40.00	65.00	90.00	125.00	175.00	375.00	400.00
1863S	100,000	7.50	10.00	13.00	21.00	45.00	350.00	
1864 (470)	48,470	85.00	125.00	170.00	225.00	300.00	600.00	650.00
1864S	90,000	11.00	16.00	30.00	45.00	100.00	350.00	
1865 (500)	13,500	60.00	85.00	110.00	130.00	200.00	400.00	450.00
1865S	120,000	6.50	10.00	13.00	22.00	40.00	350.00	
1866 (725)	10,725	60.00	80.00	125.00	150.00	225.00	375.00	400.00
1866S	120,000	6.50	10.00	13.00	22.00	40.00	300.00	
1867 (625)	8,625	125.00	160.00	215.00	250.00	300.00	400.00	400.00
1867S	120,000	6.50	10.00	13.00	25.00	40.00	200.00	
1868 (600)	89,200	10.00	18.00	30.00	50.00	110.00	250.00	300.00
1868S	280,000	5.00	6.50	8.00	10.00	19.00	150.00	
1869 (600)	208,600	5.00	5.50	6.50	9.00	17.00	100.00	300.00
1869S	230,000	5.00	6.50	8.00	10.00	19.00	175.00	
1870 (1,000)	536,000	4.00	4.50	5.50	7.50	15.00	75.00	300.00
1870S	Unique							
1871 (960)	1,873,960	4.00	4.50	5.50	7.50	15.00	75.00	300.00
1871S	161,000	5.50	9.00	15.00	25.00	40.00	125.00	
1872 (950)	2,947,950	4.00	4.50	5.50	7.50	15.00	75.00	300.00
1872S	837,000	4.00	4.50	5.50	7.50	15.00	75.00	
1873 (600)	712,600	4.00	4.50	5.50	7.50	15.00	75.00	300.00
1873S	324,000	4.00	4.50	5.50	7.50	15.00	75.00	

DIMES — 1796 to Date

The designs of the dimes, first coined in 1796, follow closely those of the half dimes up through the Liberty seated type. The dimes in each instance weigh twice as much as the half dimes.

DRAPED BUST TYPE, SMALL EAGLE REVERSE 1796-1797

AG-3 ABOUT GOOD—*Details clear enough to identify.*
G-4 GOOD—*Date readable. Bust outlined, but no detail.*
VG-8 VERY GOOD—*All but deepest drapery folds worn smooth. Hairlines nearly gone and curls lack detail.*
F-12 FINE—*All drapery lines visible. Hair partly worn.*
VF-20 VERY FINE—*Only left side of drapery is indistinct.*
EF-40 EXTREMELY FINE—*Hair well outlined and shows details.*
MS-60 UNCIRCULATED—*No trace of wear. Light blemishes.*

1797, 16 Stars

1797, 13 Stars

	Quan. Minted	*AG-3*	*G-4*	*VG-8*	*F-12*	*VF-20*	*EF-40*	*MS-60*
1796	22,135	$200.00	$450.00	$750.00	$900.00	$1,500	$2,500	$4,500
1797 16 stars	} 25,261	200.00	450.00	750.00	900.00	1,500	2,500	4,500
1797 13 stars	}	200.00	450.00	750.00	900.00	1,500	2,500	4,500

DRAPED BUST TYPE, HERALDIC EAGLE REVERSE 1798-1807

1798 All kinds	27,550							
1798 over 97, 16 stars on rev.		100.00	225.00	250.00	425.00	600.00	1,000	2,700
1798 over 97, 13 stars		225.00	500.00	900.00	1,400	2,500	—	
1798		90.00	210.00	225.00	400.00	550.00	900.00	2,300
1800	21,760	100.00	210.00	225.00	400.00	550.00	900.00	2,500
1801	34,640	100.00	210.00	250.00	400.00	550.00	1,000	3,000
1802	10,975	100.00	250.00	350.00	550.00	1,000	1,900	6,000
1803	33,040	90.00	200.00	250.00	400.00	550.00	900.00	2,800
1804	8,265	225.00	450.00	650.00	1,000	1,800	3,750	6,000
1805	120,780	65.00	150.00	225.00	325.00	450.00	750.00	1,800
1807	165,000	65.00	150.00	225.00	325.00	450.00	750.00	1,800

CAPPED BUST TYPE 1809-1837

G-4 GOOD—*Date, letters and stars discernible. Bust outlined, no details.*
VG-8 VERY GOOD—*Legends and date plain. Minimum of 3 letters in LIBERTY.*
F-12 FINE—*Full LIBERTY. Ear and shoulder clasp visible. Part of rim shows both sides.*
VF-20 VERY FINE—*LIBERTY distinct. Full rim. Ear and clasp plain and distinct.*
EF-40 EXTREMELY FINE—*LIBERTY sharp. Ear distinct. Hair above eye well defined.*
MS-60 UNCIRCULATED—*No trace of wear. Light blemishes.*

DIMES

Wide Border 1809-1828

	Quan. Minted	G-4	VG-8	F-12	VF-20	EF-40	MS-60
1809	51,065	$45.00	$65.00	$100.00	$200.00	$425.00	$1,600
1811 over 9	65,180	25.00	40.00	60.00	110.00	275.00	1,500
1814	421,500	12.00	15.00	25.00	70.00	175.00	650.00
1820	942,587	8.00	10.00	18.00	45.00	150.00	500.00
1821	1,186,512	8.00	10.00	18.00	45.00	150.00	500.00
1822	100,000	100.00	200.00	325.00	500.00	1,000	3,200
1823, 3 over 2, all kinds	440,000						
1823, 3 over 2, small E's		8.00	10.00	18.00	45.00	150.00	500.00
1823, 3 over 2, large E's		8.00	10.00	18.00	45.00	150.00	500.00

1823, 3 over 2

1824, 4 over 2

1828 Large Date

1828 Small Date

	Quan. Minted	G-4	VG-8	F-12	VF-20	EF-40	MS-60
1824, 4 over 2 }	510,000	9.00	12.00	22.50	65.00	200.00	750.00
1825 }		8.00	10.00	18.00	45.00	125.00	450.00
1827	1,215,000	8.00	10.00	18.00	45.00	125.00	450.00
1828 Both vars	125,000						
1828 Large date, curl base 2		13.00	18.00	35.00	70.00	200.00	800.00

Modified Design 1828-1837

1829 Small 10c

Large 10c

1830, 30 over 29

	Quan. Minted	G-4	F-12	VF-20	EF-40	MS-60
1828 Small date, sq. base 2		$12.00	$25.00	$45.00	$135.00	$600.00
1829 Small 10c }	770,000	7.00	12.00	25.00	90.00	400.00
1829 Medium 10c }		7.00	12.00	23.00	90.00	325.00
1829 Large 10c }		10.00	18.00	30.00	100.00	400.00
1830, 30 over 29 }	510,000	15.00	40.00	80.00	175.00	500.00
1830 Large 10c }		7.00	11.00	23.00	90.00	325.00
1830 Small 10c }		7.00	11.00	23.00	90.00	325.00
1831	771,350	7.00	11.00	23.00	90.00	325.00
1832	522,500	7.00	11.00	23.00	90.00	325.00
1833	485,000	7.00	11.00	23.00	90.00	325.00
1834	635,000	7.00	11.00	23.00	90.00	325.00
1835	1,410,000	7.00	11.00	23.00	90.00	325.00
1836	1,190,000	7.00	11.00	23.00	90.00	325.00
1837	359,500	7.00	11.00	23.00	90.00	325.00

DIMES

LIBERTY SEATED TYPE 1837-1891

No Stars on Obverse 1837-1838

G-4 GOOD—*LIBERTY on shield smooth. Date and letters readable.*
F-12 FINE—*Entire LIBERTY visible, weak spots.*
VF-20 VERY FINE—*Entire LIBERTY strong and even.*
EF-40 EXTREMELY FINE—*LIBERTY and scroll edges distinct.*
MS-60 UNCIRCULATED—*No trace of wear. Light blemishes.*

No Drapery from Elbow
No Stars on Obverse

Mint marks on Liberty seated dimes are placed on the reverse, within or below the wreath.

	Quan. Minted	*G-4*	*F-12*	*VF-20*	*EF-40*	*MS-60*
1837	682,500	$12.00	$30.00	$100.00	$200.00	$600.00
1838O	406,034	15.00	50.00	125.00	275.00	1,500

Stars on Obverse 1838-1853

No Drapery from Elbow
Tilted Shield

1838 Small Stars **1838 Large Stars**

1838 Small stars	1,992,500	6.50	16.00	35.00	70.00	400.00
1838 Large stars		4.00	6.50	10.00	30.00	150.00
1838 Partial drapery		6.50	15.00	25.00	55.00	400.00
1839	1,053,115	3.25	5.50	9.00	25.00	135.00
1839O	1,323,000	4.00	7.00	14.00	27.00	175.00
1840	981,500	3.25	5.50	9.00	20.00	135.00
1840O	1,175,000	3.50	7.00	15.00	30.00	475.00

Drapery from Elbow
Upright Shield

	Quan. Minted	*G-4*	*F-12*	*VF-20*	*EF-40*	*MS-60*	*Proof-63*
1840	377,500	$10.00	$25.00	$50.00	$125.00	$400.00	
1841	1,622,500	3.00	4.00	7.00	18.00	135.00	
1841O	2,007,500	3.50	7.00	12.00	25.00	425.00	
1842	1,887,500	3.00	4.00	7.00	18.00	135.00	
1842O	2,020,000	3.00	4.00	10.00	50.00	1,200	
1843	1,370,000	3.00	4.00	7.00	18.00	135.00	
1843O	150,000	13.00	40.00	90.00	175.00	650.00	
1844	72,500	35.00	125.00	175.00	310.00	1,000	

DIMES

	Quan. Minted	G-4	F-12	VF-20	EF-40	MS-60	Proof-63
1845	1,755,000	$3.00	$4.00	$7.00	$18.00	$135.00	
1845O	230,000	7.00	20.00	65.00	150.00	625.00	
1846	31,300	25.00	60.00	135.00	325.00	1,100	
1847	245,000	5.00	14.00	25.00	50.00	350.00	
1848	451,500	3.25	5.50	12.00	30.00	200.00	
1849	839,000	3.00	4.00	7.00	18.00	175.00	
1849O	300,000	5.00	10.00	40.00	100.00	1,000	
1850	1,931,500	3.00	4.00	7.00	18.00	135.00	
1850O	510,000	4.00	8.00	30.00	65.00	425.00	
1851	1,026,500	3.00	4.00	7.00	18.00	160.00	
1851O	400,000	5.00	10.00	25.00	75.00	750.00	
1852	1,535,500	3.00	4.00	7.00	18.00	150.00	
1852O	430,000	5.00	12.00	40.00	90.00	850.00	
1853 No arrows	95,000	17.50	32.50	50.00	135.00	350.00	

Arrows at Date 1853-1855

1853-1855
Arrows at Date

1856-1860
Small Date, Arrows Removed

	Quan. Minted	G-4	F-12	VF-20	EF-40	MS-60	Proof-63
1853 With arrows	12,078,010	2.50	4.00	7.00	20.00	150.00	
1853O	1,100,000	3.00	4.50	10.00	40.00	300.00	
1854	4,470,000	2.50	4.00	7.00	20.00	150.00	$5,000
1854O	1,770,000	3.00	4.50	9.00	35.00	275.00	
1855	2,075,000	2.50	4.00	7.00	20.00	175.00	3,000

No Arrows at Date 1856-1860

	Quan. Minted	G-4	F-12	VF-20	EF-40	MS-60	Proof-63
1856 Lg. date }	5,780,000	2.50	3.75	7.00	16.00	140.00	
1856 Sm. date }		2.50	3.75	7.00	16.00	140.00	1,100
1856O	1,180,000	2.50	4.00	9.00	20.00	135.00	
1856S	70,000	22.00	80.00	125.00	250.00	—	
1857	5,580,000	2.50	3.75	7.00	15.00	135.00	700.00
1857O	1,540,000	2.50	3.75	7.00	15.00	150.00	
1858 (300+)	1,540,000	2.50	3.75	7.00	15.00	135.00	700.00
1858O	290,000	5.00	12.00	30.00	75.00	300.00	
1858S	60,000	22.00	50.00	100.00	225.00	—	
1859 (800)	430,000	2.50	5.00	10.00	25.00	135.00	600.00
1859O	480,000	2.50	6.00	17.00	35.00	150.00	
1859S	60,000	25.00	70.00	150.00	275.00	1,200	
1860S	140,000	6.00	17.00	45.00	100.00	—	

Legend on Obverse 1860-1873

DIMES

	Quan. Minted	G-4	F-12	VF-20	EF-40	MS-60	Proof-63
1860 ....(1,000)	607,000	$2.50	$4.00	$6.50	$11.00	$100.00	$250.00
1860O	40,000	150.00	350.00	550.00	1,100	—	
1861 ....(1,000)	1,884,000	2.50	4.00	6.50	11.00	100.00	300.00
1861S	172,500	8.00	22.00	50.00	110.00	550.00	
1862 ....(550)	847,550	2.50	4.00	6.50	13.00	110.00	300.00
1862S	180,750	7.00	18.00	40.00	100.00	525.00	
1863 ....(460)	14,460	65.00	135.00	220.00	300.00	500.00	375.00
1863S	157,500	8.50	20.00	40.00	65.00	450.00	
1864 ....(470)	11,470	60.00	125.00	180.00	300.00	500.00	375.00
1864S	230,000	5.50	15.00	30.00	60.00	500.00	
1865 ....(500)	10,500	65.00	140.00	210.00	310.00	525.00	375.00
1865S	175,000	5.50	15.00	30.00	100.00	600.00	
1866 ....(725)	8,725	110.00	200.00	375.00	400.00	600.00	375.00
1866S	135,000	6.50	15.00	30.00	100.00	550.00	
1867 ....(625)	6,625	120.00	225.00	325.00	400.00	675.00	400.00
1867S	140,000	5.50	14.00	30.00	65.00	600.00	
1868 ....(600)	464,600	2.75	6.00	14.00	30.00	175.00	300.00
1868S	260,000	5.00	10.00	30.00	60.00	175.00	
1869 ....(600)	256,600	3.50	8.00	18.00	35.00	185.00	300.00
1869S	450,000	4.00	7.00	15.00	35.00	200.00	
1870 ....(1,000)	471,500	2.50	4.00	8.00	17.00	110.00	275.00
1870S	50,000	75.00	100.00	135.00	175.00	700.00	
1871 ....(960)	907,710	2.50	4.00	6.50	13.00	100.00	275.00
1871CC	20,100	240.00	550.00	850.00	1,500	—	
1871S	320,000	5.00	14.00	25.00	60.00	250.00	
1872 ....(950)	2,396,450	2.50	4.00	6.50	13.00	75.00	275.00
1872CC	35,480	120.00	250.00	600.00	1,200	—	
1872S	190,000	7.50	20.00	35.00	90.00	500.00	
1873 Closed 3 (1,100)	1,508,000	2.50	4.00	6.50	13.00	100.00	275.00
1873 Open 3	60,000	8.00	20.00	30.00	60.00	175.00	
1873CC (Unique)	12,400					—	

Arrows at Date 1873-1874

In 1873 the dime was increased in weight to 2.50 grams. Arrows at date in 1873 and 1874 indicate this change.

	Quan. Minted	G-4	F-12	VF-20	EF-40	MS-60	Proof-63
1873 ....(800)	2,378,500	$4.00	$9.00	$20.00	$50.00	$275.00	$700.00
1873CC	18,791	275.00	700.00	1,000	2,000	—	
1873S	455,000	6.00	15.00	28.00	55.00	400.00	
1874 ....(700)	2,940,000	4.00	9.00	20.00	50.00	275.00	700.00
1874CC	10,817	500.00	1,750	2,500	4,000	—	
1874S	240,000	8.50	20.00	40.00	70.00	340.00	

No Arrows at Date 1875-1891

	Quan. Minted	G-4	F-12	VF-20	EF-40	MS-60	Proof-63
1875 ....(700)	10,350,700	2.25	3.50	5.00	10.00	75.00	275.00
1875CC	4,645,000	2.25	3.50	5.00	15.00	100.00	
1875S	9,070,000	2.25	3.50	5.00	11.00	75.00	
1876 ....(1,150)	11,461,150	2.25	3.50	5.00	10.00	75.00	275.00
1876CC	8,270,000	2.25	3.50	5.00	12.00	100.00	
1876S	10,420,000	2.25	3.50	5.00	11.00	75.00	
1877 ....(510)	7,310,510	2.25	3.50	5.00	11.00	75.00	300.00
1877CC	7,700,000	2.25	3.50	5.00	11.00	100.00	
1877S	2,340,000	2.25	3.50	5.00	11.00	100.00	

DIMES

	Quan. Minted	G-4	F-12	VF-20	EF-40	MS-60	Proof-63
1878 ....(800)	1,678,000	$2.25	$3.50	$5.00	$11.00	$80.00	$275.00
1878CC	200,000	13.00	40.00	55.00	135.00	375.00	
1879 ....(1,100)	15,100	50.00	110.00	150.00	200.00	350.00	250.00
1880 ....(1,355)	37,355	35.00	75.00	95.00	150.00	275.00	300.00
1881 ....(975)	24,975	40.00	85.00	120.00	175.00	300.00	300.00
1882 ....(1,100)	3,911,100	2.25	3.50	5.00	10.00	75.00	250.00
1883 ....(1,039)	7,675,712	2.25	3.50	5.00	10.00	75.00	250.00
1884 ....(875)	3,366,380	2.25	3.50	5.00	10.00	75.00	250.00
1884S	564,969	4.50	10.00	20.00	30.00	325.00	
1885 ....(930)	2,533,427	2.25	3.50	5.00	10.00	75.00	250.00
1885S	43,690	110.00	220.00	425.00	850.00	2,500	
1886 ....(886)	6,377,570	2.25	3.50	5.00	10.00	75.00	250.00
1886S	206,524	6.00	14.00	25.00	35.00	250.00	
1887 ....(710)	11,283,939	2.25	3.50	5.00	10.00	75.00	250.00
1887S	4,454,450	2.25	3.50	5.00	10.00	75.00	
1888 ....(832)	5,496,487	2.25	3.50	5.00	10.00	75.00	250.00
1888S	1,720,000	2.25	3.50	5.00	12.00	100.00	
1889 ....(711)	7,380,711	2.25	3.50	5.00	10.00	75.00	250.00
1889S	972,678	4.50	10.00	20.00	35.00	200.00	
1890 ....(590)	9,911,541	2.25	3.50	5.00	10.00	75.00	250.00
1890S	1,423,076	3.00	7.00	14.00	24.00	125.00	
1891 ....(600)	15,310,600	2.25	3.50	5.00	10.00	75.00	250.00
1891O	4,540,000	2.25	3.50	5.00	12.00	100.00	
1891S	3,196,116	2.25	3.50	5.00	13.00	100.00	

BARBER or LIBERTY HEAD TYPE 1892-1916

This type was designed by Charles E. Barber, Chief Engraver of the Mint. His initial B is at the truncation of the neck. He also designed quarters and half dollars of the same period.

G-4 GOOD—*Date and letters plain. LIBERTY Is obliterated.*
VG-8 VERY GOOD—*At least 3 letters visible in LIBERTY.*
F-12 FINE—*All letters in LIBERTY visible, though some are weak.*
VF-20 VERY FINE—*All letters of LBERTY evenly plain.*
EF-40 EXTREMELY FINE—*All letters in LIBERTY are sharp, distinct. Headband edges are distinct.*
MS-60 UNCIRCULATED—*No trace of wear. Light blemishes.*

Mint mark location is on the reverse below the wreath.

	Quan. Minted	G-4	VG-8	F-12	VF-20	EF-40	MS-60	Proof-63
1892 ....(1,245)	12,121,245	$1.00	$1.25	$4.00	$6.50	$10.00	$50.00	$250.00
1892O	3,841,700	2.25	3.50	6.00	10.00	18.00	80.00	
1892S ....(792)	990,710	14.00	25.00	50.00	65.00	85.00	200.00	
1893, 3 over 2 }					—	55.00	200.00	450.00
1893 }	3,340,792	2.00	3.00	5.00	8.00	14.00	80.00	200.00
1893O	1,760,000	7.00	10.00	30.00	45.00	50.00	150.00	
1893S	2,491,401	3.00	6.00	8.00	12.00	20.00	120.00	
1894 ....(972)	1,330,972	3.50	7.00	25.00	40.00	50.00	125.00	200.00
1894O	720,000	18.00	28.00	70.00	90.00	160.00	575.00	
1894S	24						90,000	
1895 ....(880)	690,880	30.00	35.00	100.00	150.00	175.00	310.00	250.00
1895O	440,000	100.00	135.00	285.00	450.00	750.00	1,500	
1895S	1,120,000	8.00	13.00	40.00	50.00	65.00	180.00	
1896 ....(762)	2,000,762	2.00	5.00	10.00	15.00	25.00	80.00	200.00
1896O	610,000	24.00	35.00	80.00	110.00	160.00	425.00	
1896S	575,056	22.00	32.00	75.00	100.00	135.00	340.00	

DIMES

	Quan. Minted	G-4	VG-8	F-12	VF-20	EF-40	MS-60	Proof-63
1897	(731) 10,869,264	*$.60*	*$.75*	$2.00	$3.50	$10.00	$65.00	$200.00
1897O	666,000	20.00	30.00	100.00	125.00	170.00	400.00	
1897S	1,342,844	3.00	6.00	20.00	35.00	50.00	200.00	
1898	(735) 16,320,735	*.50*	*.70*	1.35	3.50	10.00	60.00	200.00
1898O	2,130,000	1.25	4.00	22.00	37.00	55.00	200.00	
1898S	1,702,507	1.00	3.00	8.00	12.00	20.00	125.00	
1899	(846) 19,580,846	*.50*	*.70*	1.35	3.50	10.00	60.00	200.00
1899O	2,650,000	*1.00*	3.00	15.00	25.00	50.00	175.00	
1899S	1,867,493	*1.00*	2.00	5.00	9.00	15.00	110.00	
1900	(912) 17,600,912	*.60*	*.75*	1.35	3.50	10.00	60.00	200.00
1900O	2,010,000	2.00	3.50	20.00	35.00	75.00	250.00	
1900S	5,168,270	*.80*	1.25	2.50	4.00	12.00	90.00	
1901	(813) 18,860,478	*.60*	*.75*	1.35	3.50	10.00	50.00	200.00
1901O	5,620,000	*.80*	1.25	2.50	6.00	20.00	180.00	
1901S	593,022	22.00	30.00	100.00	160.00	200.00	450.00	
1902	(777) 21,380,777	*.50*	*.70*	1.35	3.50	10.00	50.00	200.00
1902O	4,500,000	*.80*	1.25	3.00	8.00	16.00	150.00	
1902S	2,070,000	2.00	3.00	8.00	17.00	35.00	160.00	
1903	(755)...19,500,755	*.50*	*.70*	1.35	3.50	10.00	50.00	200.00
1903O	8,180,000	*.80*	1.25	2.00	4.00	13.00	135.00	
1903S	613,300	18.00	28.00	125.00	175.00	300.00	550.00	
1904	(670) 14,601,027	*.50*	*.70*	1.35	3.50	10.00	50.00	200.00
1904S	800,000	12.00	18.00	45.00	65.00	100.00	300.00	
1905	(727) 14,552,350	*.50*	*.70*	1.35	3.50	10.00	50.00	200.00
1905O	3,400,000	*.50*	1.50	8.00	12.00	20.00	110.00	
1905S	6,855,199	*.50*	1.25	2.50	4.50	12.00	110.00	
1906	(675) 19,958,406	*.50*	*.70*	1.35	3.50	10.00	50.00	200.00
1906D	4,060,000	*.50*	1.25	2.50	4.50	11.00	80.00	
1906O	2,610,000	*.80*	2.25	12.00	20.00	30.00	115.00	
1906S	3,136,640	*.70*	1.25	3.00	6.00	14.00	110.00	
1907	(575) 22,220,575	*.50*	*.70*	1.35	3.50	10.00	50.00	200.00
1907D	4,080,000	*.50*	1.00	2.25	4.25	13.00	115.00	
1907O	5,058,000	*.50*	1.00	6.00	10.00	18.00	90.00	
1907S	3,178,470	*.80*	1.25	2.50	5.00	15.00	135.00	
1908	(545) 10,600,545	*.50*	*.70*	1.35	3.50	10.00	50.00	200.00
1908D	7,490,000	*.50*	1.00	2.25	3.00	11.00	75.00	
1908O	1,789,000	*.80*	3.00	16.00	20.00	28.00	140.00	
1908S	3,220,000	*.50*	1.00	2.25	4.00	12.00	110.00	
1909	(650) 10,240,650	*.60*	*.75*	1.35	2.75	10.00	50.00	200.00
1909D	954,000	1.25	3.00	12.00	25.00	40.00	175.00	
1909O	2,287,000	*.70*	1.50	3.00	7.00	15.00	90.00	
1909S	1,000,000	1.25	4.00	22.00	30.00	60.00	220.00	
1910	(551) 11,520,551	*.50*	*.70*	1.35	2.75	10.00	50.00	200.00
1910D	3,490,000	*.50*	1.25	2.25	4.00	14.00	100.00	
1910S	1,240,000	*.50*	1.25	15.00	25.00	32.00	160.00	
1911	(543) 18,870,543	*.50*	*.70*	1.35	2.75	10.00	50.00	200.00
1911D	11,209,000	*.50*	*.70*	1.35	2.75	10.00	50.00	
1911S	3,520,000	*.50*	1.25	2.25	4.00	12.00	85.00	
1912	(700) 19,350,000	*.50*	*.70*	1.35	2.75	10.00	50.00	200.00
1912D	11,760,000	*.50*	*.70*	1.35	2.75	10.00	50.00	
1912S	3,420,000	*.50*	1.25	2.25	4.00	12.00	100.00	
1913	(622) 19,760,622	*.50*	*.70*	1.35	2.75	10.00	50.00	200.00
1913S	510,000	4.00	8.00	32.00	45.00	75.00	200.00	
1914	(425) 17,360,655	*.50*	*.70*	1.35	2.75	10.00	50.00	200.00
1914D	11,908,000	*.50*	*.70*	1.35	2.75	10.00	50.00	
1914S	2,100,000	*.50*	1.25	2.25	4.00	10.00	90.00	
1915	(450) 5,620,450	*.50*	*.70*	1.35	2.75	10.00	50.00	200.00
1915S	960,000	*.70*	1.50	8.00	11.00	20.00	100.00	
1916	18,490,000	*.50*	*.70*	1.35	2.75	10.00	50.00	
1916S	5,820,000	*.50*	*.70*	1.35	2.75	10.00	50.00	

Italic prices indicate unsettled values due to fluctuating bullion market. See Bullion Chart.

DIMES

WINGED LIBERTY HEAD or "MERCURY" TYPE 1916-1945

Although this coin is commonly called the "Mercury Dime," the main device is in fact a representation of Liberty. The wings crowning her cap are intended to symbolize liberty of thought. The designer's monogram AW is right of neck.

Mint mark location is on reverse left of fasces.

G-4 GOOD—*Letters and date clear. Lines and bands in fasces are obliterated.*
VG-8 VERY GOOD—*One-half of sticks discernible in fasces.*
F-12 FINE—*All sticks in fasces are defined. Diagonal bands worn nearly flat.*
VF-20 VERY FINE—*The two crossing diagonal bands must show.*
EF-40 EXTREMELY FINE—*Diagonal bands show only slight wear. Braids and hair before ear show clearly.*
MS-60 UNCIRCULATED—*No trace of wear. Light blemishes.*
MS-63 SELECT UNCIRCULATED—*No trace of wear. Slight blemishes.*

Uncirculated values shown are for average pieces with minimum blemishes, those with sharp strikes and split bands on reverse are worth much more.

	Quan. Minted	*G-4*	*VG-8*	*F-12*	*VF-20*	*EF-40*	*MS-60*	*MS-63*
1916	22,180,080	*$.75*	*$1.00*	*$1.25*	$2.00	$3.00	$14.00	$20.00
1916D	264,000	260.00	410.00	650.00	950.00	1,600	2,600	3,500
1916S	10,450,000	*1.00*	*1.25*	1.50	3.00	7.00	15.00	26.00
1917	55,230,000	*.35*	*.40*	*.50*	1.25	2.50	10.00	20.00
1917D	9,402,000	*1.00*	*1.25*	2.00	5.00	15.00	50.00	150.00
1917S	27,330,000	*.35*	*.50*	*.50*	1.50	3.50	20.00	65.00
1918	26,680,000	*.35*	*.40*	*.75*	3.00	10.00	27.00	60.00
1918D	22,674,800	*.35*	*.40*	*.50*	3.00	9.00	40.00	100.00
1918S	19,300,000	*.35*	*.40*	*.50*	2.00	5.00	30.00	100.00
1919	35,740,000	*.35*	*.40*	*.50*	1.50	2.50	15.00	45.00
1919D	9,939,000	*.35*	*.50*	1.00	6.00	15.00	65.00	225.00
1919S	8,850,000	*.35*	*.40*	*.75*	4.50	10.00	70.00	225.00
1920	59,030,000	*.35*	*.40*	*.45*	2.00	3.00	10.00	30.00
1920D	19,171,000	*.35*	*.40*	*.45*	3.00	8.00	40.00	140.00
1920S	13,820,000	*.35*	*.40*	*.45*	2.50	7.00	30.00	115.00
1921	1,230,000	12.00	20.00	40.00	85.00	250.00	550.00	850.00
1921D	1,080,000	20.00	28.00	52.00	125.00	275.00	575.00	950.00
1923	50,130,000	*.35*	*.40*	*.45*	1.00	1.75	10.00	20.00
1923S	6,440,000	*.35*	*.40*	*.60*	2.50	10.00	55.00	175.00
1924	24,010,000	*.35*	*.40*	*.45*	1.25	3.00	20.00	45.00
1924D	6,810,000	*.35*	*.40*	1.00	2.50	10.00	75.00	150.00
1924S	7,120,000	*.35*	*.40*	1.00	2.25	10.00	70.00	250.00
1925	25,610,000	*.35*	*.40*	*.45*	1.25	2.25	12.00	30.00
1925D	5,117,000	1.50	2.00	4.00	12.00	40.00	130.00	250.00
1925S	5,850,000	*.35*	*.40*	1.00	2.50	15.00	65.00	200.00
1926	32,160,000	*.35*	*.40*	*.45*	1.25	2.00	10.00	20.00
1926D	6,828,000	*.35*	*.40*	*.45*	2.00	6.00	35.00	100.00
1926S	1,520,000	2.50	3.50	7.50	17.00	86.00	400.00	820.00
1927	28,080,000	*.35*	*.40*	*.45*	1.00	1.75	9.00	18.00
1927D	4,812,000	*.35*	*.40*	1.00	5.00	12.00	75.00	200.00
1927S	4,770,000	*.35*	*.40*	*.45*	1.30	6.00	100.00	200.00
1928	19,480,000	*.35*	*.40*	*.45*	1.00	1.75	8.00	20.00
1928D	4,161,000	*.35*	*.40*	1.75	5.00	12.00	65.00	150.00

Italic prices indicate unsettled values due to fluctuating bullion market. See Bullion Chart.

DIMES

	Quan. Minted	G-4	VG-8	F-12	VF-20	EF-40	MS-60	MS-63
1928S	7,400,000	$.35	$.40	$.45	$1.25	$4.00	$30.00	$80.00
1929	25,970,000	.35	.40	.45	1.00	1.50	7.00	10.00
1929D	5,034,000	.35	.40	.45	1.75	3.00	12.00	15.00
1929S	4,730,000	.35	.40	.45	1.25	2.00	15.00	18.00
1930	6,770,000	.35	.40	.45	1.00	2.00	10.00	18.00
1930S	1,843,000	.50	1.00	1.25	1.50	3.00	30.00	45.00
1931	3,150,000	.35	.40	.45	1.50	3.50	15.00	30.00
1931D	1,260,000	2.00	2.50	3.50	6.00	11.00	40.00	50.00
1931S	1,800,000	.50	1.00	1.50	2.00	4.00	30.00	40.00

1942, 2 over 1

1942D, 2 over 1

	Quan. Minted	VG-8	F-12	VF-20	EF-40	MS-60	MS-63	Proof-63
1934	24,080,000	$.30	$.30	$.40	$.45	$6.00	$8.00	
1934D	6,772,000	.30	.30	.40	.45	15.00	18.00	
1935	58,830,000	.30	.30	.40	.45	5.00	7.00	
1935D	10,477,000	.30	.30	.40	.45	15.00	18.00	
1935S	15,840,000	.30	.30	.40	.45	9.00	12.00	
1936 (4,130)	87,504,130	.30	.30	.40	.45	6.00	9.00	$275.00
1936D	16,132,000	.30	.30	.40	.45	11.00	13.00	
1936S	9,210,000	.30	.30	.40	.45	8.00	10.00	
1937 (5,756)	56,865,756	.30	.30	.40	.45	4.00	7.00	135.00
1937D	14,146,000	.30	.30	.40	.45	10.00	13.00	
1937S	9,740,000	.30	.30	.40	.45	7.00	10.00	
1938 (8,728)	22,198,728	.30	.30	.40	.45	4.00	7.00	90.00
1938D	5,537,000	.30	.30	.40	.45	7.00	8.00	
1938S	8,090,000	.30	.30	.40	.45	6.00	7.00	
1939 (9,321)	67,749,321	.30	.30	.40	.45	3.00	5.00	90.00
1939D	24,394,000	.30	.30	.40	.45	3.00	5.00	
1939S	10,540,000	.30	.30	.40	.45	8.00	12.00	
1940 (11,827)	65,361,827	.30	.30	.40	.45	3.00	4.00	70.00
1940D	21,198,000	.30	.30	.40	.45	3.00	6.00	
1940S	21,560,000	.30	.30	.40	.45	3.00	5.00	
1941 (16,557)	175,106,557	.30	.30	.40	.45	3.00	4.00	65.00
1941D	45,634,000	.30	.30	.40	.45	3.00	6.00	
1941S	43,090,000	.30	.30	.40	.45	3.00	5.00	
1942, 2 over 1	205,432,329	110.00	125.00	170.00	200.00	800.00	1,300	
1942 (22,329)		.30	.30	.40	.45	3.00	4.00	65.00
1942D, 2 over 1	60,740,000	110.00	140.00	180.00	250.00	775.00	1,200	
1942D		.30	.30	.40	.45	4.00	6.00	
1942S	49,300,000	.30	.30	.40	.45	5.00	7.00	
1943	191,710,000	.30	.30	.40	.45	3.00	4.00	
1943D	71,949,000	.30	.30	.40	.45	4.00	5.00	
1943S	60,400,000	.30	.30	.40	.45	4.00	5.00	
1944	231,410,000	.30	.30	.40	.45	3.00	4.00	
1944D	62,224,000	.30	.30	.40	.45	3.00	4.00	
1944S	49,490,000	.30	.30	.40	.45	3.00	4.00	
1945	159,130,000	.30	.30	.40	.45	3.00	4.00	

Italic prices indicate unsettled values due to fluctuating bullion market. See Bullion Chart.

DIMES

	Quan. Minted	VG-8	F-12	VF-20	EF-40	MS-60	MS-63	Proof-63
1945D	40,245,000	*$.30*	*$.30*	*$.40*	*$.45*	$3.00	$4.00	
1945S Normal S	41,920,000	*.30*	*.30*	*.40*	*.45*	3.00	5.00	
1945S Micro S		*.30*	*.30*	*.40*	*.45*	7.00	12.00	

ROOSEVELT TYPE 1946 to Date

John R. Sinnock (whose initials JS are at the truncation of the neck) designed this dime showing a portrait of Franklin D. Roosevelt. The design has heavier lettering and a more modernistic character than preceding types.

VF-20 VERY FINE—*Hair above ear slightly worn. All vertical lines on torch plain.*
EF-40 EXTREMELY FINE—*All lines of torch, flame and hair very plain.*
MS-63 SELECT UNCIRCULATED—*No trace of wear. Slight blemishes.*

SILVER COINAGE — 1946-1964

Mint mark on reverse 1946-1964.

	Quan. Minted	VF-20	EF-40	MS-63	Proof-63
1946	255,250,000	*$.30*	*$.32*	$.50	
1946D	61,043,500	*.30*	*.32*	.45	
1946S	27,900,000	*.30*	*.32*	.60	
1947	121,520,000	*.30*	*.32*	.60	
1947D	46,835,000	*.30*	*.32*	.75	
1947S	34,840,000	*.30*	*.32*	.50	
1948	74,950,000	*.30*	*.32*	1.10	
1948D	52,841,000	*.30*	*.32*	1.00	
1948S	35,520,000	*.30*	*.32*	1.00	
1949	30,940,000	*.30*	*.32*	6.00	
1949D	26,034,000	*.30*	*.32*	2.00	
1949S	13,510,000	*.30*	*.32*	10.00	
1950 ....(51,386)	50,181,500	*.30*	*.32*	1.00	$10.00
1950D	46,803,000	*.30*	*.32*	.75	
1950S	20,440,000	*.30*	*.32*	5.00	
1951 ....(57,500)	103,937,602	*.30*	*.32*	.50	7.00
1951D	56,529,000	*.30*	*.32*	.50	
1951S	31,630,000	*.30*	*.32*	2.75	
1952 ....(81,980)	99,122,073	*.30*	*.32*	.50	6.00
1952D	122,100,000	*.30*	*.32*	.50	
1952S	44,419,500	*.30*	*.32*	2.00	
1953 ....(128,800)	53,618,920	*.30*	*.32*	.50	3.50
1953D	136,433,000	*.30*	*.32*	.60	
1953S	39,180,000	*.30*	*.32*	.60	
1954 ....(233,300)	114,243,503	*.30*	*.32*	.50	1.25
1954D	106,397,000	*.30*	*.32*	.50	
1954S	22,860,000	*.30*	*.32*	.50	
1955 ....(378,200)	12,828,381	*.30*	*.32*	.75	1.25
1955D	13,959,000	*.30*	*.32*	.50	
1955S	18,510,000	*.30*	*.32*	.50	
1956 ....(669,384)	109,309,384	*.30*	*.32*	.50	.65
1956D	108,015,100	*.30*	*.32*	.50	
1957 ....(1,247,952)	161,407,952	*.30*	*.32*	.45	.65
1957D	113,354,330	*.30*	*.32*	.45	

Italic prices indicate unsettled values due to fluctuating bullion market. See Bullion Chart.

DIMES

	Quan. Minted	VF-20	EF-40	MS-63	Proof-63
1958........................(875,652)	32,785,652	*$.30*	*$.32*	*$.40*	$.65
1958D	136,564,600	*.30*	*.32*	*.40*	
1959....................(1,149,291)	86,929,291	*.30*	*.32*	*.40*	.65
1959D	164,919,790	*.30*	*.32*	*.40*	
1960....................(1,691,602)	72,081,602	*.30*	*.32*	*.40*	.65
1960D	200,160,400	*.30*	*.32*	*.40*	
1961....................(3,028,244)	96,758,244	*.30*	*.32*	*.40*	.50
1961D	209,146,550	*.30*	*.32*	*.40*	
1962....................(3,218,019)	75,668,019	*.30*	*.32*	*.40*	.50
1962D	334,948,380	*.30*	*.32*	*.40*	
1963....................(3,075,645)	126,725,645	*.30*	*.32*	*.40*	.50
1963D	421,476,530	*.30*	*.32*	*.40*	
1964....................(3,950,762)	933,310,762	*.30*	*.32*	*.40*	.50
1964D	1,357,517,180	*.30*	*.32*	*.40*	

Clad Coinage

Mint mark on obverse starting 1968

	Quan. Minted	MS-63	Proof-63
1965	1,652,140,570	$.12	
1966	1,382,734,540	.12	
1967	2,244,007,320	.12	
1968	424,470,400	.11	
1968D	480,748,280	.11	
1968S Proof	(3,041,506)		$.20
1969	145,790,000	.15	
1969D	563,323,870	.12	
1969S Proof	(2,934,631)		.20
1970	345,570,000	.12	
1970D	754,942,100	.12	
1970S Proof	(2,632,810)		.20
1971	162,690,000	.15	
1971D	377,914,240	.14	
1971S Proof	(3,220,733)		.20
1972	431,540,000	.13	
1972D	330,290,000	.12	
1972S Proof	(3,260,996)		.20
1973	315,670,000	.12	
1973D	455,032,426	.12	
1973S Proof	(2,760,339)		.20
1974	470,248,000	.12	
1974D	571,083,000	.12	
1974S Proof	(2,612,568)		.25
1975	585,673,900	.13	
1975D	313,705,300	.12	
1975S Proof	(2,845,450)		.30
1976	568,760,000	.13	
1976D	695,222,774	.13	
1976S Proof	(4,149,730)		.20
1977	796,930,000	.12	
1977D	376,607,228	.12	
1977S Proof	(3,251,152)		.20

	Quan. Minted	MS-63	Proof-63
1978	663,980,000	$.12	
1978D	282,847,540	.12	
1978S Proof	(3,127,781)		$.20
1979	315,440,000	.12	
1979D	390,921,184	.12	
1979S Proof	(3,677,175)		
Filled S			.25
Clear S			.50
1980P	735,170,000	.15	
1980D	719,354,321	.12	
1980S Proof	(3,554,806)		.20
1981P	676,650,000	.12	
1981D	712,284,143	.12	
1981S Proof	(4,063,083)		.20
1982 (no mint mark)		60.00	
1982P	519,475,000	.30	
1982D	542,713,584	.20	
1982S Proof	(3,857,479)		.20
1983P	647,025,000	.15	
1983D	730,129,224	.10	
1983S Proof	(3,279,126)		.25
1984P	856,669,000	.12	
1984D	704,803,976	.15	
1984S Proof	(3,065,110)		.25
1985P	705,200,962	.10	
1985D	587,979,970	.10	
1985S Proof	(3,362,821)		.20
1986P	682,649,693	.15	
1986D	473,326,970	.15	
1986S Proof	(3,010,497)		.75
1987P	762,709,481	.10	
1987D	653,203,402	.10	
1987S Proof	(4,227,728)		.30

Italic prices indicate unsettled values due to fluctuating bullion market. See Bullion Chart.

DIMES

	Quan. Minted	MS-63	Proof-63
1988P	1,030,550,000	$.12	
1988D	962,385,489	.12	
1988S Proof	(3,262,948)		$.30
1989P	1,298,400,000	.10	
1989D	896,535,597	.10	
1989S Proof	(3,220,194)		.30
1990P	1,034,340,000	.10	
1990D	839,995,824	.10	
1990S Proof	(3,299,559)		.30
1991P	927,220,000	.10	
1991D	601,241,114	.12	
1991S Proof	(2,867,787)		1.00
1992P	593,500,000	.10	
1992D	616,273,932	.10	
1992S Proof	(2,858,981)		1.00
1992S Silver Prf	(1,317,579)		1.50
1993P	766,180,000	.10	
1993D	750,110,166	.10	
1993S Proof	(2,633,439)		1.00
1993S Silver Prf	(761,353)		1.50
1994P	1,189,000,000	.10	
1994D	1,303,268,110	.10	
1994S Proof	(2,484,594)		1.00
1994S Silver Prf	(785,329)		1.50
1995P	1,125,500,000	.10	
1995D	1,274,890,000	.15	
1995S Proof	(2,117,496)		2.00
1995S Silver Prf	(679,985)		3.00

	Quan. Minted	MS-63	Proof-63
1996P	1,421,163,000	$.10	
1996D	1,400,300,000	.10	
1996W	1,457,000	2.00	
1996S Proof	(1,750,244)		$1.00
1996S Silver Proof	(775,021)		1.50
1997P	991,640,000	.10	
1997D	979,810,000	.10	
1997S Proof	(2,055,000)		1.00
1997S Silver Proof	(741,678)		3.00
1998P	1,163,000,000	.10	
1998D	1,172,250,000	.10	
1998S Proof			1.00
1998S Silver Proof	(878,792)		1.50
1999P	2,164,000,000	.10	
1999D	1,397,750,000	.10	
1999S Proof			.75
1999S Silver Proof	(800,000)		1.25
2000P	1,842,500,000	.10	
2000D	1,818,700,000	.10	
2000S Proof	(2,968,900)		.75
2000S Silver Proof	(856,400)		1.25
2001P	1,369,590,000	.10	
2001D	1,412,800,000	.10	
2001S Proof			.75
2001S Silver Proof			1.25
2002P		.10	
2002D		.10	
2002S Proof			.75
2002S Silver Proof			1.25

TWENTY-CENT PIECES — 1875-1878

This short-lived coin was authorized by the Act of March 3, 1875. The edge of the coin is plain. Most of the 1876CC coins were melted at the Mint and never released. Mint mark is on the reverse below the eagle.

G-4 GOOD—*LIBERTY on shield obliterated. Letters and date legible.*
VG-8 VERY GOOD—*One or two letters in LIBERTY may show. Other details will be bold.*
F-12 FINE—*At least 3 letters of LIBERTY show.*
VF-20 VERY FINE—*LIBERTY completely readable, but partly weak.*
EF-40 EXTREMELY FINE—*LIBERTY sharp. Only slight wear on high points of coin.*
MS-60 UNCIRCULATED—*No trace of wear. Light blemishes.*

	Quan. Minted	*G-4*	*VG-8*	*F-12*	*VF-20*	*EF-40*	*MS-60*	*Proof-63*
1875 ....(2,790)	39,700	$25.00	$30.00	$40.00	$60.00	$100.00	$350.00	$1,000
1875CC	133,290	25.00	30.00	40.00	65.00	110.00	400.00	
1875S	1,155,000	23.00	28.00	38.00	55.00	80.00	300.00	—
1876 ....(1,260)	15,900	40.00	50.00	75.00	100.00	170.00	425.00	1,100
1876CC	10,000						35,000	
1877 ....(350)	350				550.00	850.00		1,500
1878 ....(600)	600				450.00	750.00		1,300

QUARTER DOLLARS — 1796 to Date

Authorized in 1792, this denomination was not issued until four years later. The first type weighed 104 grains which remained standard until modified to 103 1/8 grains by the Act of January 18, 1837. As with the dime and half dime, the weight was reduced and arrows placed at the date in 1853. Rays were placed in the field of the reverse during that year only.

DRAPED BUST TYPE, SMALL EAGLE REVERSE 1796

AG-3 ABOUT GOOD—*Details clear enough to identify.*
G-4 GOOD—*Date readable. Bust outlined, but no detail.*
VG-8 VERY GOOD—*All but deepest drapery folds worn smooth. Hairlines nearly gone and curls lack detail.*
F-12 FINE—*All drapery lines visible. Hair partly worn.*
VF-20 VERY FINE—*Only left side of drapery is indistinct.*
EF-40 EXTREMELY FINE—*Hair well outlined and detailed.*
MS-60 UNCIRCULATED—*No trace of wear. Light blemishes.*

	Quan. Minted	*AG-3*	*G-4*	*VG-8*	*F-12*	*VF-20*	*EF-40*	*MS-60*
1796	6,146	$1,000	$2,000	$2,750	$4,300	$6,500	$8,500	$14,000

DRAPED BUST TYPE, HERALDIC EAGLE REVERSE 1804-1807

1804	6,738	190.00	450.00	600.00	1,300	2,100	4,500	—
1805	121,394	45.00	90.00	130.00	200.00	400.00	800.00	2,600
1806 6 over 5	} 206,124	45.00	90.00	130.00	200.00	400.00	900.00	2,850
1806		45.00	90.00	130.00	200.00	400.00	800.00	2,600
1807	220,643	45.00	90.00	130.00	200.00	400.00	800.00	2,600

CAPPED BUST TYPE 1815-1838
Large Size 1815-1828

AG-3 ABOUT GOOD—*Details clear enough to identify.*
G-4 GOOD—*Date, letters and stars readable. Hair under headband smooth. Cap lines worn smooth.*
VG-8 VERY GOOD—*Rim well defined. Main details visible. Full LIBERTY on cap. Hair above eye nearly smooth.*
F-12 FINE—*All hairlines show but drapery has only part details. Shoulder clasp distinct.*
VF-20 VERY FINE—*All details show, but some wear. Clasp and ear sharp.*
EF-40 EXTREMELY FINE—*All details show distinctly. Hair well outlined.*
MS-60 UNCIRCULATED—*No trace of wear. Light blemishes.*

QUARTER DOLLARS

	Quan. Minted	*AG-3*	*G-4*	*VG-8*	*F-12*	*VF-20*	*EF-40*	*MS-60*
1815	89,235	$13.00	$25.00	$35.00	$55.00	$150.00	$450.00	$1,100
1818 8 over 5 }	361,174	13.00	25.00	35.00	55.00	150.00	425.00	1,300
1818 Normal }		13.00	25.00	30.00	50.00	135.00	375.00	1,000
1819	144,000	13.00	25.00	30.00	50.00	135.00	375.00	1,000
1820	127,444	13.00	25.00	30.00	50.00	135.00	375.00	1,000
1821	216,851	13.00	25.00	30.00	50.00	135.00	375.00	1,000
1822 All kinds	64,080	13.00	25.00	35.00	60.00	150.00	400.00	1,200
1822, 25 over 50c		200.00	425.00	850.00	1,200	2,000	3,500	5,500
1823, 3 over 2	17,800	1,300	3,500	5,500	9,500	14,000	19,000	—
1824, 4 over 2 }	168,000	15.00	30.00	37.00	75.00	200.00	500.00	1,800
1825 }		13.00	25.00	27.50	45.00	125.00	385.00	1,100
1827 Original (Curled base 2 in 25c) 4,000 Minted								—
1827 Restrike (Square base 2 in 25c)								—
1828 All kinds	102,000	13.00	25.00	27.50	45.00	125.00	385.00	1,200
1828, 25 over 50c		20.00	40.00	75.00	140.00	300.00	550.00	2,300

Reduced Size, No Motto on Reverse 1831-1838

G-4 GOOD—*Bust well defined. Hair under headband smooth. Date, letters, stars readable. Scant rims.*
VG-8 VERY GOOD—*Details apparent but worn on high spots. Rims strong. Full LIBERTY.*
F-12 FINE—*All hairlines visible. Drapery partly worn. Shoulder clasp distinct.*
VF-20 VERY FINE—*Only top spots worn. Clasp sharp. Ear distinct.*
EF-40 EXTREMELY FINE—*Hair details and clasp are bold and clear.*
MS-60 UNCIRCULATED—*No trace of wear. Light blemishes.*

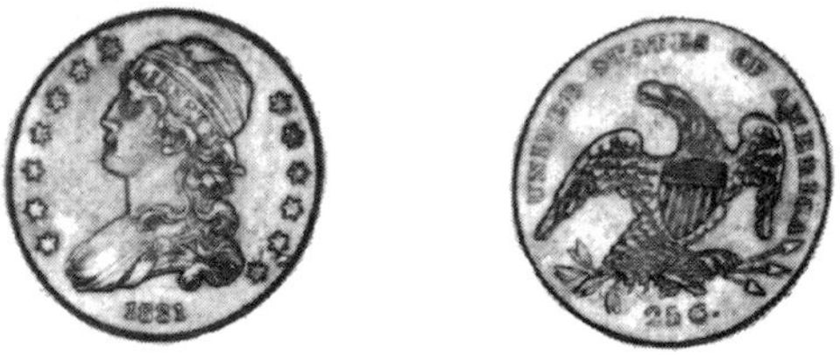

	Quan. Minted	*G-4*	*VG-8*	*F-12*	*VF-20*	*EF-40*	*MS-60*
1831	398,000	$17.00	$21.00	$26.00	$50.00	$100.00	$450.00
1832	320,000	17.00	21.00	26.00	50.00	100.00	450.00
1833	156,000	18.00	23.00	30.00	60.00	125.00	600.00
1834	286,000	17.00	21.00	26.00	50.00	100.00	450.00
1835	1,952,000	17.00	21.00	26.00	50.00	100.00	450.00
1836	472,000	17.00	21.00	26.00	50.00	100.00	450.00
1837	252,400	17.00	21.00	26.00	50.00	100.00	450.00
1838	366,000	17.00	21.00	26.00	50.00	100.00	450.00

QUARTER DOLLARS

LIBERTY SEATED TYPE 1838-1891

No Motto Above Eagle 1838-1853

G-4 GOOD—*Scant rim. LIBERTY on shield worn off. Date and letters readable.*
VG-8 VERY GOOD—*Rim fairly defined, at least 3 letters in LIBERTY evident.*
F-12 FINE—*LIBERTY complete, but partly weak.*
VF-20 VERY FINE—*LIBERTY strong.*
EF-40 EXTREMELY FINE—*Complete LIBERTY and edges of scroll. Clasp shows plainly.*
MS-60 UNCIRCULATED—*No trace of wear. Light blemishes.*

Mint mark location is on the reverse below the eagle.

	Quan. Minted	*G-4*	*VG-8*	*F-12*	*VF-20*	*EF-40*	*MS-60*
1838	466,000	$4.50	$6.00	$11.00	$21.00	$90.00	$600.00
1839	491,146	4.50	6.00	11.00	21.00	90.00	550.00
1840	188,127	7.00	9.00	20.00	35.00	70.00	550.00
1840O	425,200	4.50	6.00	15.00	30.00	70.00	550.00
1841	120,000	15.00	25.00	40.00	60.00	110.00	425.00
1841O	452,000	4.50	6.00	12.00	25.00	80.00	425.00

Small Date

Large Date

1842 Small date. Proof only							12,000
1842 Large date	88,000	30.00	40.00	70.00	130.00	175.00	800.00
1842O Small date	769,000	100.00	175.00	300.00	500.00	1,000	—
1842O Large date		5.00	7.00	11.00	15.00	60.00	650.00
1843	645,600	4.50	6.00	9.00	14.00	25.00	275.00
1843O	968,000	7.00	12.00	20.00	35.00	100.00	600.00
1844	421,200	4.50	6.00	11.00	15.00	35.00	225.00
1844O	740,000	4.50	6.00	15.00	25.00	70.00	550.00
1845	922,000	4.50	6.00	9.00	14.00	30.00	225.00
1846	510,000	4.50	6.00	11.00	15.00	30.00	225.00
1847	734,000	4.50	6.00	11.00	14.00	30.00	225.00
1847O	368,000	9.00	14.00	24.00	45.00	100.00	550.00
1848	146,000	8.00	12.00	24.00	40.00	80.00	450.00
1849	340,000	7.00	9.00	15.00	25.00	70.00	400.00
1849O	†incl. below	140.00	230.00	410.00	800.00	1,300	—
1850	190,800	8.00	12.00	20.00	28.00	60.00	500.00
1850O	412,000	12.00	16.00	22.00	35.00	65.00	550.00
1851	160,000	10.00	15.00	25.00	30.00	70.00	400.00
1851O	88,000	65.00	100.00	200.00	300.00	650.00	1,400
1852	177,060	12.00	18.00	28.00	45.00	70.00	400.00
1852O	96,000	80.00	120.00	175.00	350.00	550.00	2,000
1853 No arrows or rays	44,200	100.00	120.00	150.00	250.00	350.00	1,300

†Coinage for 1849O included with 1850O.

Arrows at Date, Rays Around Eagle 1853 Only

1853, 3 over 4

QUARTER DOLLARS

	Quan. Minted	G-4	VG-8	F-12	VF-20	EF-40	MS-60
1853	15,210,020	$4.00	$6.00	$9.00	$16.00	$60.00	$500.00
1853, 3 over 4		20.00	35.00	75.00	125.00	250.00	900.00
1853O	1,332,000	5.00	7.00	11.00	22.00	80.00	700.00

Arrows at Date, No Rays 1854-1855

1854	12,380,000	4.00	5.00	8.00	15.00	35.00	250.00
1854O	1,484,000	4.00	5.00	8.00	15.00	35.00	300.00
1855	2,857,000	4.00	5.00	8.00	15.00	35.00	275.00
1855O	176,000	18.00	28.00	40.00	85.00	150.00	900.00
1855S	396,400	16.00	25.00	30.00	60.00	125.00	850.00

No Motto Above Eagle 1856-1865

	Quan. Minted	G-4	VG-8	F-12	VF-20	EF-40	MS-60	Proof-63
1856	7,264,000	$4.00	$5.00	$7.00	$10.00	$21.00	$150.00	$1,100
1856O	968,000	5.00	7.00	11.00	17.00	40.00	500.00	
1856S	286,000	10.00	14.00	25.00	65.00	140.00	1,000	
1857	9,644,000	4.00	5.00	7.00	10.00	21.00	150.00	1,000
1857O	1,180,000	4.00	6.00	8.00	11.00	21.00	325.00	
1857S	82,000	20.00	32.00	50.00	130.00	225.00	1,200	
1858 *(300+)*	7,368,000	4.00	5.00	7.00	10.00	20.00	150.00	800.00
1858O	520,000	4.00	6.00	8.00	12.00	25.00	500.00	
1858S	121,000	17.00	25.00	40.00	100.00	200.00	1,500	
1859 (800)	1,344,000	4.00	5.00	7.00	10.00	21.00	165.00	600.00
1859O	260,000	6.00	10.00	16.00	25.00	40.00	450.00	
1859S	80,000	27.00	45.00	80.00	140.00	250.00	1,500	
1860 (1,000)	805,400	4.00	5.00	7.00	10.00	21.00	175.00	600.00
1860O	388,000	5.00	7.00	10.00	15.00	32.00	425.00	
1860S	56,000	40.00	65.00	120.00	225.00	900.00	3,000	
1861 (1,000)	4,854,600	4.00	5.00	7.00	10.00	21.00	165.00	600.00
1861S	96,000	15.00	25.00	50.00	80.00	190.00	1,500	
1862 (550)	932,550	4.00	5.00	7.00	10.00	21.00	165.00	600.00
1862S	67,000	12.00	20.00	30.00	70.00	175.00	1,000	
1863 (460)	192,060	8.00	10.00	15.00	22.00	45.00	350.00	625.00
1864 (470)	94,070	12.00	20.00	30.00	50.00	95.00	475.00	625.00
1864S	20,000	55.00	100.00	150.00	235.00	550.00	—	
1865 (500)	59,300	16.00	21.00	35.00	50.00	90.00	400.00	625.00
1865S	41,000	17.00	25.00	40.00	85.00	170.00	1,200	

Motto Above Eagle 1866-1873

1866 (725)	17,525	60.00	100.00	150.00	250.00	350.00	750.00	500.00
1866S	28,000	60.00	80.00	125.00	175.00	300.00	1,300	
1867 (625)	20,625	30.00	50.00	80.00	115.00	200.00	450.00	500.00
1867S	48,000	35.00	50.00	80.00	115.00	200.00	1,300	
1868 (600)	30,000	25.00	40.00	65.00	90.00	125.00	400.00	500.00
1868S	96,000	16.00	25.00	50.00	80.00	150.00	1,100	
1869 (600)	16,600	50.00	75.00	150.00	175.00	250.00	600.00	475.00
1869S	76,000	15.00	25.00	60.00	100.00	160.00	700.00	
1870 (1,000)	87,400	12.00	20.00	30.00	60.00	80.00	450.00	475.00

QUARTER DOLLARS

	Quan. Minted	G-4	VG-8	F-12	VF-20	EF-40	MS-60	Proof-63
1870CC	8,340	$600.00	$1,000	$2,200	$3,600	$4,800	—	
1871 (960)	119,160	6.00	12.00	16.00	35.00	60.00	$250.00	$400.00
1871CC	10,890	385.00	700.00	1,200	2,700	4,500	—	
1871S	30,900	60.00	125.00	170.00	210.00	325.00	1,300	
1872 (950)	182,950	4.00	6.00	9.00	14.00	35.00	225.00	400.00
1872CC	22,850	130.00	185.00	350.00	700.00	1,500	3,300	
1872S	83,000	75.00	125.00	175.00	300.00	425.00	2,500	
1873 (600)	212,600	6.00	10.00	15.00	30.00	50.00	200.00	400.00
1873CC	4,000				—		—	

Arrows at Date 1873-1874

	Quan. Minted	G-4	VG-8	F-12	VF-20	EF-40	MS-60	Proof-63
1873 (540)	1,271,700	6.00	8.00	14.00	35.00	90.00	425.00	700.00
1873CC	12,462	375.00	600.00	950.00	1,600	2,700	8,500	
1873S	156,000	9.00	12.00	21.00	45.00	110.00	600.00	
1874 (700)	471,900	6.00	8.00	14.00	35.00	90.00	450.00	700.00
1874S	392,000	9.00	10.00	18.00	40.00	100.00	475.00	

No Arrows at Date 1875-1891

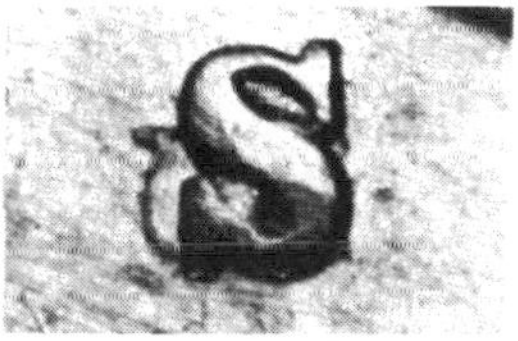

1877S, S over horizontal S

	Quan. Minted	G-4	VG-8	F-12	VF-20	EF-40	MS-60	Proof-63
1875 (700)	4,293,500	4.00	5.00	6.00	10.00	20.00	150.00	350.00
1875CC	140,000	18.00	25.00	55.00	80.00	175.00	650.00	
1875S	680,000	6.00	10.00	15.00	35.00	60.00	260.00	
1876 (1,150)	17,817,150	4.00	5.00	6.00	10.00	20.00	150.00	350.00
1876CC	4,944,000	4.00	5.00	7.00	14.00	30.00	200.00	
1876S	8,596,000	4.00	5.00	6.00	10.00	20.00	150.00	
1877 (510)	10,911,710	4.00	5.00	6.00	10.00	20.00	150.00	350.00
1877CC	4,192,000	4.00	5.00	7.00	14.00	30.00	200.00	
1877S }	8,996,000	4.00	5.00	6.00	10.00	20.00	150.00	
1877S over horizontal S }		4.00	6.00	40.00	50.00	90.00	300.00	
1878 (800)	2,260,800	4.00	5.00	6.00	10.00	20.00	150.00	350.00
1878CC	996,000	4.00	5.00	7.00	11.00	25.00	200.00	
1878S	140,000	27.00	40.00	75.00	100.00	150.00	800.00	
1879 *(1,100)*	14,700	35.00	40.00	55.00	80.00	100.00	325.00	400.00
1880 (1,355)	14,955	35.00	40.00	55.00	80.00	100.00	325.00	350.00
1881 (975)	12,975	35.00	40.00	55.00	80.00	100.00	300.00	400.00
1882 (1,100)	16,300	35.00	40.00	55.00	80.00	100.00	300.00	350.00
1883 (1,039)	15,439	35.00	40.00	55.00	80.00	100.00	300.00	350.00
1884 (875)	8,875	50.00	80.00	100.00	135.00	160.00	350.00	350.00

QUARTER DOLLARS

	Quan. Minted	G-4	VG-8	F-12	VF-20	EF-40	MS-60	Proof-63
1885 ....(930)	14,530	$35.00	$40.00	$55.00	$80.00	$110.00	$325.00	$350.00
1886 ....(886)	5,886	70.00	90.00	125.00	150.00	200.00	375.00	350.00
1887 ....(710)	10,710	40.00	55.00	70.00	100.00	150.00	325.00	350.00
1888 ....(832)	10,833	40.00	55.00	70.00	100.00	150.00	325.00	350.00
1888S	1,216,000	4.00	5.00	6.00	11.00	20.00	180.00	
1889 ....(711)	12,711	35.00	40.00	50.00	75.00	100.00	325.00	400.00
1890 ....(590)	80,590	20.00	25.00	33.00	45.00	70.00	275.00	325.00
1891 ....(600)	3,920,600	4.00	5.00	6.00	10.00	20.00	180.00	325.00
1891O	68,000	50.00	65.00	100.00	150.00	275.00	1,500	
1891S	2,216,000	4.00	5.00	7.00	12.00	23.00	180.00	

BARBER or LIBERTY HEAD TYPE 1892-1916

Like other silver coins of this type the quarter dollars minted from 1892 to 1916 were designed by Charles E. Barber. His initial B is found at the truncation of the neck of Liberty.

G-4 GOOD—*Date and legends readable. LIBERTY worn off headband.*

VG-8 VERY GOOD—*Minimum of 3 letters in LIBERTY readable.*

F-12 FINE—*LIBERTY completely readable but not sharp.*

VF-20 VERY FINE—*All letters in LIBERTY evenly plain.*

EF-40 EXTREMELY FINE—*LIBERTY bold, and its ribbon distinct.*

MS-60 UNCIRCULATED—*No trace of wear. Light blemishes.*

Mint mark location is on the reverse below the eagle.

	Quan. Minted	G-4	VG-8	F-12	VF-20	EF-40	MS-60	Proof-63
1892 ....(1,245)	8,237,245	$1.50	$2.00	$7.00	$12.00	$27.00	$115.00	$280.00
1892O	2,640,000	2.00	4.00	8.00	13.00	30.00	150.00	
1892S	964,079	6.00	9.00	15.00	22.00	50.00	200.00	
1893 ....(792)	5,444,815	1.25	1.75	6.00	12.00	30.00	115.00	280.00
1893O	3,396,000	1.50	2.00	8.00	13.00	35.00	160.00	
1893S	1,454,535	1.50	4.00	12.00	25.00	45.00	175.00	
1894 ....(972)	3,432,972	1.25	1.50	8.00	13.00	30.00	110.00	280.00
1894O	2,852,000	1.25	1.50	10.00	15.00	35.00	160.00	
1894S	2,648,821	1.25	1.50	10.00	15.00	35.00	160.00	
1895 ....(880)	4,440,880	1.25	1.50	8.00	13.00	30.00	110.00	280.00
1895O	2,816,000	1.25	2.50	12.00	25.00	38.00	185.00	
1895S	1,764,681	1.25	4.50	15.00	20.00	40.00	175.00	
1896 ....(762)	3,874,762	1.50	2.00	8.00	13.00	32.00	125.00	280.00
1896O	1,484,000	2.00	4.00	18.00	70.00	125.00	450.00	
1896S	188,039	130.00	200.00	325.00	500.00	950.00	2,100	
1897 ....(731)	8,140,731	1.50	2.00	6.00	11.00	28.00	90.00	280.00
1897O	1,414,800	2.25	6.00	15.00	60.00	120.00	425.00	
1897S	542,229	8.00	15.00	50.00	75.00	125.00	375.00	
1898 ....(735)	11,100,735	1.50	2.00	7.50	12.00	30.00	90.00	280.00
1898O	1,868,000	2.00	3.50	15.00	35.00	80.00	325.00	
1898S	1,020,592	1.50	3.00	10.00	15.00	30.00	225.00	
1899 ....(846)	12,624,846	1.25	2.00	7.00	12.00	24.00	100.00	280.00
1899O	2,644,000	2.00	4.00	8.00	15.00	32.00	225.00	
1899S	708,000	3.50	7.00	12.00	21.00	35.00	225.00	
1900 ....(912)	10,016,912	*1.25*	1.50	7.00	11.00	24.00	100.00	280.00
1900O	3,416,000	2.00	7.00	15.00	25.00	45.00	250.00	
1900S	1,858,585	1.25	3.00	9.00	15.00	30.00	175.00	

Italic prices indicate unsettled values due to fluctuating bullion market. See Bullion Chart.

QUARTER DOLLARS

	Quan. Minted	G-4	VG-8	F-12	VF-20	EF-40	MS-60	Proof-63
1901 ....(813)	8,892,813	*$1.25*	$2.00	$6.00	$10.00	$30.00	$100.00	$280.00
1901O..........................	1,612,000	8.00	15.00	30.00	75.00	125.00	400.00	
1901S	72,664	800.00	1,600	2,400	3,000	4,200	8,250	
1902 ....(777)	12,197,744	*1.25*	*1.50*	6.00	11.00	30.00	90.00	280.00
1902O..........................	4,748,000	*1.50*	*2.50*	9.00	19.00	35.00	200.00	
1902S	1,524,612	2.00	5.00	10.00	20.00	40.00	220.00	
1903 ....(755)	9,670,064	*1.25*	*1.50*	6.00	12.00	25.00	90.00	280.00
1903O..........................	3,500,000	*2.00*	*2.50*	10.00	15.00	30.00	150.00	
1903S	1,036,000	2.00	3.00	14.00	20.00	35.00	210.00	
1904 ....(670)	9,588,813	*1.25*	*1.50*	6.00	11.00	24.00	90.00	280.00
1904O..........................	2,456,000	1.50	3.00	15.00	25.00	70.00	350.00	
1905 ....(727)	4,968,250	*1.25*	*1.50*	7.00	11.00	25.00	90.00	280.00
1905O..........................	1,230,000	2.50	5.00	20.00	40.00	75.00	200.00	
1905S	1,884,000	*1.50*	*2.00*	12.00	18.00	30.00	175.00	
1906 ....(675)	3,656,435	*1.50*	*2.00*	6.00	11.00	24.00	90.00	280.00
1906D..........................	3,280,000	*1.50*	*2.00*	8.00	12.00	25.00	110.00	
1906O..........................	2,056,000	*1.50*	*2.00*	10.00	15.00	30.00	135.00	
1907 ....(575)	7,192,575	*1.50*	*2.00*	6.00	11.00	24.00	90.00	280.00
1907D..........................	2,484,000	*1.50*	*2.00*	8.00	15.00	26.00	125.00	
1907O..........................	4,560,000	*1.50*	*2.00*	6.00	11.00	24.00	100.00	
1907S	1,360,000	*1.50*	*2.00*	10.00	16.00	40.00	200.00	
1908 ....(545)	4,232,545	*1.50*	*2.00*	6.00	11.00	24.00	90.00	280.00
1908D..........................	5,788,000	*1.50*	*2.00*	6.00	11.00	25.00	110.00	
1908O..........................	6,244,000	*1.25*	*1.50*	6.00	11.00	24.00	100.00	
1908S	784,000	2.50	8.00	20.00	38.00	90.00	325.00	
1909 ....(650)	9,268,650	*1.25*	*1.50*	6.00	11.00	24.00	90.00	280.00
1909D..........................	5,114,000	*1.25*	*1.50*	6.00	11.00	24.00	110.00	
1909O............................	712,000	4.00	8.00	25.00	50.00	110.00	375.00	
1909S	1,348,000	*1.25*	*1.50*	8.00	14.00	25.00	150.00	
1910 ....(551)	2,244,551	*1.25*	*1.50*	7.00	12.00	25.00	90.00	280.00
1910D..........................	1,500,000	*1.25*	*1.50*	8.00	14.00	30.00	175.00	
1911 ....(543)	3,720,543	*1.25*	*1.50*	6.00	11.00	24.00	90.00	280.00
1911D............................	933,600	*1.25*	*1.50*	25.00	60.00	125.00	300.00	
1911S	988,000	*1.25*	*1.50*	11.00	15.00	40.00	160.00	
1912 ....(700)	4,400,700	*1.25*	*1.50*	6.00	11.00	24.00	90.00	280.00
1912S	708,000	*1.25*	*1.50*	12.00	18.00	35.00	175.00	
1913 ....(613)	484,613	5.00	7.00	22.00	65.00	185.00	550.00	325.00
1913D..........................	1,450,800	*1.25*	*1.50*	8.00	13.00	30.00	140.00	
1913S	40,000	225.00	350.00	900.00	1,500	1,900	2,500	
1914 ....(380)	6,244,610	*1.25*	*1.50*	6.00	11.00	24.00	90.00	325.00
1914D..........................	3,046,000	*1.25*	*1.50*	6.00	11.00	24.00	90.00	
1914S	264,000	20.00	33.00	55.00	75.00	175.00	420.00	
1915 ....(450)	3,480,450	*1.25*	*1.50*	6.00	11.00	24.00	90.00	325.00
1915D..........................	3,694,000	*1.25*	*1.50*	6.00	11.00	24.00	90.00	
1915S	704,000	*1.25*	*1.50*	7.00	12.00	30.00	125.00	
1916	1,788,000	*1.25*	*1.50*	6.00	11.00	24.00	90.00	
1916D..........................	6,540,800	*1.25*	*1.50*	6.00	11.00	24.00	90.00	

Italic prices indicate unsettled values due to fluctuating bullion market. See Bullion Chart.

STANDING LIBERTY TYPE 1916-1930

This design is by Hermon A. MacNeil, whose initial M is above and to the right of the date. Liberty bears a shield of protection in her left arm, while the right hand holds the olive branch of peace. There was a modification in 1917. The reverse has a new arrangement of stars and the eagle is higher. After 1924 the date was "recessed," thereby giving it greater protection from the effects of circulation.

G-4 GOOD—*Date and lettering readable. Top of date worn. Liberty's right leg and toes worn off. Left leg and drapery lines show much wear.*

VG-8 VERY GOOD—*Distinct date. Toes show faintly. Drapery lines visible above her left leg.*

QUARTER DOLLARS

F-12 FINE—*High curve of right leg flat from thigh to ankle. Left leg shows only slight wear. Drapery lines over right thigh seen only at sides of leg.*
VF-20 VERY FINE—*Garment line across right leg will be worn but show at sides.*
EF-40 EXTREMELY FINE—*Flattened only at high spots. Her toes are sharp. Drapery lines across right leg are evident.*
MS-60 UNCIRCULATED—*No trace of wear. Light blemishes.*

No stars below eagle 1916-1917

	Quan. Minted	*G-4*	*VG-8*	*F-12*	*VF-20*	*EF-40*	*MS-60*
1916	52,000	$650.00	$850.00	$1,000	$1,500	$1,800	$2,500
1917	8,740,000	5.00	7.00	12.00	16.00	27.00	100.00
1917D	1,509,200	7.00	9.00	15.00	30.00	45.00	110.00
1917S	1,952,000	7.00	9.00	15.00	31.00	60.00	125.00

Stars below eagle 1917-1930

1918S, 8 over 7

Mint mark position is on obverse at left of date.

	Quan. Minted	*G-4*	*VG-8*	*F-12*	*VF-20*	*EF-40*	*MS-60*
1917	13,880,000	5.00	7.00	9.00	12.00	20.00	65.00
1917D	6,224,400	10.00	12.00	20.00	30.00	47.50	85.00
1917S	5,552,000	9.50	11.00	15.00	22.00	35.00	80.00
1918	14,240,000	5.00	7.00	10.00	15.00	20.00	65.00
1918D	7,380,000	13.00	15.00	20.00	25.00	40.00	100.00
1918S Norm. date	} 11,072,000	7.00	11.00	12.00	14.00	25.00	80.00
1918S, 8 over 7		450.00	750.00	1,100	1,400	2,250	6,200
1919	11,324,000	13.00	15.00	21.00	25.00	30.00	70.00
1919D	1,944,000	25.00	35.00	55.00	80.00	150.00	275.00
1919S	1,836,000	25.00	35.00	50.00	85.00	175.00	300.00
1920	27,860,000	5.00	7.00	9.00	13.00	18.00	65.00
1920D	3,586,400	15.00	20.00	30.00	40.00	55.00	110.00
1920S	6,380,000	6.00	8.00	12.00	15.00	20.00	100.00
1921	1,916,000	40.00	50.00	70.00	90.00	135.00	250.00
1923	9,716,000	4.00	5.00	6.00	10.00	18.00	65.00
1923S	1,360,000	65.00	100.00	150.00	175.00	225.00	350.00
1924	10,920,000	4.00	5.00	6.00	10.00	16.00	65.00
1924D	3,112,000	12.00	18.00	27.00	32.00	45.00	75.00
1924S	2,860,000	8.00	10.00	13.00	16.00	35.00	110.00

Recessed Date 1925-1930

	Quan. Minted	*G-4*	*VG-8*	*F-12*	*VF-20*	*EF-40*	*MS-60*
1925	12,280,000	*1.00*	*1.25*	2.50	6.00	12.00	60.00
1926	11,316,000	*1.00*	*1.25*	2.50	6.00	12.00	60.00
1926D	1,716,000	*1.00*	*1.25*	6.00	10.00	18.00	65.00
1926S	2,700,000	*1.00*	*1.25*	4.00	8.00	35.00	130.00
1927	11,912,000	*1.00*	*1.35*	2.50	5.00	12.00	60.00
1927D	976,000	*1.50*	*1.75*	6.00	13.00	27.00	80.00
1927S	396,000	3.50	6.00	23.00	75.00	500.00	1,650
1928	6,336,000	*1.00*	*1.25*	2.50	5.00	12.00	60.00

QUARTER DOLLARS

	Quan. Minted	*G-4*	*VG-8*	*F-12*	*VF-20*	*EF-40*	*MS-60*
1928D	1,627,600	*$1.00*	*$1.25*	$2.50	$6.00	$13.00	$60.00
1928S	2,644,000	*1.00*	*1.25*	2.50	6.00	12.00	60.00
1929	11,140,000	*1.00*	*1.25*	2.50	5.00	12.00	60.00
1929D	1,358,000	*1.00*	*1.25*	2.50	5.00	12.00	60.00
1929S	1,764,000	*1.00*	*1.25*	2.50	5.00	12.00	60.00
1930	5,632,000	*1.00*	*1.25*	2.50	5.00	12.00	60.00
1930S	1,556,000	*1.00*	*1.25*	2.50	5.00	12.00	60.00

WASHINGTON TYPE 1932 to Date

This type was intended to be a commemorative issue marking the two-hundredth anniversary of Washington's birth. John Flanagan, a New York sculptor, was the designer. The initals JF are found at the base of the neck. Mint mark is on reverse below wreath. 1932 to 1964. Starting in 1968 mint mark is on obverse at right of ribbon.

VG-8 VERY GOOD—*Wing tips outlined. Rims are fine and even. Tops of letters at rim are flattened.*
F-12 FINE—*Hairlines about ear are visible. Tiny feathers on eagle's breast are faintly visible.*
VF-20 VERY FINE—*Hair details worn but plain. Feathers at sides of eagle's breast are plain.*
EF-40 EXTREMELY FINE—*Hairlines sharp. Wear spots confined to top of eagle's legs and center of breast.*
MS-60 UNCIRCULATED—*No trace of wear. Light blemishes.*
MS-63 SELECT UNCIRCULATED—*No trace of wear. Very few noticeable blemishes.*

Starting in 1968 mint mark is on obverse at right of ribbon.

Silver Coinage—1932-1964

	Quan. Minted	*VG-8*	*F-12*	*VF-20*	*EF-40*	*MS-60*	*MS-63*	*Proof-63*
1932	5,404,000	*$1.50*	*$1.75*	$2.00	$4.00	$10.00	$18.00	
1932D	436,800	30.00	35.00	45.00	75.00	275.00	700.00	
1932S	408,000	30.00	32.00	40.00	45.00	135.00	250.00	
1934	31,912,052	*.75*	*1.25*	1.40	3.00	9.00	15.00	
1934D	3,527,200	*1.00*	*1.25*	1.40	5.00	50.00	95.00	
1935	32,484,000	*.75*	*1.00*	1.25	2.00	8.00	12.00	
1935D	5,780,000	*1.00*	*1.25*	2.00	5.00	70.00	90.00	
1935S	5,660,000	*1.00*	*1.25*	1.40	4.00	23.00	35.00	
1936	(3,837) 41,303,837		*.75*	*.75*	*1.00*	8.00	10.00	$300.00
1936D	5,374,000		*1.00*	5.00	18.00	140.00	190.00	
1936S	3,828,000		*.75*	*1.50*	4.00	25.00	35.00	
1937	(5,542) 19,701,542		*.75*	*.75*	*.85*	8.00	12.00	120.00
1937D	7,189,600		*.75*	*1.50*	*3.00*	18.00	25.00	
1937S	1,652,000		*.75*	*2.00*	6.00	45.00	60.00	
1938	(8,045) 9,480,045		*.75*	*2.00*	5.00	25.00	30.00	55.00
1938S	2,832,000		*.75*	*1.50*	4.00	25.00	30.00	
1939	(8,795) 33,548,795		*.75*	*.75*	*.85*	5.00	8.00	55.00
1939D	7,092,000		*.75*	*1.00*	*2.00*	12.00	15.00	
1939S	2,628,000		*.75*	*1.00*	4.00	25.00	30.00	
1940	(11,246) 35,715,246		*.75*	*.75*	*.85*	4.00	7.00	30.00
1940D	2,797,600		*.75*	*1.00*	5.00	25.00	35.00	
1940S	8,244,000		*.75*	*.75*	*1.00*	5.00	8.00	
1941	(15,287) 79,047,287		*.75*	*.75*	*.85*	*1.50*	3.00	25.00
1941D	16,714,800		*.75*	*.75*	*.85*	6.00	10.00	

Italic prices indicate unsettled values due to fluctuating bullion market. See Bullion Chart.

QUARTER DOLLARS

	Quan. Minted	*F-12*	*VF-20*	*EF-40*	*MS-60*	*MS-63*	*Proof-63*
1941S	16,080,000	*$.75*	*$.75*	*$.85*	$5.00	$10.00	
1942 (21,123)	102,117,123	*.75*	*.75*	*.85*	*1.50*	2.25	$22.00
1942D	17,487,200	*.75*	*.75*	*1.00*	4.00	6.00	
1942S	19,384,000	*.75*	*.75*	*1.00*	17.00	25.00	
1943	99,700,000	*.75*	*.75*	*.85*	*1.25*	2.00	
1943D	16,095,600	*.75*	*.75*	*.85*	6.00	10.00	
1943S	21,700,000	*.75*	*.75*	*1.00*	8.00	13.00	
1944	104,956,000	*.75*	*.75*	*.85*	*1.25*	2.00	
1944D	14,600,800	*.75*	*.75*	*.85*	*2.00*	5.00	
1944S	12,560,000	*.75*	*.75*	*.85*	*2.00*	5.00	
1945	74,372,000	*.75*	*.75*	*.85*	*1.25*	2.00	
1945D	12,341,600	*.75*	*.75*	*.85*	*3.00*	7.00	
1945S	17,004,001	*.75*	*.75*	*.85*	*2.00*	4.00	
1946	53,436,000	*.75*	*.75*	*.85*	*1.25*	2.00	
1946D	9,072,800	*.75*	*.75*	*.85*	*1.25*	2.00	
1946S	4,204,000	*.75*	*.75*	*.85*	*1.25*	2.50	
1947	22,556,000	*.75*	*.75*	*.85*	*1.25*	3.00	
1947D	15,338,400	*.75*	*.75*	*.85*	*1.25*	2.50	
1947S	5,532,000	*.75*	*.75*	*.85*	*1.25*	3.00	
1948	35,196,000	*.75*	*.75*	*.85*	*1.25*	2.00	
1948D	16,766,800	*.75*	*.75*	*.85*	*1.25*	2.50	
1948S	15,960,000	*.75*	*.75*	*.85*	*1.25*	2.50	
1949	9,312,000	*.75*	*.75*	*.85*	8.00	12.00	
1949D	10,068,400	*.75*	*.75*	*.85*	*2.00*	7.00	
1950 (51,386)	24,971,512	*.75*	*.75*	*.85*	*1.25*	2.00	18.00
1950D	21,075,600	*.75*	*.75*	*.85*	*1.25*	2.00	
1950D, D over S			25.00	60.00	100.00	150.00	
1950S	10,284,004	*.75*	*.75*	*.85*	*2.00*	4.00	
1950S, S over D			25.00	70.00	120.00	175.00	
1951 (57,500)	43,505,602	*.75*	*.75*	*.85*	*1.25*	2.00	13.00
1951D	35,354,800	*.75*	*.75*	*.85*	*1.25*	2.00	
1951S	9,048,000	*.75*	*.75*	*.85*	*1.25*	6.00	
1952 (81,980)	38,862,073	*.75*	*.75*	*.85*	*1.25*	2.00	9.00
1952D	49,795,200	*.75*	*.75*	*.85*	*1.25*	2.00	
1952S	13,707,800	*.75*	*.75*	*.85*	*1.25*	4.00	
1953 (122,800)	18,664,920	*.75*	*.75*	*.85*	*1.25*	2.00	8.00
1953D	56,112,400	*.75*	*.75*	*.85*	*1.25*	2.00	
1953S	14,016,000	*.75*	*.75*	*.85*	*1.25*	2.00	
1954 (233,300)	54,645,503	*.75*	*.75*	*.85*	*1.25*	2.00	3.00
1954D	42,305,500	*.75*	*.75*	*.85*	*1.00*	*1.50*	
1954S	11,834,722	*.75*	*.75*	*.85*	*1.25*	2.25	
1955 (378,200)	18,558,381	*.75*	*.75*	*.85*	*1.25*	2.00	3.00
1955D	3,182,400	*.75*	*.75*	*.85*	*1.25*	2.25	
1956 (669,384)	44,813,384	*.75*	*.75*	*.75*	*.85*	*1.00*	1.50
1956D	32,334,500	*.75*	*.75*	*.75*	*.85*	*1.00*	
1957 (1,247,952)	47,779,952	*.75*	*.75*	*.75*	*.85*	*1.00*	1.25
1957D	77,924,160	*.75*	*.75*	*.75*	*.85*	*1.00*	
1958 (875,652)	7,235,652	*.75*	*.75*	*.75*	*.85*	*1.25*	1.50
1958D	78,124,900	*.75*	*.75*	*.75*	*.85*	*1.00*	
1959 (1,149,291)	25,533,291	*.75*	*.75*	*.75*	*.85*	*1.00*	1.25
1959D	62,054,232	*.75*	*.75*	*.75*	*.85*	*1.00*	
1960 (1,691,602)	30,855,602	*.75*	*.75*	*.75*	*.85*	*1.00*	1.25
1960D	63,000,324	*.75*	*.75*	*.75*	*.85*	*1.00*	
1961 (3,028,244)	40,064,244	*.75*	*.75*	*.75*	*.85*	*1.00*	1.10
1961D	83,656,928	*.75*	*.75*	*.75*	*.85*	*1.00*	
1962 (3,218,019)	39,374,019	*.75*	*.75*	*.75*	*.85*	*1.00*	1.10
1962D	127,554,756	*.75*	*.75*	*.75*	*.85*	*.90*	
1963 (3,075,645)	77,391,645	*.75*	*.75*	*.75*	*.85*	*.90*	1.00
1963D	135,288,184	*.75*	*.75*	*.75*	*.85*	*.90*	
1964 (3,950,762)	564,341,347	*.75*	*.75*	*.75*	*.85*	*.90*	1.00
1964D	704,135,528	*.75*	*.75*	*.75*	*.85*	*.90*	

Italic prices indicate unsettled values due to fluctuating bullion market. See Bullion Chart.

QUARTER DOLLARS

Clad Coinage—1965 to Date

	Quan. Minted	*MS-63*	*Proof-63*
1965	1,819,717,540	$.30	
1966	821,101,500	.30	
1967	1,524,031,848	.30	
1968	220,731,500	.30	
1968D	101,534,000	.30	
1968S Proof	(3,041,506)		$.35
1969	176,212,000	.60	
1969D	114,372,000	.35	
1969S Proof	(2,934,631)		.35
1970	136,420,000	.30	
1970D	417,341,364	.30	
1970S Proof	(2,632,810)		.35
1971	109,284,000	$.30	
1971D	258,634,428	.30	
1971S Proof	(3,220,733)		$.35
1972	215,048,000	.30	
1972D	311,067,732	.30	
1972S Proof	(3,260,996)		.35
1973	346,924,000	.30	
1973D	232,977,400	.30	
1973S Proof	(2,760,339)		.35
1974	801,456,000	.30	
1974D	353,160,300	.30	
1974S Proof	(2,612,568)		.35

BICENTENNIAL COINAGE DATED 1776-1976

	Quan. Minted	*MS-63*	*Proof-63*
1776-1976 Copper-nickel clad	809,784,016	$.30	
1776-1976D Copper-nickel clad	860,118,839	.30	
1776-1976S Copper-nickel clad	(7,059,099)		$.40
1776-1976S Silver clad	**11,000,000*	*1.00*	
1776-1976S Silver clad	*(*4,000,000)*		1.35

*Approximate mintage.

Eagle Reverse Resumed (Dies slightly modified to lower relief)

	Quan. Minted	*MS-63*	*Proof-63*
1977	468,556,000	$.27	
1977D	256,524,978	.27	
1977S Proof	(3,251,152)		$.35
1978	521,452,000	.27	
1978D	287,373,152	.27	
1978S Proof	(3,127,781)		.35
1979	515,708,000	.28	
1979D	489,789,780	.27	
1979S Proof	(3,677,175)		
Filled S			.35
Clear S			.60
1980P	635,832,000	.27	
1980D	518,327,487	.27	
1980S Proof	(3,554,806)		.35
1981P	601,716,000	.27	
1981D	575,722,833	.27	
1981S Proof	(4,063,083)		.35
1982P	500,931,000	1.50	
1982D	480,042,788	.35	
1982S Proof	(3,857,479)		.50
1983P	673,535,000	4.00	
1983D	617,806,446	2.50	
1983S Proof	(3,279,126)		.75
1984P	676,545,000	.27	
1984D	546,483,064	.35	
1984S Proof	(3,065,110)		.75
1985P	775,818,962	.50	
1985D	519,962,888	$.35	
1985S Proof	(3,362,821)		$.50
1986P	551,199,333	1.00	
1986D	504,298,660	2.00	
1986S Proof	(3,010,497)		.80
1987P	582,499,481	.27	
1987D	655,594,696	.27	
1987S Proof	(4,227,728)		.50
1988P	562,052,000	.50	
1988D	596,810,688	.27	
1988S Proof	(3,262,948)		.60
1989P	512,868,000	.27	
1989D	896,535,597	.27	
1989S Proof	(3,220,194)		.50
1990P	613,792,000	.27	
1990D	927,638,181	.27	
1990S Proof	(3,299,559)		.50
1991P	570,968,000	.27	
1991D	630,966,693	.27	
1991S Proof	(2,867,787)		.50
1992P	384,764,000	.27	
1992D	389,777,107	.35	
1992S Proof	(2,858,981)		.50
1992S Silver Prf.	(1,317,579)		1.25
1993P	639,276,000	.30	
1993D	645,476,128	.30	
1993S Proof	(2,633,439)		1.00

Italic prices indicate unsettled values due to fluctuating bullion market. See Bullion Chart.

QUARTER DOLLARS

	Quan. Minted	MS-63	Proof-63
1993S Silver Prf	(761,353)		$2.00
1994P	825,600,000	$.30	
1994D	800,034,110	.30	
1994S Proof	(2,484,594)		1.00
1994S Silver Prf	(785,329)		2.50
1995P	1,004,336,000	.30	
1995D	1,103,216,000	.30	
1995S Proof	(2,117,496)		2.50
1995S Silver Prf	(679,985)		3.50
1996P	925,040,000	.25	
1996D	906,868,000	.25	
1996S Proof	(1,750,244)		$1.00
1996S Silver Prf	(775,021)		2.25
1997P	595,740,000	$.25	
1997D	599,680,000	.25	
1997S Proof	(2,055,000)		1.50
1997S Silver Prf	(741,678)		5.00
1998P	896,268,000	.25	
1998D	821,000,000	.25	
1998S Proof			2.00
1998S Silver Prf	(878,792)		1.75

STATEHOOD QUARTER DOLLARS 1999-

The United States Mint 50 State Quarters Program begun in 1999 will produce a series of 50 quarter dollar coins with special designs honoring each state. Five different designs will be issued each year during the period 1999-2008. States are being commemorated in the order of their entrance into statehood.

These are all legal tender coins of standard weight and composition. The obverse side depicting President George Washington has been modified slightly to include some of the wording previously used on the reverse. The modification was authorized by special legislation, and carried out by Mint Sculptor-Engraver William Cousins, whose initials have been added to the truncation of Washington's neck adjacent to those of the original designer, John Flanagan.

Each state theme is being proposed, and approved, by the governor of the state. Final designs will be created by mint personnel.

Circulation coins are made at the Philadelphia and Denver mints. Proof coins are made in San Francisco. Both copper-nickel and silver proof coins are made each year.

	Quan. Minted	AU-50	MS-63	Proof-63
1999P Delaware	373,400,000	$.25	$.60	
1999D Delaware	401,424,000	.25	.60	
1999S Delaware Proof				$1.50
1999S Delaware Silver Proof	(800,000)			2.50
1999P Pennsylvania	349,000,000	.25	.60	
1999D Pennsylvania	358,332,000	.25	.60	
1999S Pennsylvania Proof				1.50
1999S Pennsylvania Silver Proof	(800,000)			2.50
1999P New Jersey	363,200,000	.25	.30	
1999D New Jersey	299,028,000	.25	.35	
1999S New Jersey Proof				1.50
1999S New Jersey Silver Proof	(800,000)			2.50
1999P Georgia	451,188,000	.25	.30	
1999D Georgia	488,744,000	.25	.30	
1999S Georgia Proof				1.50
1999S Georgia Silver Proof	(800,000)			2.50
1999P Connecticut	688,744,000	.25	.30	
1999D Connecticut	657,880,000	.25	.30	
1999S Connecticut Proof				1.50
1999S Connecticut Silver Proof	(800,000)			2.50

QUARTER DOLLARS
Statehood Quarters

	Quan. Minted	*AU-50*	*MS-63*	*Proof-63*
2000P Massachusetts	628,600,000	$.25	$.30	
2000D Massachusetts	535,184,000	.25	.30	
2000S Massachusetts Proof	(937,600)			$1.50
2000S Massachusetts Silver Proof	(856,400)			2.50
2000P Maryland	678,200,000	.25	.30	
2000D Maryland	556,532,000	.25	.30	
2000S Maryland Proof	(937,600)			1.50
2000S Maryland Silver Proof	(856,400)			2.50
2000P South Carolina	742,576,000	.25	30	
2000D South Carolina	566,208,000	.25	.30	
2000S South Carolina Proof	(937,600)			1.50
2000S South Carolina Silver Proof	(856,400)			2.50
2000P New Hampshire	673,040,000	.25	.30	
2000D New Hampshire	495,976,000	.25	.30	
2000S New Hampshire Proof	(937,600)			1.50
2000S New Hampshire Silver Proof	(856,400)			2.50
2000P Virginia	943,000,000	.25	.30	
2000D Virginia	651,616,000	.25	.30	
2000S Virginia Proof	(937,600)			1.50
2000S Virginia Silver Proof	(856,400)			2.50
2001P New York	655,400,000	.25	.30	
2001D New York	619,640,000	.25	.30	
2001S New York Proof				1.50
2001S New York Silver Proof				2.50
2001P North Carolina	627,600,000	.25	.30	
2001D North Carolina	427,876,000	.25	.30	
2001S North Carolina Proof				1.50
2001S North Carolina Silver Proof				2.50
2001P Rhode Island	423,000,000	.25	.30	
2001D Rhode Island	447,100,000	.25	.30	
2001S Rhode Island Proof				1.50
2001S Rhode Island Silver Proof				2.50
2001P Vermont	423,400,000	.25	.30	
2001D Vermont	459,404,000	.25	.30	
2001S Vermont Proof				1.50
2001S Vermont Silver Proof				2.50
2001P Kentucky	353,000,000	.25	.30	
2001D Kentucky	370,564,000	.25	.30	
2001S Kentucky Proof				1.50
2001S Kentucky Silver Proof				2.50
2002P Tennessee		.25	.30	
2002D Tennessee		.25	.30	
2002S Tennessee Proof				1.50
2002S Tennessee Silver Proof				2.50
2002P Ohio		.25	.30	
2002D Ohio		.25	.30	
2002S Ohio Proof				1.50
2002S Ohio Silver Proof				2.50

QUARTER DOLLARS
Statehood Quarters

	Quan. Minted	AU-50	MS-63	Proof-63
2002P Louisiana		$.25	$.30	
2002D Louisiana		.25	.30	
2002S Louisiana Proof				$1.50
2002S Louisiana Silver Proof				2.50
2002P Indiana		.25	.30	
2002D Indiana		.25	.30	
2002S Indiana Proof				1.50
2002S Indiana Silver Proof				2.50
2002P Mississippi		.25	.30	
2002D Mississippi		.25	.30	
2002S Mississippi Proof				1.50
2002S Mississippi Silver Proof				2.50

2003 Illinois
2003 Alabama
2003 Maine
2003 Missouri
2003 Arkansas

2004 Michigan
2004 Florida
2004 Texas
2004 Iowa
2004 Wisconsin

2005 California
2005 Minnesota
2005 Oregon
2005 Kansas
2005 West Virginia

2006 Nevada
2006 Nebraska
2006 Colorado
2006 North Dakota
2006 South Dakota

2007 Montana
2007 Washington
2007 Idaho
2007 Wyoming
2007 Utah

2008 Oklahoma
2008 New Mexico
2008 Arizona
2008 Alaska
2008 Hawaii

QUARTER DOLLARS
Statehood Quarters

HALF DOLLARS — 1794 to Date

The half dollar, authorized by the Act of April 2, 1792, was not minted until December, 1794.

The weight of the half dollar was 208 grains and its fineness .8924 when first issued. This standard was not changed until 1837 when the law of January 18, 1837 specified 206 1/4 grains, .900 fine. This fineness continued in use until 1965.

Arrows at the date in 1853 indicate the reduction of weight to 192 grains. During that year only, rays were added to the field on the reverse side. Arrows remained in 1854 and 1855.

In 1873 the weight was raised to 192.9 grains and arrows were again placed at the date.

FLOWING HAIR TYPE 1794-1795

AG-3 ABOUT GOOD—*Clear enough to identify.*
G-4 GOOD—*Date and letters sufficient to be readable. Main devices outlined, but lack details.*
VG-8 VERY GOOD—*Major details discernible. Letters well formed but worn.*
F-12 FINE—*Hair ends distinguishable. Top hairlines show, but otherwise worn smooth.*
VF-20 VERY FINE—*Hair in center shows some detail. Other details more bold.*
EF-40 EXTREMELY FINE—*Hair above head and down neck detailed with slight wear.*

2 Leaves under wings **3 Leaves under wings**

Quan. Minted	*AG-3*	*G-4*	*VG-8*	*F-12*	*VF-20*	*EF-40*
1794 23,464	$275.00	$550.00	$1,000	$1,500	$3,000	$6,000
1795 All kinds 299,680	125.00	250.00	325.00	450.00	850.00	2,400
1795 Recut date.........................	125.00	250.00	325.00	450.00	850.00	2,200
1795 3 leaves under each wing.	185.00	400.00	675.00	1,300	2,500	5,000

DRAPED BUST TYPE, SMALL EAGLE REVERSE 1796-1797

Grading same as above for About Good to Fine.

VF-20 VERY FINE—*Right side of drapery slightly worn. Left side to curls is smooth.*
EF-40 EXTREMELY FINE—*All lines in drapery on bust will show distinctly around to hair curls.*
MS-60 UNCIRCULATED—*No trace of wear. Light blemishes.*

1796, 15 Stars **1796, 16 Stars**

HALF DOLLARS

DRAPED BUST TYPE, SMALL EAGLE REVERSE 1796-1797

	Quan. Minted	*AG-3*	*G-4*	*VG-8*	*F-12*	*VF-20*	*EF-40*
1796, 15 Stars		$3,600	$6,000	$8,000	$10,000	$15,000	$25,000
1796, 16 stars	*3,918*	3,600	6,000	8,000	10,000	16,000	28,000
1797, 15 stars		3,600	6,000	8,000	10,000	15,000	27,000

DRAPED BUST TYPE, HERALDIC EAGLE REVERSE 1801-1807

	Quan. Minted	*G-4*	*VG-8*	*F-12*	*VF-20*	*EF-40*	*MS-60*
1801	30,289	$95.00	$140.00	$250.00	$500.00	$900.00	$5,100
1802	29,890	80.00	110.00	200.00	375.00	800.00	5,000
1803	188,234	60.00	75.00	110.00	250.00	475.00	3,500

1805, 5 over 4

1806, 6 over 5

1805, 5 over 4	211,722	65.00	100.00	150.00	300.00	800.00	6,000
1805 Normal date		55.00	70.00	90.00	200.00	350.00	2,500
1806		55.00	70.00	90.00	175.00	350.00	2,500
1806, 6 over 5	839,576	55.00	70.00	90.00	175.00	350.00	2,500
1806, 6 over inverted 6		60.00	85.00	150.00	300.00	600.00	3,750
1807	301,076	55.00	70.00	90.00	175.00	350.00	2,500

CAPPED BUST TYPE, Lettered Edge 1807-1836

John Reich designed this Capped Head concept of Liberty. The head of Liberty facing left was used on all U.S. coin denominations for the next thirty years.

G-4 GOOD—*Date and letters readable. Bust worn smooth with outline distinct.*
VG-8 VERY GOOD—*LIBERTY visible but faint. Legends distinguishable. Clasp at shoulder visible. Curl above it nearly smooth.*
F-12 FINE—*Clasp and adjacent curl clearly outlined with slight details.*
VF-20 VERY FINE—*Clasp at shoulder clear. Curl has wear only on highest point. Hair over brow distinguishable.*
EF-40 EXTREMELY FINE—*Clasp and adjacent curl fairly sharp. Brow and hair above distinct. Curls well defined.*
MS-60 UNCIRCULATED—*No trace of wear. Light blemishes.*

HALF DOLLARS

First style 1807-1808

	Quan. Minted	G-4	VG-8	F-12	VF-20	EF-40	MS-60
1807	750,500	$20.00	$26.00	$35.00	$75.00	$150.00	$900.00
1808, 8 over 7	}	20.00	25.00	30.00	60.00	125.00	750.00
1808	} 1,368,600	19.00	22.00	27.00	40.00	90.00	500.00

Remodeled Portrait and Eagle 1809-1834

	Quan. Minted	G-4	VG-8	F-12	VF-20	EF-40	MS-60
1809	1,405,810	17.00	21.00	24.00	32.00	75.00	425.00
1810	1,276,276	16.00	20.00	22.00	28.00	55.00	450.00
1811	1,203,644	16.00	19.00	22.00	28.00	55.00	425.00

1812, 2 over 1

1813, 50 C. over UNI

1814, 4 over 3

	Quan. Minted	G-4	VG-8	F-12	VF-20	EF-40	MS-60
1812, 2 over 1	} 1,628,059	17.00	20.00	30.00	60.00	120.00	800.00
1812 Normal	}	16.00	19.00	22.00	28.00	55.00	425.00
1813	} 1,241,903	16.00	19.00	22.00	28.00	55.00	400.00
1813, 50C over UNI.	}	18.00	22.00	35.00	50.00	90.00	475.00
1814, 4 over 3	} 1,039,075	16.00	20.00	25.00	30.00	65.00	400.00
1814 Normal	}	16.00	19.00	22.00	28.00	55.00	400.00

HALF DOLLARS

1817, 7 over 3

1817, 7 over 4

1817 Punctuated Date

	Quan. Minted	*G-4*	*VG-8*	*F-12*	*VF-20*	*EF-40*	*MS-60*
1815, 5 over 2	47,150	$300.00	$460.00	$650.00	$850.00	$1,500	$3,500
1817 All kinds	1,215,567						
1817, 7 over 3		17.00	27.00	75.00	125.00	210.00	675.00
1817, 7 over 4				25,000	40,000	70,000	
1817 dated 181.7		16.00	19.00	22.00	40.00	80.00	450.00
1817 Normal		16.00	18.00	20.00	26.00	55.00	400.00

1818, 2nd 8 over 7

1819, 9 over 8

1820, 20 over 19

	Quan. Minted	*G-4*	*VG-8*	*F-12*	*VF-20*	*EF-40*	*MS-60*
1818, 8 over 7	1,960,322	15.00	18.00	20.00	26.00	55.00	450.00
1818 Normal		15.00	18.00	20.00	26.00	55.00	400.00
1819 9 over 8	2,208,000	15.00	18.00	20.00	26.00	55.00	400.00
1819 Normal		15.00	18.00	20.00	26.00	55.00	400.00
1820, 20 over 19	751,122	15.00	19.00	21.00	30.00	60.00	460.00
1820 Normal		14.00	17.00	20.00	26.00	50.00	425.00
1821	1,305,797	14.00	17.00	20.00	26.00	50.00	400.00
1822	1,559,573	14.00	17.00	20.00	26.00	50.00	425.00
1823	1,694,200	14.00	17.00	20.00	26.00	50.00	300.00

"Various Dates" 1828 Square Base 2 (probably 4 over 2 over 0)

1824, 4 over 1

1828 Curl Base, Knob 2

1828 Square Base 2

	Quan. Minted	*G-4*	*VG-8*	*F-12*	*VF-20*	*EF-40*	*MS-60*
1824 All kinds	3,504,954						
1824 over various dates		14.00	17.00	20.00	26.00	50.00	300.00
1824, 4 over 1		15.00	18.00	20.00	26.00	55.00	310.00
1824 Normal		14.00	17.00	20.00	26.00	50.00	350.00
1825	2,943,166	14.00	17.00	20.00	26.00	50.00	275.00
1826	4,004,180	14.00	17.00	20.00	26.00	50.00	275.00
1827, 7 over 6	5,493,400	16.00	19.00	22.00	26.00	55.00	350.00
1827 Normal		14.00	17.00	20.00	26.00	50.00	275.00
1828 All kinds	3,075,200						
1828 Curl base no knob 2		14.00	17.00	20.00	26.00	50.00	275.00
1828 Curl base knob 2		18.00	22.00	27.00	40.00	60.00	475.00
1828 Square base		14.00	17.00	20.00	26.00	50.00	325.00

HALF DOLLARS

	Quan. Minted	G-4	VG-8	F-12	VF-20	EF-40	MS-60
1829, 9 over 7	3,712,156	$16.00	$18.00	$21.00	$27.00	$55.00	$350.00
1829 Normal		14.00	17.00	20.00	25.00	50.00	325.00
1830	4,764,800	14.00	17.00	20.00	25.00	50.00	275.00
1831	5,873,660	14.00	17.00	20.00	25.00	50.00	275.00
1832	4,797,000	14.00	17.00	20.00	25.00	50.00	275.00
1833	5,206,000	14.00	17.00	20.00	25.00	50.00	275.00
1834	6,412,004	14.00	17.00	20.00	25.00	50.00	275.00
1835	5,352,006	14.00	17.00	20.00	25.00	50.00	275.00
1836	6,545,000	14.00	17.00	20.00	25.00	50.00	275.00
1836, 50 over 00		17.00	21.00	25.00	38.00	70.00	500.00

Reeded Edge, Reverse "50 CENTS" 1836-1837

G-4 GOOD—*LIBERTY discernible on headband.*
VG-8 VERY GOOD—*Minimum of 3 letters in LIBERTY must be clear.*
F-12 FINE—*LIBERTY complete.*
VF-20 VERY FINE—*LIBERTY is sharp. Shoulder clasp is clear.*
EF-40 EXTREMELY FINE—*LIBERTY sharp and strong. Hair details show.*
MS-60 UNCIRCULATED—*No trace of wear. Light blemishes.*

1836	1,200	275.00	350.00	450.00	600.00	900.00	3,250
1837	3,629,820	18.00	20.00	25.00	40.00	70.00	400.00

Reeded Edge, Reverse "HALF DOL." 1838-1839

In 1838-39 the mint mark appears on the obverse; thereafter it is on the reverse below the eagle.

1838	3,546,000	17.00	19.00	25.00	40.00	70.00	400.00
1838O	(20)						40,000
1839	1,392,976	17.00	19.00	25.00	40.00	70.00	500.00
1839O	178,976	55.00	80.00	110.00	165.00	300.00	1,300

LIBERTY SEATED TYPE 1839-1891
No Motto Above Eagle 1839-1853

G-4 GOOD—*Scant rim. LIBERTY on shield worn off. Date and letters readable.*
VG-8 VERY GOOD—*Rim fairly defined. At least 3 letters in LIBERTY are evident.*
F-12 FINE—*LIBERTY complete, but weak.*
VF-20 VERY FINE—*LIBERTY mostly sharp.*
EF-40 EXTREMELY FINE—*LIBERTY entirely sharp. Scroll edges and clasp distinct.*
MS-60 UNCIRCULATED—*No trace of wear. Light blemishes.*

HALF DOLLARS

	Quan. Minted	G-4	VG-8	F-12	VF-20	EF-40	MS-60
1839 No drapery from elbow		$17.00	$25.00	$45.00	$125.00	$300.00	$2,500

Drapery from Elbow starting 1839

1842 Small Date

	Quan. Minted	G-4	VG-8	F-12	VF-20	EF-40	MS-60
1839	1,972,400	9.00	11.00	16.00	25.00	40.00	250.00
1840	1,435,008	8.00	12.00	17.00	30.00	50.00	250.00
1840O	855,100	8.00	10.00	15.00	25.00	37.00	275.00
1841	310,000	9.00	12.00	17.00	60.00	100.00	450.00
1841O	401,000	8.00	10.00	15.00	25.00	40.00	300.00
1842 Small date }	2,012,764	8.00	10.00	15.00	30.00	45.00	300.00
1842 Med. date }		8.00	10.00	15.00	25.00	40.00	275.00
1842O Small date	203,000	175.00	300.00	500.00	950.00	1,750	—
1842O Med. date	754,000	8.00	9.00	13.00	23.00	35.00	250.00
1843	3,844,000	8.00	9.00	13.00	23.00	35.00	250.00
1843O	2,268,000	8.00	9.00	13.00	23.00	35.00	250.00
1844	1,766,000	8.00	9.00	13.00	23.00	35.00	250.00
1844O	2,005,000	8.00	9.00	13.00	23.00	35.00	250.00
1845	589,000	8.00	9.00	15.00	24.00	40.00	250.00
1845O	2,094,000	8.00	9.00	13.00	23.00	35.00	250.00
1846 All kinds	2,210,000	8.00	9.00	13.00	18.00	35.00	250.00
1846 over horizontal 6 (error)		27.00	60.00	90.00	120.00	200.00	750.00
1846O	2,304,000	8.00	9.00	13.00	18.00	35.00	250.00
1847	1,156,000	8.00	9.00	13.00	18.00	35.00	250.00
1847O	2,584,000	8.00	9.00	13.00	18.00	35.00	250.00
1848	580,000	12.00	17.00	25.00	35.00	60.00	400.00
1848O	3,180,000	8.00	9.00	13.00	18.00	35.00	250.00
1849	1,252,000	8.00	9.00	13.00	18.00	35.00	250.00
1849O	2,310,000	8.00	9.00	13.00	18.00	35.00	250.00
1850	227,000	35.00	70.00	110.00	150.00	200.00	675.00
1850O	2,456,000	8.00	9.00	13.00	18.00	35.00	250.00
1851	200,750	35.00	70.00	130.00	175.00	250.00	675.00
1851O	402,000	8.00	9.00	13.00	18.00	35.00	250.00
1852	77,130	65.00	100.00	150.00	250.00	350.00	750.00
1852O	144,000	15.00	21.00	35.00	45.00	125.00	600.00
1853O		10,000	20,000	30,000	50,000		

HALF DOLLARS

Arrows at Date, Rays Around Eagle 1853 Only

	Quan. Minted	G-4	VG-8	F-12	VF-20	EF-40	MS-60
1853	3,532,708	$7.00	$9.00	$15.00	$45.00	$100.00	$900.00
1853O All kinds	1,328,000	7.00	9.00	15.00	45.00	110.00	1,200

Arrows at Date, No Rays 1854-1855

	Quan. Minted	G-4	VG-8	F-12	VF-20	EF-40	MS-60
1854	2,982,000	6.00	8.00	12.00	21.00	50.00	400.00
1854O	5,240,000	6.00	8.00	12.00	21.00	50.00	400.00
1855 over 1854	} 759,500	10.00	25.00	50.00	100.00	200.00	700.00
1855 Normal date		6.00	8.00	12.00	21.00	50.00	400.00
1855O	3,688,000	6.00	8.00	12.00	21.00	50.00	400.00
1855S	129,950	125.00	175.00	250.00	500.00	1,100	—

No Arrows at Date 1856-1866

	Quan. Minted	G-4	VG-8	F-12	VF-20	EF-40	MS-60
1856	938,000	7.00	8.00	12.00	17.00	35.00	200.00
1856O	2,658,000	7.00	8.00	12.00	17.00	35.00	200.00
1856S	211,000	9.00	11.00	17.00	40.00	85.00	750.00
1857	1,988,000	7.00	8.00	12.00	17.00	35.00	200.00
1857O	818,000	7.00	8.00	12.00	17.00	35.00	200.00
1857S	158,000	11.00	16.00	20.00	45.00	110.00	750.00

	Quan. Minted	G-4	VG-8	F-12	VF-20	EF-40	MS-60	Proof-63
1858	*(300+)* 4,226,000	$7.00	$8.00	$12.00	$17.00	$35.00	$200.00	$1,200
1858O	7,294,000	7.00	8.00	12.00	17.00	35.00	200.00	
1858S	476,000	9.00	11.00	15.00	24.00	45.00	500.00	
1859	(800) 748,000	7.00	8.00	12.00	17.00	35.00	200.00	800.00
1859O	2,834,000	7.00	8.00	12.00	17.00	35.00	200.00	
1859S	566,000	9.00	11.00	15.00	25.00	70.00	450.00	
1860	(1,000) 303,700	9.00	11.00	14.00	22.00	40.00	200.00	500.00
1860O	1,290,000	7.00	8.00	12.00	17.00	35.00	200.00	
1860S	472,000	9.00	11.00	14.00	20.00	35.00	275.00	
1861	(1,000) 2,888,400	7.00	8.00	12.00	17.00	35.00	200.00	500.00
1861O	2,532,633	7.00	8.00	12.00	17.00	35.00	200.00	
1861S	939,500	7.00	8.00	12.00	17.00	35.00	250.00	
1862	(550) 253,550	10.00	14.00	18.00	35.00	50.00	400.00	500.00
1862S	1,352,000	7.00	8.00	12.00	17.00	35.00	250.00	
1863	(460) 503,660	9.00	11.00	14.00	22.00	40.00	275.00	500.00
1863S	916,000	7.00	8.00	12.00	17.00	35.00	250.00	
1864	(470) 379,570	10.00	12.00	15.00	25.00	45.00	275.00	500.00
1864S	658,000	7.00	8.00	12.00	17.00	35.00	250.00	
1865	(500) 511,900	9.00	11.00	14.00	22.00	40.00	275.00	500.00
1865S	675,000	7.00	8.00	12.00	17.00	35.00	250.00	
1866S No motto	60,000	23.00	39.00	70.00	120.00	175.00	2,000	

HALF DOLLARS
Motto "In God We Trust" Added Above Eagle 1866-1873

	Quan. Minted	G-4	VG-8	F-12	VF-20	EF-40	MS-60	Proof-63
1866 ....(725)	745,625	$5.00	$6.00	$11.00	$15.00	$30.00	$200.00	$400.00
1866S	994,000	5.00	6.00	11.00	15.00	30.00	200.00	
1867 ....(625)	449,925	7.00	9.00	14.00	17.00	40.00	250.00	400.00
1867S	1,196,000	5.00	6.00	11.00	15.00	30.00	275.00	
1868 ....(600)	418,200	7.00	10.00	15.00	20.00	50.00	200.00	400.00
1868S	1,160,000	5.00	6.00	11.00	15.00	30.00	275.00	
1869 ....(600)	795,900	5.00	6.00	11.00	15.00	30.00	250.00	400.00
1869S	656,000	5.00	6.00	11.00	15.00	30.00	275.00	
1870 ....(1,000)	634,900	5.00	6.00	11.00	15.00	30.00	250.00	400.00
1870CC	54,617	175.00	350.00	600.00	1,100	2,500	—	
1870S	1,004,000	5.00	6.00	11.00	15.00	30.00	275.00	
1871 ....(960)	1,204,560	5.00	6.00	11.00	15.00	30.00	250.00	400.00
1871CC	153,950	35.00	60.00	100.00	180.00	400.00	2,000	
1871S	2,178,000	5.00	6.00	11.00	15.00	30.00	275.00	
1872 ....(950)	881,550	5.00	6.00	11.00	15.00	30.00	200.00	400.00
1872CC	257,000	17.00	30.00	60.00	110.00	200.00	1,500	
1872S	580,000	6.00	7.00	12.00	15.00	30.00	325.00	
1873 ....(600)	801,800	5.00	6.00	11.00	15.00	30.00	325.00	400.00
1873CC	122,500	35.00	65.00	110.00	200.00	350.00	2,750	

Arrows at Date 1873-1874

	Quan. Minted	G-4	VG-8	F-12	VF-20	EF-40	MS-60	Proof-63
1873 ....(550)	1,815,700	10.00	14.00	18.00	45.00	125.00	525.00	1,100
1873CC	214,560	30.00	55.00	100.00	180.00	400.00	2,000	
1873S	228,000	14.00	20.00	30.00	50.00	125.00	525.00	
1874 ....(700)	2,360,300	10.00	14.00	18.00	45.00	125.00	525.00	1,100
1874CC	59,000	85.00	125.00	225.00	350.00	650.00	3,000	
1874S	394,000	14.00	20.00	30.00	50.00	125.00	750.00	

No Arrows at Date 1875-1891

	Quan. Minted	G-4	VG-8	F-12	VF-20	EF-40	MS-60	Proof-63
1875 ....(700)	6,027,500	5.00	6.00	11.00	15.00	27.00	200.00	350.00
1875CC	1,008,000	5.00	7.00	12.00	20.00	35.00	235.00	

HALF DOLLARS

	Quan. Minted	G-4	VG-8	F-12	VF-20	EF-40	MS-60	Proof-63
1875S	3,200,000	$5.00	$6.00	$11.00	$15.00	$27.00	$200.00	
1876 (1,150)	8,419,150	5.00	6.00	11.00	15.00	27.00	200.00	$350.00
1876CC	1,956,000	5.00	6.00	11.00	16.00	30.00	350.00	
1876S	4,528,000	5.00	6.00	11.00	15.00	27.00	200.00	
1877 (510)	8,304,510	5.00	6.00	11.00	15.00	27.00	200.00	350.00
1877CC	1,420,000	5.00	6.00	11.00	16.00	32.00	235.00	
1877S	5,356,000	5.00	6.00	11.00	15.00	27.00	200.00	
1878 (800)	1,378,400	5.00	6.00	11.00	15.00	27.00	200.00	350.00
1878CC	62,000	85.00	140.00	200.00	300.00	500.00	1,900	
1878S	12,000	2,300	3,500	4,500	6,800	8,750	14,000	
1879 (1,100)	5,900	65.00	80.00	100.00	125.00	180.00	400.00	350.00
1880 (1,355)	9,755	55.00	70.00	95.00	125.00	150.00	350.00	350.00
1881 (975)	10,975	55.00	70.00	95.00	125.00	150.00	350.00	350.00
1882 (1,100)	5,500	65.00	80.00	100.00	125.00	180.00	400.00	350.00
1883 (1,039)	9,039	55.00	70.00	95.00	125.00	150.00	350.00	350.00
1884 (875)	5,275	65.00	80.00	100.00	125.00	180.00	450.00	400.00
1885 (930)	6,130	55.00	70.00	95.00	125.00	150.00	450.00	400.00
1886 (886)	5,886	55.00	70.00	95.00	125.00	150.00	450.00	400.00
1887 (710)	5,710	55.00	70.00	95.00	125.00	150.00	450.00	400.00
1888 (832)	12,833	50.00	65.00	80.00	125.00	140.00	400.00	400.00
1889 (711)	12,711	50.00	65.00	80.00	125.00	140.00	400.00	400.00
1890 (590)	12,590	50.00	65.00	80.00	125.00	140.00	400.00	400.00
1891 (600)	200,600	10.00	15.00	20.00	25.00	50.00	250.00	350.00

BARBER or LIBERTY HEAD TYPE 1892-1915

Like the dime and quarter dollar, this type was designed by Charles E. Barber, whose initial B is on the truncation of the neck.

G-4 GOOD—*Date and legends readable. LIBERTY worn off headband.*
VG-8 VERY GOOD—*Minimum of 3 letters readable in LIBERTY.*
F-12 FINE—*LIBERTY completely readable, but not sharp.*
VF-20 VERY FINE—*All letters in LIBERTY evenly plain.*
EF-40 EXTREMELY FINE—*LIBERTY bold, and its ribbon distinct.*
MS-60 UNCIRCULATED—*No trace of wear. Light blemishes.*

Mint mark location on reverse below eagle.

	Quan. Minted	G-4	VG-8	F-12	VF-20	EF-40	MS-60	Proof-63
1892 (1,245)	935,245	$7.00	$11.00	$16.00	$32.00	$100.00	$200.00	$375.00
1892O	390,000	45.00	60.00	100.00	150.00	235.00	450.00	
1892S	1,029,028	50.00	60.00	100.00	150.00	225.00	435.00	
1893 (792)	1,826,792	5.00	7.00	18.00	30.00	90.00	250.00	375.00
1893O	1,389,000	8.00	12.00	25.00	55.00	150.00	275.00	
1893S	740,000	30.00	40.00	70.00	140.00	200.00	600.00	
1894 (972)	1,148,972	5.00	8.00	22.00	38.00	100.00	250.00	375.00
1894O	2,138,000	4.00	6.00	22.00	36.00	125.00	275.00	
1894S	4,048,690	4.00	6.00	20.00	30.00	100.00	250.00	
1895 (880)	1,835,218	4.00	6.00	20.00	35.00	90.00	275.00	375.00
1895O	1,766,000	4.00	7.00	21.00	35.00	100.00	275.00	

Italic prices indicate unsettled values due to fluctuating bullion market. See Bullion Chart.

HALF DOLLARS

	Quan. Minted	G-4	VG-8	F-12	VF-20	EF-40	MS-60	Proof-63
1895S	1,108,086	$8.00	$11.00	$25.00	$50.00	$125.00	$275.00	
1896	(762) 950,762	5.00	7.00	20.00	35.00	100.00	275.00	$375.00
1896O	924,000	7.00	10.00	35.00	80.00	175.00	575.00	
1896S	1,140,948	25.00	35.00	60.00	100.00	200.00	600.00	
1897	(731) 2,480,731	*2.50*	*3.50*	10.00	25.00	65.00	200.00	375.00
1897O	632,000	22.00	35.00	120.00	225.00	360.00	800.00	
1897S	933,900	40.00	50.00	110.00	175.00	300.00	675.00	
1898	(735) 2,956,735	*2.50*	*3.50*	10.00	25.00	75.00	200.00	375.00
1898O	874,000	6.50	10.00	25.00	65.00	160.00	375.00	
1898S	2,358,550	3.50	5.00	16.00	30.00	90.00	350.00	
1899	(846) 5,538,846	*2.50*	*3.50*	10.00	25.00	60.00	200.00	375.00
1899O	1,724,000	3.00	4.50	20.00	35.00	130.00	325.00	
1899S	1,686,411	3.00	4.50	20.00	35.00	100.00	325.00	
1900	(912) 4,762,912	*2.50*	*3.50*	10.00	25.00	65.00	200.00	375.00
1900O	2,744,000	3.00	5.00	20.00	35.00	125.00	325.00	
1900S	2,560,322	3.00	5.00	18.00	35.00	100.00	275.00	
1901	(813) 4,268,813	*2.50*	*3.50*	10.00	25.00	60.00	200.00	375.00
1901O	1,124,000	3.00	5.00	20.00	45.00	140.00	675.00	
1901S	847,044	5.50	8.50	37.00	80.00	275.00	800.00	
1902	(777) 4,922,777	*2.50*	*3.50*	10.00	25.00	60.00	200.00	375.00
1902O	2,526,000	3.00	4.50	12.00	30.00	90.00	300.00	
1902S	1,460,670	3.00	4.50	12.00	30.00	90.00	275.00	
1903	(755) 2,278,755	*2.50*	*3.50*	10.00	25.00	60.00	200.00	375.00
1903O	2,100,000	3.00	5.00	12.00	30.00	90.00	300.00	
1903S	1,920,772	3.00	5.00	12.00	30.00	95.00	300.00	
1904	(670) 2,992,670	*2.50*	*3.50*	10.00	25.00	60.00	200.00	375.00
1904O	1,117,600	4.00	6.50	16.00	40.00	140.00	500.00	
1904S	553,038	5.50	9.00	40.00	120.00	275.00	950.00	
1905	(727) 662,727	*2.50*	*3.50*	15.00	30.00	75.00	225.00	375.00
1905O	505,000	4.00	6.50	16.00	40.00	135.00	350.00	
1905S	2,494,000	3.00	4.50	12.00	30.00	85.00	300.00	
1906	(675) 2,638,675	*2.50*	*3.50*	10.00	25.00	65.00	200.00	375.00
1906D	4,028,000	3.00	4.50	12.00	35.00	75.00	200.00	
1906O	2,446,000	*2.50*	*3.50*	11.00	30.00	75.00	275.00	
1906S	1,740,154	*2.50*	*3.50*	11.00	35.00	80.00	275.00	
1907	(575) 2,598,575	*2.50*	*3.50*	10.00	25.00	65.00	200.00	375.00
1907D	3,856,000	*2.50*	*3.50*	11.00	30.00	70.00	200.00	
1907O	3,946,600	*2.50*	*3.50*	11.00	30.00	70.00	200.00	
1907S	1,250,000	*2.50*	4.00	18.00	45.00	115.00	375.00	
1908	(545) 1,354,545	*2.50*	*3.50*	10.00	25.00	65.00	200.00	375.00
1908D	3,280,000	*2.50*	*3.50*	10.00	30.00	65.00	200.00	
1908O	5,360,000	*2.50*	*3.50*	10.00	30.00	65.00	200.00	
1908S	1,644,828	*2.50*	*3.50*	15.00	37.00	90.00	325.00	
1909	(650) 2,368,650	*2.50*	*3.50*	11.00	30.00	65.00	200.00	375.00
1909O	925,400	4.00	5.00	15.00	37.00	110.00	325.00	
1909S	1,764,000	*2.50*	*3.50*	12.00	30.00	85.00	250.00	
1910	(551) 418,551	4.00	6.00	15.00	40.00	125.00	285.00	375.00
1910S	1,948,000	*2.50*	*3.50*	12.00	30.00	85.00	250.00	
1911	(543) 1,406,543	*2.50*	*3.50*	10.00	25.00	65.00	225.00	375.00
1911D	695,080	*2.50*	*3.50*	10.00	25.00	70.00	275.00	
1911S	1,272,000	*2.50*	*3.50*	10.00	25.00	70.00	280.00	
1912	(700) 1,550,700	*2.50*	*3.50*	10.00	22.00	65.00	200.00	375.00
1912D	2,300,800	*2.50*	*3.50*	10.00	25.00	70.00	200.00	
1912S	1,370,000	*2.50*	*3.50*	10.00	25.00	70.00	275.00	

Italic prices indicate unsettled values due to fluctuating bullion market. See Bullion Chart.

HALF DOLLARS

	Quan. Minted	G-4	VG-8	F-12	VF-20	EF-40	MS-60	Proof-63
1913 ....(627)	188,627	$7.50	$12.00	$30.00	$75.00	$130.00	$450.00	$500.00
1913D.....................	534,000	*2.50*	*3.50*	12.00	25.00	80.00	225.00	
1913S.....................	604,000	*2.50*	*3.50*	15.00	35.00	75.00	275.00	
1914 ....(380)	124,610	11.00	18.00	70.00	120.00	200.00	450.00	500.00
1914S.....................	992,000	*2.50*	*3.50*	12.00	25.00	70.00	325.00	
1915 ....(450)	138,450	8.00	12.50	32.00	80.00	150.00	475.00	500.00
1915D.....................	1,170,400	*2.50*	*3.50*	10.00	22.00	65.00	200.00	
1915S.....................	1,604,000	*2.50*	*3.50*	10.00	22.00	65.00	210.00	

LIBERTY WALKING TYPE 1916-1947

This type was designed by A. A. Weinman. The designer's monogram AAW appears under the tip of the wing feathers. On the 1916 coins and some of the 1917 coins the mint mark is located on the obverse below the motto.

G-4 GOOD—*Rims are defined. Motto IN GOD WE TRUST readable.*
VG-8 VERY GOOD—*Motto is distinct. About half of skirt lines at left are clear.*
F-12 FINE—*All skirt lines evident, but worn in spots. Details in sandal below motto are clear.*
VF-20 VERY FINE—*Skirt lines sharp including leg area. Little wear on breast and right arm.*
EF-40 EXTREMELY FINE—*All skirt lines bold.*
MS-60 UNCIRCULATED—*No trace of wear. Light blemishes.*
MS-63 SELECT UNCIRCULATED—*No trace of wear. Slight blemishes. Attractive mint luster.*

1916-1917

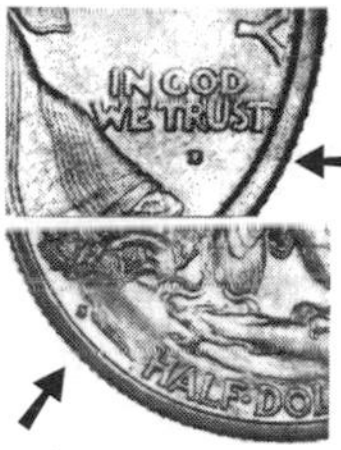

1917-1947

Mint mark locations.

Choice uncirculated well struck specimens are worth more than values listed.

	Quan. Minted	G-4	VG-8	F-12	VF-20	EF-40	MS-60
1916..................................	608,000	$11.00	$14.00	$24.00	$50.00	$70.00	$135.00
1916D...............(Obv.)	1,014,400	8.00	9.00	15.00	35.00	65.00	125.00
1916S ....(Obv.)	508,000	30.00	35.00	55.00	135.00	210.00	450.00
1917..................................	12,292,000	*2.00*	*2.50*	3.50	8.00	12.00	50.00
1917D...............(Obv.)	765,400	5.50	7.00	16.00	35.00	55.00	180.00
1917D ....(Rev.)	1,940,000	3.00	3.50	9.00	25.00	70.00	300.00
1917S ....(Obv.)	952,000	7.00	9.00	22.00	110.00	270.00	825.00
1917S...............(Rev.)	5,554,000	*2.50*	3.00	5.00	12.00	20.00	120.00
1918..................................	6,634,000	*2.00*	3.00	5.00	24.00	55.00	210.00
1918D................................	3,853,040	*2.00*	3.00	5.00	25.00	70.00	400.00
1918S................................	10,282,000	*2.00*	3.00	5.00	12.00	25.00	160.00
1919..................................	962,000	7.00	9.00	14.00	60.00	180.00	550.00
1919D................................	1,165,000	5.00	7.00	15.00	75.00	210.00	1,000
1919S................................	1,552,000	5.00	7.00	10.00	60.00	235.00	925.00
1920..................................	6,372,000	*1.60*	*1.60*	4.00	12.00	25.00	95.00
1920D................................	1,551,000	*3.00*	*4.00*	11.00	60.00	135.00	500.00
1920S................................	4,624,000	*1.60*	*3.00*	7.50	20.00	60.00	275.00
1921..................................	246,000	40.00	60.00	95.00	275.00	725.00	1,500
1921D................................	208,000	60.00	75.00	140.00	325.00	950.00	1,400
1921S................................	548,000	10.00	15.00	45.00	225.00	1,800	4,200
1923S................................	2,178,000	*3.00*	*3.50*	7.00	22.50	80.00	450.00

Italic prices indicate unsettled values due to fluctuating bullion market. See Bullion Chart.

HALF DOLLARS

	Quan. Minted	G-4	VG-8	F-12	VF-20	EF-40	MS-60	Proof-63
1927S	2,392,000	*$1.60*	*$1.75*	$4.00	$13.00	$40.00	$325.00	
1928S	1,940,000	*1.60*	*1.75*	4.00	15.00	50.00	300.00	
1929D	1,001,200	*1.60*	*1.75*	3.50	9.00	30.00	125.00	
1929S	1,902,000	*1.60*	*1.75*	3.50	8.50	35.00	125.00	
1933S	1,786,000	*1.60*	*1.75*	3.00	6.00	21.00	200.00	
1934	6,964,000	*1.50*	*1.50*	*1.60*	*2.00*	4.00	20.00	
1934D	2,361,400	*1.50*	*1.50*	*1.60*	*2.50*	12.00	50.00	
1934S	3,652,000	*1.50*	*1.50*	*1.60*	*2.25*	12.50	120.00	
1935	9,162,000	*1.50*	*1.50*	*1.60*	*2.00*	3.00	20.00	
1935D	3,003,800	*1.50*	*1.50*	*1.60*	*2.25*	12.00	60.00	
1935S	3,854,000	*1.50*	*1.50*	*1.60*	*2.25*	12.00	65.00	
1936	(3,901) 12,617,901	*1.50*	*1.50*	*1.60*	*2.00*	3.00	20.00	$675.00
1936D	4,252,400	*1.50*	*1.50*	*1.60*	*2.25*	7.00	40.00	
1936S	3,884,000	*1.50*	*1.50*	*1.60*	*2.25*	7.00	65.00	
1937	(5,728) 9,527,728	*1.50*	*1.50*	*1.60*	*2.00*	3.00	20.00	250.00
1937D	1,676,000	*1.50*	*1.50*	*2.00*	*3.00*	12.00	80.00	
1937S	2,090,000	*1.50*	*1.50*	*1.60*	*2.25*	7.00	60.00	
1938	(8,152) 4,118,152	*1.50*	*1.50*	*1.60*	*2.00*	4.00	27.00	225.00
1938D	491,600	10.00	12.00	16.00	20.00	50.00	200.00	
1939	(8,808) 6,820,808	*1.50*	*1.50*	*1.60*	*2.00*	3.00	18.00	225.00
1939D	4,267,800	*1.50*	*1.50*	*1.60*	*2.00*	4.00	20.00	
1939S	2,552,000	*1.50*	*1.50*	*1.60*	*2.00*	6.00	45.00	

	Quan. Minted	VG-8	F-12	VF-20	EF-40	MS-60	MS-63	Proof-63
1940	(11,279) 9,167,279	*$1.50*	*$1.50*	*$1.60*	*$2.00*	$13.00	$15.00	$175.00
1940S	4,550,000	*1.50*	*1.50*	*1.60*	*2.00*	15.00	18.00	
1941	(15,412) 24,207,412	*1.50*	*1.50*	*1.60*	*2.00*	12.00	15.00	160.00
1941D	11,248,400	*1.50*	*1.50*	*1.60*	*2.00*	15.00	20.00	
1941S	8,098,000	*1.50*	*1.50*	*1.60*	*2.00*	30.00	45.00	
1942	(21,120) 47,839,120	*1.50*	*1.50*	*1.60*	*2.00*	12.00	15.00	160.00
1942D	10,973,800	*1.50*	*1.50*	*1.60*	*2.00*	14.00	22.00	
1942S	12,708,000	*1.50*	*1.50*	*1.60*	*2.00*	15.00	23.00	
1943	53,190,000	*1.50*	*1.50*	*1.60*	*2.00*	12.00	15.00	
1943D	11,346,000	*1.50*	*1.50*	*1.60*	*2.00*	16.00	25.00	
1943S	13,450,000	*1.50*	*1.50*	*1.60*	*2.00*	15.00	20.00	
1944	28,206,000	*1.50*	*1.50*	*1.60*	*2.00*	12.00	15.00	
1944D	9,769,000	*1.50*	*1.50*	*1.60*	*2.00*	15.00	20.00	
1944S	8,904,000	*1.50*	*1.50*	*1.60*	*2.00*	14.00	23.00	
1945	31,502,000	*1.50*	*1.50*	*1.60*	*2.00*	12.00	15.00	
1945D	9,966,800	*1.50*	*1.50*	*1.60*	*2.00*	12.00	17.00	
1945S	10,156,000	*1.50*	*1.50*	*1.60*	*2.00*	12.00	18.00	
1946	12,118,000	*1.50*	*1.50*	*1.60*	*2.00*	12.00	15.00	
1946D	2,151,000	*1.50*	*1.50*	*1.60*	*2.00*	12.00	15.00	
1946S	3,724,000	*1.50*	*1.50*	*1.60*	*2.00*	12.00	15.00	
1947	4,094,000	*1.50*	*1.50*	*1.60*	*2.00*	12.00	18.00	
1947D	3,900,600	*1.50*	*1.50*	*1.60*	*2.00*	12.00	18.00	

Italic prices indicate unsettled values due to fluctuating bullion market. See Bullion Chart

FRANKLIN-LIBERTY BELL TYPE 1948-1963

The Benjamin Franklin half dollar and the Roosevelt dime were both designed by John R. Sinnock. His initials appear below the shoulder.

VF-20 VERY FINE—*At least half of the lower and upper incused lines on the rim of the bell must show.*
EF-40 EXTREMELY FINE—*Wear spots appear at top of end curls and hair back of ears. On reverse, Liberty Bell will show wear at top and on lettering.*
MS-60 UNCIRCULATED—*No trace of wear. A few noticeable blemishes.*
MS-63 SELECT UNCIRCULATED—*No trace of wear. Light blemishes. Attractive mint luster.*

HALF DOLLARS

Mint mark location

Choice, well struck uncirculated halves command higher prices.

	Quan. Minted	VF-20	EF-40	MS-60	MS-63	Proof-63
1948	3,006,814	*$1.75*	$2.00	$5.00	$8.00	
1948D	4,028,600	*1.50*	*1.50*	4.00	5.00	
1949	5,614,000	*1.50*	*1.75*	10.00	14.00	
1949D	4,120,600	*1.50*	*1.75*	12.00	16.00	
1949S	3,744,000	*1.50*	3.00	20.00	25.00	
1950 (51,386)	7,793,509	*1.50*	*1.75*	9.00	12.00	$115.00
1950D	8,031,600	*1.50*	*1.75*	8.00	12.00	
1951 (57,500)	16,859,602	*1.50*	*1.75*	3.00	5.00	65.00
1951D	9,475,200	*1.50*	*1.75*	9.00	12.00	
1951S	13,696,000	*1.50*	*1.75*	9.00	13.00	
1952 (81,980)	21,274,073	*1.50*	*1.75*	3.00	4.00	35.00
1952D	25,395,600	*1.50*	*1.75*	2.75	4.00	
1952S	5,526,000	*1.50*	*1.75*	13.00	15.00	
1953 (128,800)	2,796,920	*1.50*	*1.75*	6.00	8.00	26.00
1953D	20,900,400	*1.50*	*1.50*	3.00	4.00	
1953S	4,148,000	*1.50*	*1.50*	6.00	8.00	
1954 (233,300)	13,421,503	*1.50*	*1.50*	2.00	3.00	18.00
1954D	25,445,580	*1.50*	*1.50*	2.50	3.50	
1954S	4,993,400	*1.50*	*1.50*	3.00	4.00	
1955 (378,200)	2,876,381	2.00	3.00	4.00	5.00	14.00
1956 (669,384)	4,701,384	*1.50*	*1.50*	2.00	2.50	5.00
1957 (1,247,952)	6,361,952	*1.50*	*1.50*	2.00	3.00	5.00
1957D	19,966,850	*1.50*	*1.50*	2.00	2.10	
1958 (875,652)	4,917,652	*1.50*	*1.50*	2.00	2.10	5.00
1958D	23,962,412	*1.50*	*1.50*	2.00	2.10	
1959 (1,149,291)	7,349,291	*1.50*	*1.50*	2.00	2.10	3.00
1959D	13,053,750	*1.50*	*1.50*	2.00	2.10	
1960 (1,691,602)	7,715,602	*1.50*	*1.50*	*1.60*	1.75	3.00
1960D	18,215,812	*1.50*	*1.50*	*1.60*	1.75	
1961 (3,028,244)	11,318,244	*1.50*	*1.50*	*1.60*	1.75	2.50
1961D	20,276,442	*1.50*	*1.50*	*1.60*	1.75	
1962 (3,218,019)	12,932,019	*1.50*	*1.50*	*1.60*	1.75	2.50
1962D	35,473,281	*1.50*	*1.50*	*1.60*	1.75	
1963 (3,075,645)	25,239,645	*1.50*	*1.50*	*1.60*	1.75	2.50
1963D	67,069,292	*1.50*	*1.50*	*1.60*	1.75	

Italic prices indicate unsettled values due to fluctuating bullion market. See Bullion Chart.

KENNEDY TYPE 1964 to Date

Gilroy Roberts, former Chief Engraver of the Mint, designed the obverse of this coin. His stylized initials are on the truncation of the forceful bust of President John F. Kennedy. The reverse, which uses the presidential coat of arms for the motif, is the work of Chief Engraver Frank Gasparro.

1964 Mint mark location

1968 Mint mark location

Silver Coinage 1964

	Quan. Minted	MS-63	Proof-63
1964 ....(3,950,762)	277,254,766	*$1.50*	$2.50
1964D	156,205,446	*1.50*	

Silver Clad Coinage 1965-1970

	Quan. Minted	MS-63	Proof-63
1965	65,879,366	*.60*	
1966	108,984,932	*.60*	
1967	295,046,978	*.60*	
1968D	246,951,930	*.60*	
1968S Proof	(3,041,506)		1.00
1969D	129,881,800	*.60*	
1969S Proof	(2,934,631)		1.00
1970D (Issued only in mint sets)	2,150,000	6.00	
1970S Proof	(2,632,810)		4.00

Copper-Nickel Clad Coinage 1971-

	Quan. Minted	MS-63	Proof-63
1971	155,164,000	$.55	
1971D	302,097,424	.55	
1971S Proof	(3,220,733)		$.75
1972	153,180,000	.60	
1972D	141,890,000	.60	
1972S Proof	(3,260,996)		.75
1973	64,964,000	$.55	
1973D	83,171,400	.55	
1973S Proof	(2,760,339)		$.75
1974	201,596,000	.55	
1974D	79,066,300	.55	
1974S Proof	(2,612,568)		.75

BICENTENNIAL COINAGE DATED 1776—1976

	Quan. Minted	MS-63	Proof-63
1776-1976 Copper-nickel clad	234,308,000	$.55	
1776-1976D Copper-nickel clad	287,565,248	.55	
1776-1976S Copper-nickel clad	(7,059,099)		$.75
1776-1976S Silver clad ....*(4,000,000)	*11,000,000	1.50	2.00

Eagle Reverse Resumed

	Quan. Minted	MS-63	Proof-63
1977	43,598,000	.60	
1977D	31,449,106	.60	

*Approximate mintage.

Italic prices indicate unsettled values due to fluctuating bullion market. See Bullion Chart.

HALF DOLLARS

	Quan. Minted	MS-63	Proof-63
1977S Proof	(3,251,152)		$1.00
1978	14,350,000	$.60	
1978D	13,765,799	.90	
1978S Proof	(3,127,781)		1.00
1979	68,312,000	.55	
1979D	15,815,422	.55	
1979S Proof	(3,677,175)		
Filled S			1.00
Clear S			6.00
1980P	44,134,000	.55	
1980D	33,456,449	.55	
1980S Proof	(3,554,806)		1.00
1981P	29,544,000	.60	
1981D	27,839,533	.55	
1981S Proof	(4,063,083)		1.00
1982P	10,819,000	1.00	
1982D	13,140,102	1.00	
1982S Proof	(3,857,479)		1.00
1983P	34,139,000	1.25	
1983D	32,472,244	1.25	
1983S Proof	(3,279,126)		1.00
1984P	26,029,000	.75	
1984D	26,262,158	.75	
1984S Proof	(3,065,110)		1.00
1985P	18,706,962	.75	
1985D	19,814,034	.90	
1985S Proof	(3,362,821)		1.00
1986P	13,107,633	2.50	
1986D	15,336,145	1.50	
1986S Proof	(3,010,497)		4.00
1987P	*2,890,758	1.50	
1987D	*2,890,758	1.50	
1987S Proof	(4,227,728)		1.00
1988P	13,626,000	1.00	
1988D	12,000,096	1.00	
1988S Proof	(3,262,948)		2.00
1989P	24,542,000	.75	
1989D	23,000,216	.70	
1989S Proof	(3,220,194)		1.50
1990P	22,278,000	.75	
1990D	20,096,242	1.00	
1990S Proof	(3,299,559)		2.00
1991P	14,874,000	.60	
1991D	15,054,678	1.00	
1991S Proof	(2,867,787)		4.50
1992P	17,628,000	$.50	
1992D	17,000,106	.75	
1992S Proof	(2,858,981)		$3.50
1992S Silver Prf	(1,317,579)		5.00
1993P	15,510,000	.50	
1993D	15,000,006	.50	
1993S Proof	(2,633,439)		5.50
1993S Silver Prf	(761,353)		10.00
1994P	23,718,000	.50	
1994D	23,828,110	.50	
1994S Proof	(2,484,594)		3.00
1994S Silver Prf	(785,329)		14.00
1995P	26,496,000	.50	
1995D	26,288,000	.50	
1995S Proof	(2,117,496)		13.00
1995S Silver Prf	(679,985)		30.00
1996P	24,442,000	.50	
1996D	24,744,000	.50	
1996S Proof	(1,750,244)		3.50
1996S Silver Prf	(775,021)		15.00
1997P	20,882,000	.50	
1997D	19,876,000	.50	
1997S Proof	(2,055,000)		8.00
1997S Silver Prf	(741,678)		27.00
1998P	15,646,000	.50	
1998D	15,064,000	.50	
1998S Proof			5.00
1998S Silver Prf	(878,792)		8.00
1998S Silver Matte Prf			100.00
1999P	8,900,000	.55	
1999D	10,682,000	.55	
1999S Proof			3.00
1999S Silver Proof	(800,000)		6.00
2000P	22,600,000	.60	
2000D	19,466,000	.60	
2000S Proof	(2,968,900)		3.00
2000S Silver Proof	(856,400)		5.00
2001P	(21,200,000)	.55	
2001D	(19,504,000)	.55	
2001S Proof			3.00
2001S Silver Proof			5.00
2002P		.55	
2002D		.55	
2002S Proof			2.00
2002S Silver Proof			5.00

*Not issued for circulation; included with uncirculated and souvenir sets.

SILVER DOLLARS — 1794 to Date

The silver dollar was authorized by Congress April 2, 1792. Weight and fineness were specified at 416 grains and 892.4 fine. The first issues appeared in 1794 and until 1804 all silver dollars had the value stamped on the edge: HUNDRED CENTS, ONE DOLLAR OR UNIT. After a lapse in coinage of the silver dollar during the period 1804 to 1835, coins were made with either plain or reeded edges and the value was placed on the reverse side.

The weight was changed by the law of January 18, 1837 to 412½ grains, fineness .900. The coinage was discontinued by the Act of February 12, 1873 and reauthorized by the Act of February 28, 1878. The dollar was again discontinued after 1935, and since then only the copper-nickel pieces first authorized in 1971 have been coined for circulation.

SILVER DOLLARS

FLOWING HAIR TYPE 1794-1795

AG-3 ABOUT GOOD—*Clear enough to identify.*
G-4 GOOD—*Date and letters readable. Main devices outlined, but lack details.*
VG-8 VERY GOOD—*Major details discernible. Letters well formed but worn.*
F-12 FINE—*Hair ends distinguishable. Top hairlines show, but otherwise worn smooth.*
VF-20 VERY FINE—*Hair in center shows some detail. Other details more bold.*
EF-40 EXTREMELY FINE—*Hair well defined but will show some wear.*
MS-60 UNCIRCULATED—*No trace of wear. Light blemishes.*

	Quan. Minted	*AG-3*	*G-4*	*VG-8*	*F-12*	*VF-20*	*EF-40*	*MS-60*
1794	1,758	$2,500	$5,000	$8,000	$12,500	$24,000	$42,500	—
1795	*160,295*	250.00	450.00	600.00	850.00	1,500	3,000	$14,000

DRAPED BUST TYPE, SMALL EAGLE REVERSE 1795-1798

AG-3 ABOUT GOOD—*Clear enough to identify.*
G-4 GOOD—*Bust outlined, no detail. Date readable, some leaves evident.*
VG-8 VERY GOOD—*Drapery worn except deepest folds. Hairlines smooth.*
F-12 FINE—*All drapery lines distinguishable. Hairlines near cheek and neck show some detail.*
VF-20 VERY FINE—*Left side of drapery worn smooth.*
EF-40 EXTREMELY FINE—*Drapery shows distinctly. Hair well outlined and detailed.*
MS-60 UNCIRCULATED—*No trace of wear. Light blemishes.*

1795 Bust Type	*42,738*	$250.00	$375.00	$475.00	$700.00	$1,100	$2,000	$10,000
1796	72,920	250.00	350.00	450.00	650.00	1,000	1,900	10,000
1797	*57,776*	250.00	350.00	450.00	650.00	1,000	1,900	8,500
1798 All Kinds	*277,536*	200.00	325.00	450.00	650.00	900.00	1,900	9,000

SILVER DOLLARS

HERALDIC EAGLE REVERSE 1798-1804

G-4 GOOD—*Letters and date readable. E PLURIBUS UNUM obliterated.*
VG-8 VERY GOOD—*Motto partially readable. Only deepest drapery details visible. All other lines smooth.*
F-12 FINE—*All drapery lines distinguishable. Harlines near cheek and neck show some detail.*
VF-20 VERY FINE—*Left side of drapery worn smooth.*
EF-40 EXTREMELY FINE—*Drapery is distinct. Hair well detailed.*
MS-60 UNCIRCULATED—*No trace of wear. Light blemishes.*

Quan. Minted	*G-4*	*VG-8*	*F-12*	*VF-20*	*EF-40*	*MS-60*
1798 Heraldic eagle	$200.00	$250.00	$350.00	$500.00	$900.00	$6,000
1799 423,515	200.00	250.00	350.00	500.00	900.00	6,000
1800 220,920	200.00	250.00	350.00	500.00	900.00	6,000
1801 54,454	200.00	250.00	350.00	500.00	900.00	6,000
1802 41,650	200.00	250.00	350.00	500.00	900.00	6,000
1803 85,634	200.00	250.00	350.00	500.00	900.00	6,000
1804 Variety 1, letter O in "OF" above cloud						Proof $800,000
1804 Variety 2, letter O above space between clouds						Proof $500,000

GOBRECHT SILVER DOLLARS

Silver dollars of 1836, 1838, and 1839 were mostly made as trial pieces, but some were made in quantities for general circulation. There was no regular issue of dollars 1805 to 1835 inclusive.

	VF-20	*EF-40*	*Proof-60*
1836 C. GOBRECHT F. on base. Rev. Eagle flying upward amid stars. Plain edge. Although scarce, this is the most common variety and was issued for circulation as regular coinage	$2,000	$2,750	$5,000
1838 Similar obv., designer's name omitted, stars added around border. Rev. Eagle flying left in plain field. Reeded edge	2,100	3,000	5,200
1839 Obv. as above. Rev. Eagle in plain field. Reeded edge. Issued for circulation as regular coinage	2,200	3,250	6,000

SILVER DOLLARS
LIBERTY SEATED TYPE — REGULAR ISSUES 1840-1873

In 1840 silver dollars were again issued for general circulation, and the seated figure of Liberty device was adopted for the obverse, and a heraldic eagle on the reverse.

VG-8 VERY GOOD—*Any 3 letters of LIBERTY at least two-thirds complete.*
F-12 FINE—*All 7 letters of LIBERTY visible though weak.*
VF-20 VERY FINE—*LIBERTY is strong but its ribbon shows slight wear.*
EF-40 EXTREMELY FINE—*Horizontal lines of shield complete. Eagle's eye plain.*
MS-60 UNCIRCULATED—*No trace of wear. Light marks or blemishes.*

Mint mark location is on the reverse below eagle.

	Quan. Minted	*VG-8*	*F-12*	*VF-20*	*EF-40*	*MS-60*	*Proof-60*
1840	61,005	$65.00	$100.00	$150.00	$210.00	$700.00	$3,000
1841	173,000	50.00	80.00	120.00	200.00	600.00	3,500
1842	184,618	50.00	80.00	120.00	200.00	600.00	3,000
1843	165,100	50.00	80.00	120.00	200.00	600.00	3,000
1844	20,000	60.00	90.00	135.00	225.00	950.00	3,000
1845	24,500	60.00	90.00	135.00	225.00	1,000	3,500
1846	110,600	50.00	80.00	120.00	200.00	600.00	3,000
1846O	59,000	65.00	100.00	135.00	250.00	1,400	
1847	140,750	50.00	80.00	120.00	200.00	600.00	3,000
1848	15,000	100.00	200.00	275.00	375.00	1,000	3,000
1849	62,600	50.00	80.00	120.00	200.00	600.00	3,000
1850	7,500	125.00	210.00	250.00	450.00	2,000	3,000
1850O	40,000	90.00	120.00	225.00	450.00	2,500	
1851	1,300	1,500	2,500	4,000	5,000	8,000	8,000
1852	1,100	1,000	2,100	3,500	4,000	7,000	6,000
1853	46,110	70.00	90.00	120.00	200.00	800.00	4,000
1854	33,140	300.00	450.00	600.00	1,100	2,250	5,000
1855	26,000	200.00	400.00	500.00	800.00	2,250	5,000
1856	63,500	85.00	120.00	175.00	300.00	1,300	2,500
1857	94,000	85.00	120.00	175.00	300.00	1,000	2,100
1858 Est. (300+)		1,000	1,300	2,000	2,500		2,750
1859 (800)	256,500	100.00	135.00	185.00	250.00	900.00	1,500
1859O	360,000	50.00	80.00	120.00	200.00	600.00	
1859S	20,000	100.00	150.00	225.00	450.00	2,500	
1860 (1,330)	218,930	80.00	110.00	160.00	225.00	700.00	1,500
1860O	515,000	50.00	80.00	120.00	200.00	600.00	
1861 (1,000)	78,500	125.00	225.00	325.00	425.00	1,000	1,500
1862 (550)	12,090	100.00	125.00	250.00	425.00	1,000	1,500
1863 (460)	27,660	70.00	110.00	160.00	275.00	1,000	1,200
1864 (470)	31,170	60.00	100.00	140.00	250.00	900.00	1,200
1865 (500)	47,000	60.00	100.00	140.00	250.00	900.00	1,200

SILVER DOLLARS
Motto "In God We Trust" Added to Reverse

	Quan. Minted	VG-8	F-12	VF-20	EF-40	MS-60	Proof-60
1866 ....(725)	49,625	$55.00	$85.00	$120.00	$200.00	$700.00	$800.00
1867 ....(625)	47,525	60.00	100.00	125.00	225.00	750.00	800.00
1868 ....(600)	162,700	55.00	85.00	120.00	200.00	700.00	800.00
1869 ....(600)	424,300	55.00	85.00	120.00	200.00	700.00	800.00
1870 ....(1,000)	416,000	50.00	85.00	120.00	200.00	500.00	800.00
1870CC	11,758	120.00	225.00	350.00	600.00	3,000	
1870S..........................				45,000	55,000	90,000	
1871 ....(960)	1,074,760	50.00	85.00	120.00	200.00	500.00	800.00
1871CC	1,376	1,100	2,000	3,000	4,500	12,000	
1872 ....(950)	1,106,450	50.00	85.00	120.00	175.00	500.00	800.00
1872CC	3,150	375.00	700.00	1,150	2,000	8,000	
1872S	9,000	100.00	150.00	250.00	375.00	3,000	
1873 ....(600)	293,600	55.00	85.00	120.00	200.00	500.00	800.00
1873CC	2,300	1,500	2,750	5,000	7,000	22,000	

TRADE DOLLARS 1873-1885

This coin was issued for circulation in the Orient to compete with dollar-size coins of other countries. It weighed 420 grains compared to 412 1/2 grains, the weight of the regular silver dollar.

VG-8 VERY GOOD—*About half of mottoes IN GOD WE TRUST and E PLURIBUS UNUM will show. Rim on both sides well defined.*
F-12 FINE—*Mottoes and LIBERTY readable but worn.*
EF-40 EXTREMELY FINE—*Mottoes and LIBERTY are sharp. Only slight wear on rims.*
MS-60 UNCIRCULATED—*No trace of wear. Light blemishes.*

1875S
S over CC

TRADE DOLLARS 1873-1885

	Quan. Minted	VG-8	F-12	EF-40	MS-60	Proof-63
1873 (865)	397,500	$32.00	$42.00	$75.00	$300.00	$1,000
1873CC	124,500	35.00	50.00	100.00	500.00	
1873S	703,000	32.00	42.00	75.00	300.00	
1874 (700)	987,800	32.00	42.00	70.00	250.00	1,000
1874CC	1,373,200	35.00	45.00	75.00	400.00	
1874S	2,549,000	32.00	42.00	70.00	250.00	
1875 (700)	218,900	60.00	100.00	200.00	550.00	1,000
1875CC	1,573,700	35.00	45.00	90.00	325.00	
1875S }	4,487,000	32.00	42.00	75.00	250.00	
1875S, S over CC }		75.00	100.00	300.00	850.00	
1876 (1,150)	456,150	32.00	42.00	70.00	250.00	1,000
1876CC	509,000	40.00	50.00	90.00	400.00	
1876S	5,227,000	32.00	42.00	70.00	250.00	
1877 (510)	3,039,710	32.00	42.00	70.00	275.00	1,000
1877CC	534,000	40.00	60.00	125.00	450.00	
1877S	9,519,000	32.00	42.00	70.00	250.00	
1878 (900)		....	....	....		1,000
1878CC	97,000	110.00	235.00	700.00	3,500	
1878S	4,162,000	30.00	40.00	70.00	250.00	
1879 (1,541)		....	....	....		1,000
1880 (1,987)		....	....	....		1,000
1881 (960)		....	....	....		1,000
1882 (1,097)		....	....	....		1,000
1883 (979)		....	....	....		1,000
1884 (10)		....	....	....		50,000
1885 (5)		....	....	....		100,000

LIBERTY HEAD OR MORGAN TYPE 1878-1921

George T. Morgan, formerly a pupil of Wyon in the Royal Mint in London, designed the new dollar. His initial M is found at the truncation of the neck, at the last tress. It also appears on the reverse on the left-hand loop of the ribbon.

Sharply struck "proof-like" coins have a highly reflective surface and usually command substantial premiums.

VF-20 VERY FINE—*Two-thirds of hairlines from top of forehead to ear must show. Ear well defined. Feathers on eagle's breast worn.*

EF-40 EXTREMELY FINE—*All hairlines strong and ear bold. Eagle's feathers all plain but slight wear on breast and wing tips.*

AU-50 ABOUT UNCIRCULATED—*Slight trace of wear. Most of mint luster is present although marred by bag marks.*

MS-60 UNCIRCULATED—*No trace of wear. Has full mint luster, but may be noticeably marred by scuff marks or bag abrasions.*

MS-63 SELECT UNCIRCULATED—*No trace of wear, full mint luster, few noticeable surface marks.*

Most uncirculated silver dollars have scratches or nicks because of handling of mint bags. Choice sharply struck coins with full brilliance and without blemishes are worth more than listed values.

8 Tail Feathers, 1878 Philadelphia Only
Mint mark location on the reverse below wreath

SILVER DOLLARS

	Quan. Minted	VF-20	EF-40	AU-50	MS-60	MS-63
1878, 8 tail feathers...(500)	750,000	$9.00	$13.00	$16.00	$40.00	$50.00
1878, 7 tail feathers...(250) }	9,759,550	*7.00*	*8.00*	*9.00*	20.00	30.00
1878, doubled tail feathers. }		12.00	14.00	22.00	40.00	65.00
1878CC	2,212,000	17.00	22.00	30.00	60.00	70.00
1878S	9,774,000	*7.00*	*8.00*	*9.00*	12.00	20.00
1879 (1,100)	14,807,100	*7.00*	*8.00*	*9.00*	11.00	20.00
1879CC	756,000	45.00	135.00	275.00	800.00	1,300
1879O	2,887,000	*7.00*	*8.00*	10.00	25.00	65.00
1879S	9,110,000	*7.00*	*8.00*	*9.00*	10.00	14.00
1880 (1,355)	12,601,355	*7.00*	*8.00*	*9.00*	10.00	14.00
1880CC	591,000	32.00	55.00	70.00	100.00	120.00
1880O	5,305,000	*7.00*	*8.00*	*9.00*	22.00	150.00
1880S	8,900,000	*7.00*	*8.00*	*9.00*	10.00	14.00
1881 (984)	9,163,975	*7.00*	*8.00*	*9.00*	10.00	14.00
1881CC	296,000	60.00	70.00	80.00	100.00	130.00
1881O	5,708,000	*7.00*	*8.00*	*9.00*	10.00	16.50
1881S	11,760,000	*7.00*	*8.00*	*9.00*	10.00	14.00
1882 (1,100)	11,101,100	*7.00*	*8.00*	*9.00*	12.00	22.00
1882CC	1,133,000	20.00	25.00	31.00	45.00	55.00
1882O	6,090,000	*7.00*	*8.00*	*9.00*	10.00	14.00
1882S	9,250,000	*7.00*	*8.00*	*9.00*	10.00	14.00
1883 (1,039)	12,291,039	*7.00*	*8.00*	*9.00*	10.00	14.00
1883CC	1,204,000	21.00	26.00	35.00	45.00	55.00
1883O	8,725,000	*7.00*	*8.00*	*9.00*	10.00	14.00
1883S	6,250,000	8.00	11.00	50.00	225.00	750.00
1884 (875)	14,070,875	*7.00*	*8.00*	*9.00*	10.00	14.00
1884CC	1,136,000	24.00	28.00	33.00	40.00	50.00
1884O	9,730,000	*7.00*	*8.00*	*9.00*	10.00	14.00
1884S	3,200,000	8.00	15.00	100.00	2,200	9,500
1885 (930)	17,787,930	*7.00*	*8.00*	*9.00*	10.00	14.00
1885CC	228,000	95.00	115.00	125.00	150.00	170.00
1885O	9,185,000	*7.00*	*8.00*	*9.00*	10.00	14.00
1885S	1,497,000	*7.00*	*12.00*	25.00	55.00	90.00
1886 (886)	19,963,886	*7.00*	*8.00*	*9.00*	10.00	14.00
1886O	10,710,000	*7.00*	9.00	30.00	135.00	1,100
1886S	750,000	14.00	20.00	30.00	65.00	125.00
1887 (710)	20,290,710	*7.00*	*8.00*	*9.00*	10.00	14.00
1887O	11,550,000	*7.00*	*8.00*	*9.00*	18.00	45.00
1887S	1,771,000	*7.00*	*8.00*	14.00	35.00	85.00
1888 (832)	19,183,832	*7.00*	*8.00*	*9.00*	10.00	14.00
1888O	12,150,000	*7.00*	*8.00*	*9.00*	11.00	16.00
1888S	657,000	16.00	21.00	32.00	75.00	120.00
1889 (811)	21,726,811	*7.00*	*8.00*	*9.00*	10.00	14.00
1889CC	350,000	220.00	500.00	1,700	4,200	7,750
1889O	11,875,000	*7.00*	*8.00*	16.00	40.00	120.00
1889S	700,000	13.00	15.00	27.50	60.00	95.00
1890 (590)	16,802,590	*7.00*	*8.00*	*9.00*	11.00	17.00
1890CC	2,309,041	19.00	23.00	50.00	125.00	235.00
1890O	10,701,000	*7.00*	*8.00*	11.00	18.00	35.00

Proof Morgan Dollars where indicated in mintage records (quantity shown in parentheses) are valued approximately as follows:

Proof-60 $400.00 Proof-63 $750.00 Proof-65 $2,250

Italic prices indicate unsettled values due to fluctuating bullion market. See Bullion Chart.

SILVER DOLLARS

	Quan. Minted	VF-20	EF-40	AU-50	MS-60	MS-63
1890S	8,230,373	*$7.00*	*$8.00*	$11.00	$18.00	$35.00
1891 (650)	8,694,206	*7.00*	*8.00*	13.00	20.00	65.00
1891CC	1,618,000	21.00	26.00	50.00	100.00	160.00
1891O	7,954,529	*7.00*	11.00	20.00	40.00	110.00
1891S	5,296,000	*7.00*	*8.00*	11.00	20.00	36.00
1892 (1,245)	1,037,245	*7.00*	11.00	30.00	65.00	135.00
1892CC	1,352,000	35.00	55.00	125.00	225.00	425.00
1892O	2,744,000	*8.00*	9.00	27.00	50.00	110.00
1892S	1,200,000	22.00	75.00	850.00	7,000	20,000
1893 (792)	378,792	40.00	65.00	100.00	180.00	400.00
1893CC	677,000	80.00	240.00	400.00	750.00	1,600
1893O	300,000	55.00	110.00	240.00	800.00	2,800
1893S	100,000	900.00	2,200	7,500	20,000	37,500
1894 (972)	110,972	175.00	225.00	325.00	525.00	1,500
1894O	1,723,000	16.00	22.00	75.00	350.00	1,400
1894S	1,260,000	24.00	50.00	100.00	220.00	400.00
1895 (880)	12,880			†7,000	†10,000	†14,000
1895O	450,000	70.00	120.00	475.00	6,000	15,000
1895S	400,000	110.00	225.00	400.00	725.00	1,700
1896 (762)	9,976,762	*7.00*	*8.00*	*9.00*	10.00	16.00
1896O	4,900,000	*7.00*	8.00	50.00	400.00	3,100
1896S	5,000,000	20.00	70.00	200.00	450.00	750.00
1897 (731)	2,822,731	*7.00*	*8.00*	*9.00*	10.00	14.00
1897O	4,004,000	*7.00*	*8.00*	45.00	270.00	2,100
1897S	5,825,000	*7.00*	*8.00*	11.00	18.00	30.00
1898 (735)	5,884,735	*7.00*	*8.00*	*9.00*	10.00	14.00
1898O	4,440,000	*7.00*	*8.00*	*9.00*	10.00	14.00
1898S	4,102,000	*7.00*	12.00	35.00	75.00	125.00
1899 (846)	330,846	20.00	25.00	35.00	43.00	55.00
1899O	12,290,000	*7.00*	*8.00*	*9.00*	10.00	14.00
1899S	2,562,000	10.00	15.00	40.00	90.00	150.00
1900 (912)	8,830,912	*7.00*	*8.00*	*9.00*	10.00	14.00
1900O	12,590,000	*7.00*	*8.00*	*9.00*	10.00	14.00
1900S	3,540,000	*8.00*	15.00	30.00	65.00	100.00
1901 (813)	6,962,813	15.00	25.00	135.00	825.00	6,000
1901O	13,320,000	*7.00*	*8.00*	*9.00*	10.00	14.00
1901S	2,284,000	12.00	22.00	60.00	140.00	220.00
1902 (777)	7,994,777	*7.00*	*8.00*	10.00	16.00	28.00
1902O	8,636,000	*7.00*	*8.00*	*9.00*	10.00	14.00
1902S	1,530,000	30.00	42.00	55.00	90.00	150.00
1903 (755)	4,652,755	*8.00*	10.00	12.00	17.00	22.00
1903O	4,450,000	75.00	80.00	90.00	110.00	140.00
1903S	1,241,000	35.00	140.00	500.00	1,300	2,200
1904 (650)	2,788,650	*7.00*	*8.00*	15.00	30.00	100.00
1904O	3,720,000	*7.00*	*8.00*	*9.00*	10.00	14.00
1904S	2,304,000	22.00	80.00	275.00	500.00	900.00
1921	44,690,000	*5.50*	*7.00*	*7.50*	8.00	10.00
1921D	20,345,000	*5.50*	*7.00*	*7.50*	10.00	15.00
1921S	21,695,000	*5.50*	*7.00*	*7.50*	11.00	16.00

†Values are for proofs.

Proof Morgan Dollars where indicated in mintage records (quantity shown in parenthesis) are valued approximately as follows:

Proof-60 $400.00 Proof-63 $750.00 Proof-65 $2,250

Italic prices indicate unsettled values due to fluctuating bullion market. See Bullion Chart.

SILVER DOLLARS
PEACE TYPE 1921-1935

Anthony De Francisci, a medalist, designed this dollar. His monogram is located in the field of the coin under the neck of Liberty.

VF-20 VERY FINE—*Hair over eye well worn. Some strands over ear well defined. Some eagle feathers on top and outside edge of right wing will show.*
EF-40 EXTREMELY FINE—*Hairlines over brow and ear are strong though slightly worn. Outside wing feathers at right and those at top are visible but faint.*
AU-50 ABOUT UNCIRCULATED—*Slight trace of wear. Most of mint luster is present although marred by contact marks.*
MS-60 UNCIRCULATED—*No trace of wear. Has full mint luster but may be noticeably marred by stains, surface marks or bag abrasions.*
MS-63 SELECT UNCIRCULATED—*No trace of wear, full mint luster, few noticeable surface marks.*

Most uncirculated silver dollars have scratches or nicks because of handling of mint bags. Choice sharply struck coins with full brilliance and without blemishes are worth more than listed values.

Mint mark location is on reverse below one.

	Quan. Minted	*VF-20*	*EF-40*	*AU-50*	*MS-60*	*MS-63*
1921	1,006,473	$18.00	$22.00	$35.00	$70.00	$110.00
1922	51,737,000	*5.50*	*6.00*	*7.00*	8.00	9.00
1922D	15,063,000	*5.50*	*6.00*	*7.00*	10.00	18.00
1922S	17,475,000	*5.50*	*6.00*	*7.00*	10.00	21.00
1923	30,800,000	*5.50*	*6.00*	*7.00*	8.00	9.00
1923D	6,811,000	*5.50*	*6.00*	*7.00*	15.00	40.00
1923S	19,020,000	*5.50*	*6.00*	*7.00*	10.00	25.00
1924	11,811,000	*5.50*	*6.00*	*7.00*	8.00	10.00
1924S	1,728,000	*5.50*	*8.00*	25.00	65.00	175.00
1925	10,198,000	*5.50*	*6.00*	*7.00*	8.00	10.00
1925S	1,610,000	*5.50*	*7.00*	11.00	22.00	50.00
1926	1,939,000	*5.50*	*6.00*	8.00	11.00	18.00
1926D	2,348,700	*5.50*	*6.00*	10.00	22.00	55.00
1926S	6,980,000	*5.50*	*6.00*	8.00	13.00	24.00
1927	848,000	*7.00*	10.00	15.00	25.00	45.00
1927D	1,268,900	*5.50*	*6.00*	30.00	65.00	110.00
1927S	866,000	*5.50*	*6.00*	20.00	50.00	100.00
1928	360,649	75.00	85.00	95.00	110.00	160.00
1928S	1,632,000	*5.50*	8.00	18.00	50.00	130.00
1934	954,057	*7.00*	9.00	15.00	35.00	50.00
1934D	1,569,500	*5.50*	8.00	15.00	35.00	90.00
1934S	1,011,000	22.00	70.00	225.00	600.00	1,200
1935	1,576,000	*5.50*	*6.00*	10.00	22.00	35.00
1935S	1,964,000	*5.50*	*6.00*	25.00	60.00	120.00

Italic prices indicate unsettled values due to fluctuating bullion market. See Bullion Chart.

EISENHOWER DOLLARS 1971-1978

Honoring both President Dwight D. Eisenhower and the first landing of man on the moon, this design is the work of Chief Engraver Frank Gasparro, whose initials are on the truncation and below the eagle. The reverse is an adaptation of the official *Apollo 11* insignia.

Mint mark location is above the date.

	Quan. Minted *Proof*	*Regular*	*EF-40*	*MS-63*	*Proof-63*
1971 Copper-nickel clad		47,799,000	$1.05	$1.40	
1971D Copper-nickel clad		68,587,424	1.05	1.25	
1971S Silver clad	(4,265,234)	6,868,530		2.50	$2.50
1972 Copper-nickel clad		75,890,000	1.05	1.25	
1972D Copper-nickel clad		92,548,511	1.05	1.25	
1972S Silver clad	(1,811,631)	2,193,056		2.50	2.50
1973 Copper-nickel clad		*2,000,056	1.50	3.50	
1973D Copper-nickel clad		*2,000,000	1.50	3.50	
1973S Copper-nickel clad	(2,760,339)				3.00
1973S Silver clad	(1,013,646)	1,883,140		3.00	10.00
1974 Copper-nickel clad		27,366,000	1.05	1.30	
1974D Copper-nickel clad		45,517,000	1.05	1.30	
1974S Copper-nickel clad	(2,612,568)				2.50
1974S Silver clad	(1,306,579)	1,900,156		2.50	2.50

*1,769,258 of each sold only in sets and not released for circulation. Unissued coins destroyed at mint.

BICENTENNIAL COINAGE DATED 1776-1976

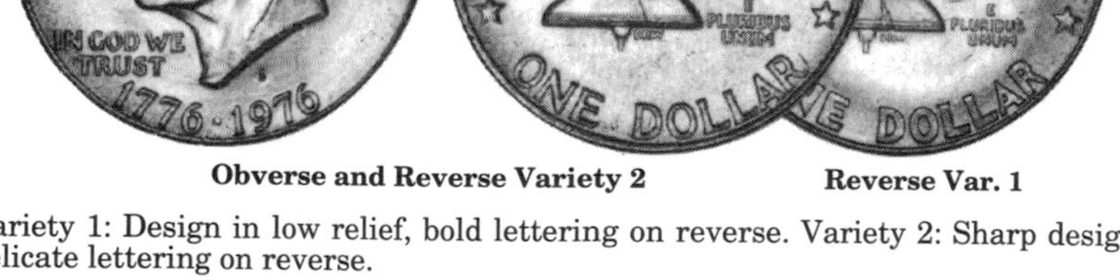

Obverse and Reverse Variety 2 **Reverse Var. 1**

Variety 1: Design in low relief, bold lettering on reverse. Variety 2: Sharp design, delicate lettering on reverse.

BICENTENNIAL DOLLARS

	Quan. Minted	*EF-40*	*MS-63*	*Proof-63*
1776-1976 Copper-nickel clad, variety 1	4,019,000	$1.10	$1.50	
1776-1976 Copper-nickel clad, variety 2	113,318,000	1.10	1.20	
1776-1976D Copper-nickel clad, variety 1	21,048,710	1.10	1.40	
1776-1976D Copper-nickel clad, variety 2	82,179,564	1.10	1.20	
1776-1976S Copper-nickel clad, variety 1	(2,845,450)			$2.50
1776-1976S Copper-nickel clad, variety 2	(4,149,730)			2.50
1776-1976S Silver clad, variety 1	* 11,000,000	1.50	4.00	
1776-1976S Silver clad, variety 1	*(4,000,000)			4.00

*Approximate mintage.

EAGLE REVERSE RESUMED

1977 Copper-nickel clad	12,596,000	1.05	1.50	
1977D Copper-nickel clad	32,983,006	1.05	1.25	
1977S Copper-nickel clad	(3,251,152)			2.50
1978 Copper-nickel clad	25,702,000	1.05	1.25	
1978D Copper-nickel clad	23,012,890	1.05	1.25	
1978S Copper-nickel clad	(3,127,781)			2.50

SUSAN B. ANTHONY DOLLARS 1979-1999

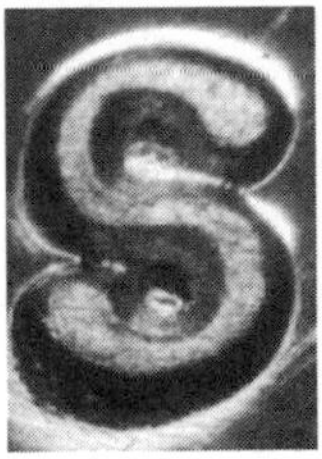

Clear S

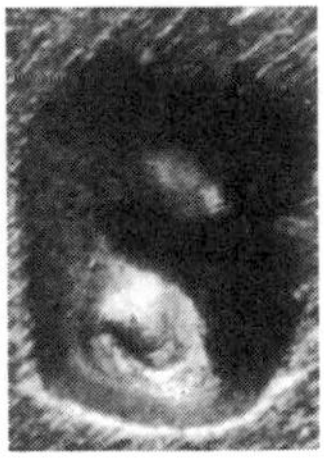

Filled S

	Quan. Minted	*MS-63*	*Proof-63*
1979P	360,222,000	$1.00	
1979P Wide rim		2.50	
1979D	288,015,744	1.00	
1979S	109,576,000	1.00	
1979S Proof	(3,677,175)		
Filled S			$2.50
Clear S			35.00
1980P	27,610,000	1.00	
1980D	41,628,708	1.00	
1980S	20,422,000	1.00	

	Quan. Minted	*MS-63*	*Proof-63*
1980S Proof	(3,554,806)		$2.50
1981P	3,000,000	$2.00	
1981D	3,250,000	2.00	
1981S	3,492,000	2.00	
1981S Proof	(4,063,083)		2.50
1981S Proof Clear S			40.00
1999P	29,592,000	1.05	
1999P Proof			6.00
1999D	11,776,000	1.15	

SACAGAWEA DOLLARS 2000-

	Quan. Minted	MS-63	Proof-63
2000P	767,140,000	$1.00	
2000D	518,916,000	1.00	
2000S Proof			$2.50
2001P	62,468,000	1.00	
2001D	70,939,500	1.00	
2001S Proof			2.50
2002P		1.10	
2002D		1.10	
2002S Proof			2.50

GOLD

GOLD DOLLARS 1849-1889

Coinage of the gold dollar was authorized by the Act of March 3, 1849. The weight was 25.8 grains, fineness .900. The first type, struck until 1854, is known as the Liberty Head or small-sized type.

In 1854 the piece was made larger in diameter and thinner. The design was changed to a feather headdress on a female, generally referred to as the Indian Head or large-sized type. In 1856 the type was changed slightly by enlarging the size of the head.

LIBERTY HEAD TYPE 1849-1854

VF-20 VERY FINE—*LIBERTY on headband complete and readable. Knobs on coronet are defined.*
EF-40 EXTREMELY FINE—*Slight wear on Liberty's hair. Knobs on coronet sharp.*
AU-50 ABOUT UNCIRCULATED—*Trace of wear over eye and on coronet.*
MS-60 UNCIRCULATED—*No trace of wear. Light marks and blemishes.*

Mint mark is below wreath.

	Quan. Minted	*VF-20*	*EF-40*	*AU-50*	*MS-60*
1849	688,567	$75.00	$100.00	$115.00	$210.00
1849C	11,634	200.00	425.00	800.00	2,500
1849D	21,588	200.00	425.00	650.00	1,800
1849O	215,000	100.00	140.00	175.00	450.00
1850	481,953	75.00	100.00	115.00	200.00
1850C	6,966	225.00	400.00	900.00	3,000
1850D	8,382	225.00	375.00	825.00	3,000
1850O	14,000	120.00	150.00	315.00	1,100
1851	3,317,671	75.00	100.00	115.00	200.00
1851C	41,267	150.00	225.00	425.00	1,400
1851D	9,882	200.00	375.00	650.00	2,100
1851O	290,000	100.00	130.00	160.00	400.00
1852	2,045,351	75.00	100.00	115.00	200.00
1852C	9,434	200.00	400.00	600.00	1,900
1852D	6,360	250.00	450.00	700.00	2,750
1852O	140,000	100.00	125.00	150.00	525.00
1853	4,076,051	75.00	100.00	115.00	200.00
1853C	11,515	200.00	275.00	500.00	2,000
1853D	6,583	225.00	300.00	650.00	2,600
1853O	290,000	100.00	125.00	150.00	350.00
1854	855,502	75.00	100.00	115.00	210.00
1854D	2,935	300.00	600.00	2,000	5,000
1854S	14,632	150.00	250.00	400.00	1,000

INDIAN HEAD TYPE, Small Head 1854-1856

VF-20 VERY FINE—*Feather curl tips outlined but details worn.*
EF-40 EXTREMELY FINE—*Slight wear on tips of feather curls on headdress.*
AU-50 ABOUT UNCIRCULATED—*Trace of wear on headdress.*
MS-60 UNCIRCULATED—*No trace of wear. Light marks and blemishes.*

	Quan. Minted	*VF-20*	*EF-40*	*AU-50*	*MS-60*
1854	783,943	$125.00	$225.00	$350.00	$1,200
1855	758,269	125.00	225.00	350.00	1,200
1855C	9,803	425.00	900.00	2,000	6,000
1855D	1,811	1,700	2,700	3,750	11,000
1855O	55,000	250.00	375.00	700.00	2,750
1856S	24,600	250.00	400.00	900.00	3,500

GOLD DOLLARS

INDIAN HEAD TYPE, Large Head 1856-1889

VF-20 VERY FINE—*Curled feathers have slight detail. Details worn smooth at eyebrow, hair below headdress and behind ear and bottom curl.*

EF-40 EXTREMELY FINE—*Slight wear above and to right of eye and on top of curled feathers.*

AU-50 ABOUT UNCIRCULATED—*Trace of wear on headdress.*

MS-60 UNCIRCULATED—*No trace of wear. Light marks and blemishes.*

	Quan. Minted	*VF-20*	*EF-40*	*AU-50*	*MS-60*	*Proof-63*
1856	1,762,936	$75.00	$100.00	$115.00	$240.00	$3,400
1856D	1,460	1,400	2,500	4,250	11,000	
1857	774,789	75.00	100.00	115.00	180.00	3,400
1857C	13,280	250.00	400.00	1,000	3,500	
1857D	3,533	325.00	600.00	1,000	3,750	
1857S	10,000	150.00	225.00	350.00	2,200	
1858	117,995	75.00	100.00	115.00	180.00	3,400
1858D	3,477	325.00	500.00	900.00	3,000	
1858S	10,000	150.00	200.00	550.00	2,000	
1859 (80)	168,324	75.00	100.00	115.00	200.00	3,400
1859C	5,235	225.00	450.00	1,000	3,000	
1859D	4,952	350.00	500.00	1,000	2,750	
1859S	15,000	125.00	175.00	475.00	2,000	
1860 (154)	36,668	75.00	100.00	115.00	200.00	2,750
1860D	1,566	1,250	2,500	4,500	9,000	
1860S	13,000	125.00	200.00	350.00	1,000	
1861 (349)	527,499	75.00	100.00	110.00	180.00	2,750
1861D		3,500	5,500	9,000	17,000	
1862 (35)	1,361,390	75.00	100.00	110.00	180.00	3,500
1863 (50)	6,250	200.00	300.00	450.00	1,800	4,000
1864 (50)	5,950	200.00	300.00	350.00	675.00	4,000
1865 (25)	3,725	140.00	300.00	375.00	750.00	4,000
1866 (30)	7,130	125.00	160.00	300.00	550.00	3,900
1867 (50)	5,250	125.00	180.00	325.00	700.00	3,900
1868 (25)	10,525	100.00	150.00	250.00	600.00	3,900
1869 (25)	5,925	125.00	165.00	300.00	650.00	3,900
1870 (35)	6,335	115.00	160.00	275.00	625.00	3,500
1870S	3,000	250.00	375.00	600.00	1,600	
1871 (30)	3,930	115.00	160.00	225.00	425.00	3,500
1872 (30)	3,530	115.00	160.00	225.00	450.00	3,900
1873 Closed 3 (25)	1,825	125.00	175.00	250.00	800.00	4,500
1873 Open 3	123,300	75.00	100.00	110.00	180.00	
1874 (20)	198,820	75.00	100.00	110.00	180.00	3,900
1875 (20)	420	1,000	1,500	2,200	4,500	10,000
1876 (45)	3,245	100.00	135.00	185.00	425.00	2,500
1877 (20)	3,920	100.00	135.00	185.00	450.00	2,500
1878 (20)	3,020	100.00	135.00	185.00	450.00	2,500
1879 (30)	3,030	100.00	135.00	185.00	400.00	2,500
1880 (36)	1,636	100.00	135.00	185.00	300.00	2,500
1881 (87)	7,707	75.00	100.00	115.00	210.00	2,000
1882 (125)	5,125	75.00	100.00	115.00	210.00	2,000
1883 (207)	11,007	75.00	100.00	115.00	210.00	2,000
1884 (1,006)	6,236	75.00	100.00	115.00	210.00	2,000
1885 (1,105)	12,261	75.00	100.00	115.00	210.00	2,000
1886 (1,016)	6,016	75.00	100.00	115.00	210.00	2,000
1887 (1,043)	8,543	75.00	100.00	115.00	210.00	2,000
1888 (1,079)	16,580	75.00	100.00	115.00	210.00	2,000
1889 (1,779)	30,729	75.00	100.00	115.00	210.00	2,000

QUARTER EAGLES—1796-1929
($2.50 GOLD PIECES)

Although authorized by the Act of April 2, 1792, coinage of quarter eagles was not begun until 1796.

CAPPED BUST TO RIGHT 1796-1807

No Stars on Obverse 1796 Only

F-12 FINE—*Hair worn smooth on high spots. E PLURIBUS UNUM weak but readable.*
VF-20 VERY FINE—*Some wear on high spots.*
EF-40 EXTREMELY FINE—*Only slight wear on hair and cheek.*
MS-60 UNCIRCULATED—*No trace of wear. Light blemishes.*

Stars on Obverse 1796-1807

	Quan. Minted	*F-12*	*VF-20*	*EF-40*	*MS-60*
1796 No stars on obverse	963	$6,250	$11,000	$20,000	$50,000
1796 Stars on obverse	432	4,750	8,000	12,000	32,000
1797	427	4,200	6,200	9,000	20,000
1798	1,094	2,000	2,800	3,500	12,000
1802, 2 over 1	3,035	1,600	2,000	3,000	9,000
1804, 13-Star reverse	} 3,327	4,500	9,000	22,000	50,000
1804, 14-Star reverse		1,500	2,100	3,500	10,000
1805	1,781	1,500	2,000	3,400	9,500
1806, 6 over 4, stars 8 + 5	1,136	1,500	2,000	3,400	9,500
1806, 6 over 5, stars 7 + 6	480	2,000	3,600	6,000	18,000
1807	6,812	1,500	2,000	3,400	9,250

CAPPED BUST TO LEFT, Large Size 1808

F-12 FINE—*E PLURIBUS UNUM and LIBERTY on headband readable but weak.*
VF-20 VERY FINE—*Motto and LIBERTY clear.*
EF-40 EXTREMELY FINE—*All details of hair are plain.*
MS-60 UNCIRCULATED—*No trace of wear. Light blemishes.*

1808	2,710	5,250	8,750	15,000	30,000

CAPPED HEAD TO LEFT 1821-1834

Those dated 1829-1834 are smaller in diameter than the 1821-1827 pieces.

1821	6,448	1,300	2,500	3,500	8,000
1824, 4 over 1	2,600	1,300	2,500	3,500	7,500
1825	4,434	1,300	2,500	3,500	6,500
1826, 6 over 5	760	2,200	3,300	4,500	14,000
1827	2,800	1,300	2,500	3,750	8,000
1829	3,403	1,300	2,000	3,000	5,000
1830	4,540	1,200	2,000	3,000	5,000

QUARTER EAGLES

	Quan. Minted	F-12	VF-20	EF-40	MS-60
1831	4,520	$1,200	$2,000	$3,000	$5,000
1832	4,400	1,200	2,000	3,000	5,000
1833	4,160	1,200	2,000	3,000	5,000
1834 (Motto)	4,000	2,750	5,500	9,000	20,000

CLASSIC HEAD TYPE, No Motto on Reverse 1834-1839

In 1834 the quarter eagle was redesigned. A ribbon binding the hair, bearing the word liberty, replaces the Liberty cap. The motto was omitted from the reverse.

F-12 FINE—*LIBERTY readable and complete. Curl under ear oulined but no detail.*
VF-20 VERY FINE—*LIBERTY plain. Hair curl has detail.*
EF-40 EXTREMELY FINE—*Small amount of wear on top of hair and below L in LIBERTY. Wear evident on wing.*
AU-50 ABOUT UNCIRCULATED—*Trace of wear on coronet and hair above ear.*
MS-60 UNCIRCULATED—*No trace of wear. Light blemishes.*

Mint mark location.

	Quan. Minted	F-12	VF-20	EF-40	AU-50	MS-60
1834 No motto	112,234	$110.00	$150.00	$275.00	$425.00	$900.00
1835	131,402	110.00	150.00	275.00	425.00	900.00
1836	547,986	110.00	150.00	275.00	425.00	900.00
1837	45,080	110.00	150.00	275.00	450.00	1,400
1838	47,030	110.00	150.00	275.00	450.00	1,300
1838C	7,880	225.00	300.00	950.00	2,200	12,000
1839	27,021	100.00	150.00	300.00	600.00	2,000
1839C	18,140	180.00	310.00	750.00	1,700	10,000
1839D	13,674	200.00	400.00	900.00	2,250	11,000
1839O	17,781	150.00	225.00	325.00	800.00	2,500

CORONET TYPE 1840-1907

Mint mark location.

4 **Plain 4**

4 **Crosslet 4**

	Quan. Minted	VF-20	EF-40	AU-50	MS-60
1840	18,859	$125.00	$175.00	$800.00	$2,200
1840C	12,822	225.00	450.00	1,400	6,500
1840D	3,532	850.00	2,200	4,500	16,000
1840O	33,580	150.00	250.00	800.00	4,000
1841 Proofs only		10,000	22,000	35,000	55,000
1841C	10,281	275.00	500.00	1,250	6,250
1841D	4,164	400.00	1,000	3,200	7,500
1842	2,823	300.00	800.00	1,700	7,000
1842C	6,729	400.00	1,000	3,500	8,000
1842D	4,643	400.00	900.00	4,000	10,000
1842O	19,800	200.00	600.00	1,000	5,000
1843	100,546	125.00	175.00	200.00	600.00
1843C	26,064	250.00	400.00	850.00	2,500
1843D	36,209	275.00	500.00	850.00	2,750
1843O	364,002	125.00	175.00	225.00	675.00
1844	6,784	160.00	275.00	800.00	2,700
1844C	11,622	275.00	600.00	2,300	6,500
1844D	17,332	200.00	310.00	675.00	3,500

QUARTER EAGLES

	Quan. Minted	VF-20	EF-40	AU-50	MS-60	Proof-63
1845	91,051	$115.00	$150.00	$175.00	$600.00	
1845D	19,460	250.00	500.00	1,000	3,000	
1845O	4,000	500.00	900.00	2,200	6,000	
1846	21,598	130.00	200.00	425.00	2,300	
1846C	4,808	325.00	700.00	1,500	7,500	
1846D	19,303	250.00	500.00	1,000	3,500	
1846O	62,000	125.00	200.00	400.00	1,750	
1847	29,814	125.00	175.00	250.00	1,200	
1847C	23,226	200.00	275.00	700.00	2,750	
1847D	15,784	200.00	275.00	750.00	3,000	
1847O	124,000	125.00	175.00	300.00	1,200	
1848	7,497	250.00	400.00	950.00	2,750	

CAL. Above Eagle on Reverse

California Gold Quarter Eagle

In 1848 about two hundred and thirty ounces of gold were sent to Secretary of War Marcy by Col. R. B. Mason, Military Governor of California. The gold was turned over to the mint and made into quarter eagles. The distinguishing mark "CAL." was punched above the eagle on the reverse side, while the coins were in the die.

	Quan. Minted	VF-20	EF-40	AU-50	MS-60	Proof-63
1848 CAL. above eagle	1,389	4,000	6,500	10,000	20,000	
1848C	16,788	250.00	400.00	950.00	4,300	
1848D	13,771	250.00	400.00	700.00	2,800	
1849	23,294	125.00	165.00	200.00	1,200	
1849C	10,220	250.00	500.00	2,200	7,000	
1849D	10,945	250.00	450.00	1,200	5,500	
1850	252,923	100.00	125.00	135.00	500.00	
1850C	9,148	250.00	500.00	1,200	6,000	
1850D	12,148	250.00	500.00	950.00	5,000	
1850O	84,000	100.00	125.00	400.00	1,500	
1851	1,372,748	100.00	125.00	135.00	200.00	
1851C	14,923	200.00	400.00	1,500	5,500	
1851D	11,264	225.00	400.00	1,250	5,200	
1851O	148,000	100.00	125.00	300.00	1,600	
1852	1,159,681	100.00	125.00	135.00	200.00	
1852C	9,772	300.00	500.00	1,000	4,500	
1852D	4,078	325.00	800.00	2,000	6,000	
1852O	140,000	120.00	150.00	250.00	1,600	
1853	1,404,668	100.00	125.00	135.00	200.00	
1853D	3,178	400.00	900.00	2,000	6,000	
1854	596,258	100.00	125.00	135.00	225.00	
1854C	7,295	300.00	500.00	1,500	6,000	
1854D	1,760	1,350	2,000	4,000	10,000	
1854O	153,000	100.00	125.00	200.00	700.00	
1854S	246	15,000	25,000	50,000	—	
1855	235,480	100.00	125.00	135.00	250.00	
1855C	3,677	400.00	750.00	2,000	9,000	
1855D	1,123	1,500	3,000	4,200	15,000	
1856	384,240	100.00	125.00	135.00	225.00	
1856C	7,913	250.00	350.00	1,250	4,750	
1856D	874	2,000	5,000	8,200	20,000	
1856O	21,100	125.00	175.00	300.00	2,200	
1856S	72,120	125.00	165.00	250.00	1,600	
1857	214,130	100.00	125.00	135.00	225.00	$8,500
1857D	2,364	350.00	500.00	1,100	4,500	
1857O	34,000	110.00	135.00	250.00	1,500	
1857S	69,200	110.00	150.00	350.00	1,800	

QUARTER EAGLES

	Quan. Minted	VF-20	EF-40	AU-50	MS-60	Proof-63
1858	47,377	$100.00	$125.00	$150.00	$700.00	$9,000
1858C	9,056	250.00	350.00	800.00	3,000	
1859 (80)	39,444	100.00	125.00	150.00	600.00	7,500
1859D	2,244	300.00	650.00	2,000	8,000	
1859S	15,200	150.00	225.00	500.00	2,100	
1860 (112)	22,675	100.00	125.00	175.00	550.00	4,500
1860C	7,469	300.00	700.00	1,500	6,700	
1860S	35,600	140.00	165.00	300.00	1,250	
1861 (90)	1,283,878	100.00	125.00	135.00	200.00	4,500
1861S	24,000	140.00	150.00	450.00	2,200	
1862, 2 over 1	} 98,543		650.00	1,600	5,000	
1862 (35)		100.00	125.00	175.00	500.00	4,750
1862S	8,000	210.00	500.00	1,700	6,000	
1863 Proofs only (30)	30					—
1863S	10,800	150.00	175.00	400.00	5,000	
1864 (50)	2,874	1,250	3,700	7,000	14,000	7,500
1865 (25)	1,545	1,000	2,000	5,500	12,000	7,500
1865S	23,376	125.00	175.00	300.00	1,400	
1866 (30)	3,110	250.00	550.00	1,750	4,500	4,750
1866S	38,960	125.00	200.00	400.00	2,500	
1867 (50)	3,250	165.00	200.00	450.00	1,550	4,000
1867S	28,000	125.00	175.00	425.00	1,500	
1868 (25)	3,625	150.00	200.00	375.00	800.00	4,000
1868S	34,000	135.00	165.00	400.00	1,400	
1869 (25)	4,345	175.00	200.00	350.00	900.00	4,000
1869S	29,500	150.00	165.00	300.00	1,100	
1870 (35)	4,555	150.00	165.00	250.00	800.00	4,000
1870S	16,000	150.00	175.00	270.00	1,100	
1871 (30)	5,350	150.00	165.00	250.00	700.00	4,000
1871S	22,000	100.00	125.00	175.00	700.00	
1872 (30)	3,030	150.00	175.00	300.00	1,000	4,000
1872S	18,000	100.00	150.00	400.00	1,200	
1873 (25)	178,025	100.00	125.00	135.00	225.00	4,000
1873S	27,000	115.00	170.00	450.00	1,200	
1874 (20)	3,940	175.00	200.00	300.00	900.00	5,250
1875 (20)	420	1,200	2,500	3,750	7,500	16,000
1875S	11,600	115.00	135.00	250.00	1,200	
1876 (45)	4,221	175.00	200.00	325.00	1,000	4,000
1876S	5,000	150.00	165.00	300.00	1,200	
1877 (20)	1,652	250.00	325.00	425.00	1,000	5,000
1877S	35,400	100.00	125.00	135.00	400.00	
1878 (20)	286,260	100.00	125.00	135.00	225.00	4,000
1878S	178,000	100.00	125.00	135.00	225.00	
1879 (30)	88,990	100.00	125.00	135.00	250.00	4,000
1879S	43,500	100.00	125.00	150.00	600.00	
1880 (36)	2,996	125.00	165.00	225.00	650.00	4,000
1881 (51)	691	600.00	1,000	1,900	3,500	5,750
1882 (67)	4,067	115.00	165.00	200.00	400.00	3,500
1883 (82)	2,002	125.00	175.00	225.00	650.00	3,500
1884 (73)	2,023	125.00	175.00	225.00	625.00	3,500
1885 (87)	887	350.00	800.00	1,200	2,200	4,500
1886 (88)	4,088	125.00	175.00	225.00	475.00	4,000
1887 (122)	6,282	115.00	150.00	200.00	450.00	3,000
1888 (97)	16,098	100.00	125.00	135.00	200.00	3,000
1889 (48)	17,648	100.00	125.00	140.00	200.00	3,000
1890 (93)	8,813	100.00	125.00	150.00	300.00	3,000
1891 (80)	11,040	100.00	125.00	140.00	200.00	3,000
1892 (105)	2,545	150.00	175.00	225.00	400.00	2,500
1893 (106)	30,106	100.00	125.00	135.00	200.00	2,500
1894 (122)	4,122	125.00	140.00	185.00	400.00	2,500
1895 (119)	6,119	100.00	125.00	140.00	200.00	2,500

QUARTER EAGLES

	Quan. Minted	VF-20	EF-40	AU-50	MS-60	Proof-63
1896 ....(132)	19,202	$90.00	$110.00	$125.00	$175.00	$2,500
1897 ....(136)	29,904	90.00	110.00	125.00	175.00	2,500
1898 ....(165)	24,165	90.00	110.00	125.00	175.00	2,500
1899 ....(150)	27,350	90.00	110.00	125.00	175.00	2,500
1900 ....(205)	67,205	90.00	110.00	125.00	175.00	2,500
1901 ....(223)	91,323	90.00	110.00	125.00	175.00	2,500
1902 ....(193)	133,733	90.00	110.00	125.00	175.00	2,500
1903 ....(197)	201,257	90.00	110.00	125.00	175.00	2,500
1904 ....(170)	160,960	90.00	110.00	125.00	175.00	2,500
1905 ....(144)	217,944	90.00	110.00	125.00	175.00	2,500
1906 ....(160)	176,490	90.00	110.00	125.00	175.00	2,500
1907 ....(154)	336,448	90.00	110.00	125.00	175.00	2,500

INDIAN HEAD TYPE 1908-1929

Bela Lyon Pratt was the designer of this and the similar half eagle piece. The coin has no raised milling and the main devices and legends are incuse.

VF-20 VERY FINE—*Hair cord knot distinct. Feathers at top of head clear. Cheekbone worn.*
EF-40 EXTREMELY FINE—*Cheekbone, war bonnet and headband feathers slightly worn.*
AU-50 ABOUT UNCIRCULATED—*Trace of wear on cheekbone and headdress.*
MS-60 UNCIRCULATED—*No trace of wear. Light blemishes.*

Mint mark location is on reverse left of fasces.

	Quan. Minted	VF-20	EF-40	AU-50	MS-60	Matte Proof-63
1908 ....(236)	565,057	$90.00	$100.00	$115.00	$150.00	$4,000
1909 ....(139)	441,899	90.00	100.00	115.00	150.00	4,000
1910 ....(682)	492,682	90.00	100.00	115.00	150.00	4,000
1911 ....(191)	704,191	90.00	100.00	115.00	150.00	4,000
1911D	55,680	350.00	575.00	950.00	1,800	
1912 ....(197)	616,197	90.00	100.00	115.00	150.00	4,200
1913 ....(165)	722,165	90.00	100.00	115.00	150.00	4,200
1914 ....(117)	240,117	90.00	100.00	115.00	200.00	4,200
1914D	448,000	90.00	100.00	115.00	175.00	
1915 ....(100)	606,100	90.00	100.00	115.00	150.00	4,500
1925D	578,000	90.00	100.00	115.00	150.00	
1926	446,000	90.00	100.00	115.00	150.00	
1927	388,000	90.00	100.00	115.00	150.00	
1928	416,000	90.00	100.00	115.00	150.00	
1929	532,000	90.00	100.00	115.00	150.00	

THREE DOLLAR GOLD PIECES—1854-1889

The three dollar gold piece was authorized by the Act of February 21, 1853. The coin was first struck in 1854. It was never popular and saw very little circulation.

VF-20 VERY FINE—*Eyebrow, hair about forehead and ear and bottom curl are worn smooth. Curled feather ends have faint details showing.*
EF-40 EXTREMELY FINE—*Light wear above and to right of eye and on top of curled feathers.*
AU-50 ABOUT UNCIRCULATED—*Trace of wear on top of curled feathers and in hair above and to right of eye.*
MS-60 UNCIRCULATED—*No trace of wear. Light blemishes.*

Mint mark location is on reverse below wreath

	Quan. Minted	VF-20	EF-40	AU-50	MS-60	Proof-63
1854	138,618	$325.00	$425.00	$525.00	$1,000	$17,500
1854D	1,120	3,500	6,000	12,000	25,000	
1854O	24,000	325.00	425.00	900.00	3,600	
1855	50,555	325.00	425.00	525.00	1,000	15,000
1855S	6,600	425.00	700.00	1,500	7,000	

THREE DOLLAR GOLD PIECES

	Quan. Minted	VF-20	EF-40	AU-50	MS-60	Proof-63
1856	26,010	$325.00	$425.00	$600.00	$1,400	$11,500
1856S	34,500	350.00	450.00	750.00	3,000	
1857	20,891	350.00	450.00	600.00	1,700	9,500
1857S	14,000	375.00	700.00	1,600	5,500	
1858	2,133	400.00	600.00	850.00	2,500	9,500
1859 (80)	15,638	325.00	425.00	500.00	1,200	8,000
1860 (119)	7,155	325.00	425.00	500.00	1,300	6,000
1860S (2,592 melted at Mint)	7,000	400.00	650.00	1,600	5,500	
1861 (113)	6,072	325.00	425.00	600.00	1,750	6,000
1862 (35)	5,785	325.00	425.00	600.00	1,750	6,000
1863 (39)	5,039	375.00	475.00	650.00	1,750	6,000
1864 (50)	2,680	375.00	475.00	650.00	1,750	6,000
1865 (25)	1,165	450.00	800.00	1,300	3,400	7,500
1866 (30)	4,030	350.00	425.00	600.00	1,750	6,000
1867 (50)	2,650	350.00	425.00	600.00	1,750	6,000
1868 (25)	4,875	350.00	425.00	600.00	1,650	6,000
1869 (25)	2,525	350.00	425.00	600.00	1,750	6,000
1870 (35)	3,535	350.00	425.00	600.00	1,750	6,000
1870S	1	(Unique)				
1871 (30)	1,330	400.00	500.00	700.00	1,750	6,000
1872 (30)	2,030	350.00	450.00	625.00	1,750	6,000
1873 Open 3 (original) (25)	25					15,000
1873 Closed 3		1,250	2,000	3,000	9,000	11,000
1874 (20)	41,820	325.00	400.00	525.00	1,000	8,000
1875 Proofs only (20)						30,000
1876 Proofs only (45)						12,500
1877 (20)	1,488	425.00	800.00	1,500	4,500	10,000
1878 (20)	82,324	325.00	425.00	525.00	1,000	5,500
1879 (30)	3,030	350.00	450.00	600.00	1,250	6,500
1880 (36)	1,036	375.00	475.00	650.00	1,350	6,500
1881 (54)	554	500.00	700.00	1,300	2,500	7,000
1882 (76)	1,576	350.00	450.00	600.00	1,500	5,000
1883 (89)	989	375.00	475.00	650.00	1,650	5,000
1884 (106)	1,106	375.00	475.00	650.00	1,400	5,000
1885 (109)	910	500.00	700.00	900.00	1,850	5,000
1886 (142)	1,142	375.00	475.00	650.00	1,400	5,000
1887 (160)	6,160	350.00	450.00	600.00	1,200	5,000
1888 (291)	5,291	350.00	450.00	600.00	1,200	5,000
1889 (129)	2,429	350.00	450.00	600.00	1,200	5,000

FOUR DOLLAR GOLD OR "STELLA"

These pattern coins were first suggested by the Hon. John A. Kasson, then U.S. Minister to Austria; and it was through the efforts of Dr. W. W. Hubbell, who patented the goloid metal used in making the goloid metric dollars, that we have these beautiful and interesting pieces. Only those struck in gold are listed.

	Quan. Minted	VF-20	EF-40	Proof-60
1879 Flowing hair	425	$10,000	$15,000	$18,000
1879 Coiled hair	10	18,000	27,000	52,000
1880 Flowing hair	15	14,000	20,000	35,000
1880 Coiled hair	10	25,000	35,000	65,000

HALF EAGLES — 1795-1929
($5.00 GOLD PIECES)

The half eagle was the first gold coin struck for the United States. The $5.00 piece was authorized to be coined by the Act of April 2, 1792, and the first type weighed 135 grains, 916 2/3 fine. The weight was changed by the Act of June 28, 1834 to 129 grains, 899.225 fine. Fineness became .900 by the Act of January 18, 1837.

CAPPED BUST TO RIGHT, SMALL EAGLE 1795-1798

F-12 FINE—*Hair worn smooth but with distinct outline. For heraldic type, E PLURIBUS UNUM is faint but readable.*
VF-20 VERY FINE—*Slight to noticeable wear on high spots such as hair, turban, eagle's head and wings.*
EF-40 EXTREMELY FINE—*Slight wear on hair and highest part of cheek.*
MS-60 UNCIRCULATED—*No trace of wear. Light blemishes.*

	Quan. Minted	*F-12*	*VF-20*	*EF-40*	*MS-60*
1795 Small eagle	8,707	$2,800	$4,500	$6,500	$18,000

1796, 6 over 5

1797, 15 Stars

1797, 16 Stars

	Quan. Minted	*F-12*	*VF-20*	*EF-40*	*MS-60*
1796, 6 over 5	6,196	2,700	4,200	7,000	25,000
1797, 15 stars		4,750	6,000	9,000	27,500
1797, 16 stars All kinds	3,609	4,750	6,000	8,500	30,000
1798 Small eagle (7 known)		—	—	—	—

CAPPED BUST TO RIGHT, HERALDIC EAGLE 1795-1807

	Quan. Minted	*F-12*	*VF-20*	*EF-40*	*MS-60*
1795 Heraldic eagle		4,000	6,500	12,000	30,000
1797, 7 over 5		3,700	6,000	11,000	25,000
1798 13 star reverse	} 24,867	650.00	900.00	2,000	4,200
1798 14 star reverse		1,000	1,800	2,700	8,000
1799	7,451	650.00	900.00	2,500	6,000
1800	37,628	650.00	900.00	1,500	3,750
1802, 2 over 1	53,176	650.00	900.00	1,500	3,750
1803, 3 over 2	33,506	650.00	900.00	1,500	3,750

HALF EAGLES

	Quan. Minted	F-12	VF-20	EF-40	MS-60
1804	30,475	$650.00	$900.00	$1,500	$4,000
1805	33,183	650.00	900.00	1,500	3,750
1806	64,093	650.00	900.00	1,500	3,750
1807	32,488	650.00	900.00	1,500	3,750

CAPPED DRAPED BUST TO LEFT 1807-1812

F-12 FINE—*LIBERTY readable but partly weak.*

VF-20 VERY FINE—*Headband edges slightly worn. LIBERTY is bold.*

EF-40 EXTREMELY FINE—*Slight wear on highest portions of hair. 80% of major curls are plain.*

MS-60 UNCIRCULATED—*No trace of wear. Light blemishes.*

	Quan. Minted	F-12	VF-20	EF-40	MS-60
1807	51,605	600.00	850.00	1,100	3,500
1808, 8 over 7 }	55,578	600.00	850.00	1,000	4,500
1808 }		550.00	800.00	900.00	3,200
1809, 9 over 8	33,875	550.00	800.00	900.00	3,300
1810	100,287	550.00	800.00	900.00	3,300
1811	99,581	550.00	800.00	900.00	3,300
1812	58,087	550.00	800.00	900.00	3,300

CAPPED HEAD TO LEFT 1813-1829

	Quan. Minted	F-12	VF-20	EF-40	MS-60
1813	95,428	650.00	950.00	1,600	3,800
1814, 4 over 3	15,454	700.00	1,200	1,800	5,000
1815	635			35,000	85,000
1818	48,588	650.00	950.00	1,600	4,000
1819	51,723			10,000	20,000
1820	263,806	650.00	1,000	2,000	4,500
1821	34,641	1,400	3,200	5,000	14,000
1822	17,796	—	—	—	
1823	14,485	1,100	1,750	2,000	7,500
1824	17,340	3,000	4,500	7,000	15,000
1825, 5 over 1 }	29,060	1,650	2,500	4,250	9,000
1825, 5 over 4 }				—	
1826	18,069	1,800	3,250	4,500	10,000
1827	24,913	2,500	4,500	6,500	17,000
1828, 8 over 7 }	28,029	2,700	5,000	10,000	27,500
1828 }		3,000	4,500	9,500	25,000
1829 Large date	57,442	—	—	—	—

CAPPED HEAD TO LEFT (reduced diameter) 1829-1834

	Quan. Minted	F-12	VF-20	EF-40	MS-60
1829 Small date	inc. above		14,000	25,000	55,000
1830	126,351	1,300	2,250	3,500	7,500
1831	140,594	1,300	2,250	3,500	7,000
1832 Curved-base 2, 12 stars (4 known) }	157,487	—	—	—	—
1832 Square-base 2, 13 stars }		2,000	3,500	4,500	8,000
1833	193,630	1,300	2,500	3,500	7,000
1834	50,141	1,300	2,500	3,500	7,500

HALF EAGLES
CLASSIC HEAD TYPE 1834-1838

	Quan. Minted	F-12	VF-20	EF-40	MS-60
1834	657,460	$120.00	$150.00	$225.00	$1,250
1835	371,534	120.00	150.00	225.00	1,250
1836	553,147	120.00	150.00	225.00	1,250
1837	207,121	120.00	150.00	225.00	1,250
1838	286,588	120.00	150.00	225.00	1,250
1838C	17,179	400.00	650.00	1,800	9,000
1838D	20,583	400.00	600.00	1,600	7,000

CORONET TYPE, No Motto Above Eagle 1839-1866

VF-20 VERY FINE—*LIBERTY bold. Major lines show in neck hair.*

EF-40 EXTREMELY FINE—*Neck hair details clear. Slight wear on top and lower part of coronet, and hair.*

AU-50 ABOUT UNCIRCULATED—*Trace of wear on coronet and hair above eye.*

MS-60 UNCIRCULATED—*No trace of wear. Light blemishes.*

Mint mark above date 1839 only, below eagle 1840-1908.

	Quan. Minted	VF-20	EF-40	AU-50	MS-60
1839	118,143	$115.00	$150.00	$300.00	$1,300
1839C	17,205	250.00	600.00	1,200	6,500
1839D	18,939	250.00	700.00	1,600	4,500
1840	137,382	100.00	120.00	300.00	1,350
1840C	18,992	200.00	500.00	1,600	6,250
1840D	22,896	200.00	450.00	1,500	4,750
1840O	40,120	125.00	200.00	550.00	2,750
1841	15,833	125.00	200.00	500.00	1,500
1841C	21,467	200.00	400.00	1,000	4,250
1841D	29,392	200.00	400.00	1,000	4,000

1842 Large Date

Large Letters

Small Letters

1842 Small Letters	27,578	95.00	120.00	600.00	3,000
1842 Large letters		95.00	120.00	600.00	3,000
1842C Small date	27,432	2,000	5,000	12,000	—
1842C Large date		200.00	400.00	1,000	4,250
1842D Small date	59,608	200.00	400.00	1,000	4,000
1842D Large date		600.00	1,000	2,000	7,000
1842O	16,400	300.00	800.00	2,000	5,500
1843	611,205	95.00	110.00	160.00	750.00
1843C	44,277	200.00	350.00	1,500	4,800

HALF EAGLES

	Quan. Minted	VF-20	EF-40	AU-50	MS-60
1843D	98,452	$200.00	$350.00	$900.00	$2,500
1843O Small letters	19,075	200.00	400.00	1,000	5,000
1843O Large letters	82,000	110.00	200.00	700.00	3,200
1844	340,330	95.00	120.00	160.00	1,000
1844C	23,631	275.00	700.00	1,800	6,000
1844D	88,982	175.00	350.00	650.00	3,500
1844O	364,600	95.00	120.00	200.00	1,400
1845	417,099	95.00	120.00	160.00	800.00
1845D	90,629	160.00	350.00	800.00	4,000
1845O	41,000	175.00	225.00	800.00	4,000
1846	395,942	95.00	120.00	160.00	800.00
1846C	12,995	300.00	750.00	2,000	6,500
1846D	80,294	200.00	450.00	900.00	3,200
1846O	58,000	150.00	300.00	800.00	2,800
1847	915,981	95.00	120.00	160.00	750.00
1847C	84,151	200.00	400.00	850.00	4,400
1847D	64,405	200.00	400.00	850.00	2,800
1847O	12,000	400.00	1,200	3,500	7,000
1848	260,775	95.00	110.00	160.00	700.00
1848C	64,472	250.00	400.00	1,000	4,200
1848D	47,465	250.00	400.00	1,000	4,000
1849	133,070	95.00	110.00	160.00	800.00
1849C	64,823	225.00	400.00	800.00	3,200
1849D	39,036	225.00	400.00	800.00	4,750
1850	64,491	95.00	110.00	160.00	1,200
1850C	63,591	175.00	250.00	700.00	4,200
1850D	43,984	210.00	450.00	800.00	5,500
1851	377,505	95.00	110.00	160.00	900.00
1851C	49,176	200.00	350.00	1,000	3,800
1851D	62,710	200.00	350.00	1,000	3,800
1851O	41,000	200.00	350.00	1,000	3,500
1852	573,901	95.00	110.00	160.00	700.00
1852C	72,574	200.00	300.00	700.00	3,000
1852D	91,584	200.00	300.00	600.00	3,750
1853	305,770	95.00	110.00	160.00	700.00
1853C	65,571	200.00	300.00	700.00	3,000
1853D	89,678	150.00	200.00	500.00	2,200
1854	160,675	95.00	110.00	160.00	725.00
1854C	39,283	200.00	400.00	800.00	4,800
1854D	56,413	175.00	375.00	900.00	3,600
1854O	46,000	100.00	200.00	500.00	2,600
1854S	268	—	—	—	—
1855	117,098	95.00	110.00	160.00	700.00
1855C	39,788	200.00	425.00	1,000	5,000
1855D	22,432	200.00	425.00	1,000	5,250
1855O	11,100	200.00	425.00	1,200	5,500
1855S	61,000	150.00	400.00	900.00	3,500
1856	197,990	95.00	110.00	160.00	700.00
1856C	28,457	200.00	400.00	1,000	4,000
1856D	19,786	200.00	400.00	1,000	3,500
1856O	10,000	225.00	500.00	1,500	4,750
1856S	105,100	95.00	110.00	250.00	1,800
1857	98,188	95.00	115.00	160.00	700.00
1857C	31,360	175.00	300.00	800.00	3,200
1857D	17,046	175.00	300.00	800.00	3,250
1857O	13,000	175.00	300.00	800.00	4,500
1857S	87,000	110.00	175.00	500.00	3,000
1858	15,136	110.00	125.00	250.00	1,100

Values of common gold coins are based on the prevailing price of gold bullion, and will vary according to current market price. See Bullion Chart.

HALF EAGLES

	Quan. Minted	*VF-20*	*EF-40*	*AU-50*	*MS-60*	*Proof-63*
1858C	38,856	$200.00	$300.00	$700.00	$4,200	
1858D	15,362	200.00	300.00	700.00	4,200	
1858S	18,600	225.00	800.00	2,000	5,500	
1859 (80)	16,814	110.00	125.00	350.00	2,000	$10,000
1859C	31,847	200.00	300.00	800.00	3,900	
1859D	10,366	175.00	300.00	600.00	3,500	
1859S	13,220	300.00	900.00	2,800	—	
1860 (62)	19,825	110.00	125.00	275.00	1,250	9,000
1860C	14,813	200.00	600.00	1,200	4,500	
1860D	14,635	200.00	600.00	1,200	5,000	
1860S	21,200	225.00	600.00	2,500	—	
1861 (66)	688,150	95.00	110.00	160.00	700.00	9,000
1861C	6,879	825.00	1,400	3,200	10,000	
1861D	1,597	2,000	3,750	7,500	20,000	
1861S	18,000	250.00	1,000	2,750	12,000	
1862 (35)	4,465	150.00	500.00	1,200	—	9,000
1862S	9,500	750.00	1,800	4,200	—	
1863 (30)	2,472	200.00	900.00	1,600	6,000	9,000
1863S	17,000	200.00	1,000	3,000	7,000	
1864 (50)	4,220	150.00	500.00	1,000	3,000	9,000
1864S	3,888	2,100	4,500	10,000	—	
1865 (25)	1,295	350.00	650.00	2,400	5,500	9,000
1865S	27,612	300.00	650.00	1,600	4,000	
1866S	9,000	400.00	1,200	4,200	—	

Motto Above Eagle 1866-1908

VF-20 VERY FINE—*Half of hairlines above coronet missing. Hair curls under ear evident, but worn. Motto and its ribbon sharp.*

EF-40 EXTREMELY FINE—*Small amount of wear on top of hair and below L in LIBERTY. Wear evident on wing tips and neck of eagle.*

AU-50 ABOUT UNCIRCULATED—*Trace of wear on tip of coronet and hair above eye.*

MS-60 UNCIRCULATED—*No trace of wear. Light blemishes.*

1866 (30)	6,730	150.00	300.00	1,000	3,000	8,000
1866S	34,920	200.00	1,000	2,500	7,000	
1867 (50)	6,920	135.00	300.00	900.00	2,500	7,500
1867S	29,000	200.00	1,000	2,500	—	
1868 (25)	5,725	135.00	250.00	600.00	2,500	8,000
1868S	52,000	135.00	300.00	1,200	—	
1869 (25)	1,785	175.00	400.00	1,000	4,000	8,000
1869S	31,000	200.00	500.00	2,000	7,000	
1870 (35)	4,035	150.00	300.00	600.00	3,000	8,000
1870CC	7,675	1,500	4,000	9,000		
1870S	17,000	200.00	500.00	2,500	—	
1871 (30)	3,230	175.00	300.00	1,800	—	8,000
1871CC	20,770	250.00	1,000	3,000	7,000	
1871S	25,000	135.00	300.00	1,000	3,000	
1872 (30)	1,690	200.00	300.00	1,000	2,750	8,000
1872CC	16,980	250.00	650.00	2,400	4,000	
1872S	36,400	125.00	250.00	950.00	2,700	
1873 (25)	112,505	95.00	100.00	140.00	175.00	8,000
1873CC	7,416	500.00	1,800	4,500	7,500	
1873S	31,000	150.00	300.00	1,500	4,500	
1874 (20)	3,508	135.00	200.00	800.00	2,700	8,500

Values of common gold coins are based on the prevailing price of gold bullion, and will vary according to current market price. See Bullion Chart.

HALF EAGLES

	Quan. Minted	VF-20	EF-40	AU-50	MS-60	Proof-63
1874CC	21,198	$120.00	$225.00	$1,500	$3,500	
1874S	16,000	250.00	800.00	2,000	—	
1875 (20)	220		—	—	—	—
1875CC	11,828	150.00	600.00	2,500	4,500	
1875S	9,000	150.00	500.00	1,500	4,000	
1876 (45)	1,477	250.00	400.00	950.00	3,000	$8,000
1876CC	6,887	300.00	900.00	2,500	4,500	
1876S	4,000	250.00	800.00	2,100	4,700	
1877 (20)	1,152	200.00	350.00	1,000	3,000	8,250
1877CC	8,680	150.00	500.00	2,000	3,500	
1877S	26,700	100.00	125.00	500.00	2,000	
1878 (20)	131,740	85.00	95.00	105.00	130.00	7,750
1878CC	9,054	700.00	2,000	5,500		
1878S	144,700	85.00	100.00	150.00	175.00	
1879 (30)	301,950	85.00	95.00	105.00	130.00	7,750
1879CC	17,281	135.00	200.00	500.00	2,500	
1879S	426,200	85.00	95.00	110.00	175.00	
1880 (36)	3,166,436	85.00	95.00	105.00	130.00	7,250
1880CC	51,017	120.00	170.00	400.00	1,800	
1880S	1,348,900	85.00	95.00	105.00	130.00	
1881 (42)	5,708,802	85.00	95.00	105.00	130.00	7,250
1881CC	13,886	140.00	350.00	1,400	4,500	
1881S	969,000	85.00	95.00	105.00	130.00	
1882 (48)	2,514,568	85.00	95.00	105.00	130.00	7,250
1882CC	82,817	110.00	120.00	200.00	1,500	
1882S	969,000	85.00	95.00	105.00	130.00	
1883 (61)	233,461	85.00	95.00	105.00	130.00	7,250
1883CC	12,958	140.00	200.00	750.00	3,000	
1883S	83,200	85.00	95.00	125.00	175.00	
1884 (48)	191,078	85.00	95.00	105.00	130.00	6,750
1884CC	16,402	140.00	200.00	650.00	2,700	
1884S	177,000	85.00	95.00	105.00	130.00	
1885 (66)	601,506	85.00	95.00	105.00	130.00	6,750
1885S	1,211,500	85.00	95.00	105.00	130.00	
1886 (72)	388,432	85.00	95.00	105.00	130.00	6,750
1886S	3,268,000	85.00	95.00	105.00	130.00	
1887 Proofs only (87)	87					20,000
1887S	1,912,000	85.00	95.00	105.00	130.00	
1888 (95)	18,296	110.00	130.00	140.00	250.00	6,750
1888S	293,900	85.00	100.00	150.00	300.00	
1889 (45)	7,565	110.00	125.00	200.00	600.00	6,500
1890 (88)	4,328	110.00	200.00	300.00	700.00	6,500
1890CC	53,800	85.00	110.00	175.00	325.00	
1891 (53)	61,413	85.00	95.00	105.00	130.00	6,500
1891CC	208,000	85.00	110.00	150.00	200.00	
1892 (92)	753,572	85.00	95.00	105.00	130.00	6,500
1892CC	82,968	85.00	110.00	175.00	375.00	
1892O	10,000	175.00	300.00	550.00	1,200	
1892S	298,400	85.00	95.00	125.00	175.00	
1893 (77)	1,528,197	85.00	95.00	105.00	130.00	6,500
1893CC	60,000	85.00	100.00	175.00	400.00	
1893O	110,000	85.00	100.00	175.00	350.00	
1893S	224,000	85.00	95.00	125.00	175.00	
1894 (75)	957,955	85.00	95.00	105.00	130.00	6,500
1894O	16,600	110.00	115.00	175.00	450.00	
1894S	55,900	100.00	125.00	225.00	900.00	
1895 (81)	1,345,936	85.00	95.00	105.00	130.00	5,500
1895S	112,000	100.00	125.00	225.00	900.00	
1896 (103)	59,063	85.00	95.00	105.00	130.00	5,500

Values of common gold coins are based on the prevailing price of gold bullion, and will vary according to current market price. See Bullion Chart.

HALF EAGLES

	Quan. Minted	VF-20	EF-40	AU-50	MS-60	Proof-63
1896S	155,400	$85.00	$95.00	$105.00	$200.00	
1897 (83)	867,883	85.00	95.00	105.00	130.00	$5,500
1897S	354,000	85.00	95.00	105.00	175.00	
1898 (75)	633,495	85.00	95.00	105.00	130.00	5,500
1898S	1,397,400	85.00	95.00	105.00	130.00	
1899 (99)	1,710,729	85.00	95.00	105.00	130.00	5,500
1899S	1,545,000	85.00	95.00	105.00	130.00	
1900 (230)	1,405,730	85.00	95.00	105.00	125.00	5,500
1900S	329,000	85.00	95.00	105.00	150.00	
1901 (140)	616,040	85.00	95.00	105.00	125.00	5,500
1901S, 1 over 0	3,648,000	85.00	95.00	105.00	125.00	
1901S		85.00	95.00	105.00	125.00	
1902 (162)	172,562	85.00	95.00	105.00	125.00	5,500
1902S	939,000	85.00	95.00	105.00	125.00	
1903 (154)	227,024	85.00	95.00	105.00	125.00	5,500
1903S	1,855,000	85.00	95.00	105.00	125.00	
1904 (136)	392,136	85.00	95.00	105.00	125.00	5,500
1904S	97,000	85.00	95.00	105.00	190.00	
1905 (108)	302,308	85.00	95.00	105.00	125.00	5,500
1905S	880,700	85.00	95.00	105.00	175.00	
1906 (85)	348,820	85.00	95.00	105.00	125.00	5,500
1906D	320,000	85.00	95.00	105.00	125.00	
1906S	598,000	85.00	95.00	105.00	125.00	
1907 (92)	626,192	85.00	95.00	105.00	125.00	5,500
1907D	888,000	85.00	95.00	105.00	125.00	
1908	421,874	85.00	95.00	105.00	125.00	

INDIAN HEAD TYPE 1908-1929

This type conforms to the quarter eagle of the same date. The incuse designs and lettering make this a unique series, along with the quarter eagle, in United States coinage.

VF-20 VERY FINE—*Noticeable wear on large middle feathers and tip of eagle's wing.*
EF-40 EXTREMELY FINE—*Cheekbone, war bonnet and headband feathers slightly worn. Feathers on eagle's upper wing show considerable wear.*
AU-50 ABOUT UNCIRCULATED—*Trace of wear on cheekbone and headdress.*
MS-60 UNCIRCULATED—*No trace of wear. Light blemishes.*

Scarcer coins with well struck mint marks command higher prices.

Mint mark location

	Quan. Minted	VF-20	EF-40	AU-50	MS-60	Matte Proof-63
1908 (167)	578,012	$115.00	$125.00	$140.00	$225.00	$5,500
1908D	148,000	115.00	125.00	140.00	225.00	
1908S	82,000	150.00	200.00	250.00	800.00	
1909 (78)	627,138	115.00	125.00	140.00	225.00	5,500
1909D	3,423,560	115.00	125.00	140.00	225.00	
1909O	34,200	275.00	500.00	725.00	3,500	
1909S	297,200	115.00	125.00	175.00	600.00	
1910 (250)	604,250	115.00	125.00	140.00	225.00	5,500
1910D	193,600	115.00	125.00	165.00	275.00	

Values of common gold coins are based on the prevailing price of gold bullion, and will vary according to current market price. See Bullion Chart.

HALF EAGLES

	Quan. Minted	VF-20	EF-40	AU-50	MS-60	Matte Proof-63
1910S	770,200	$115.00	$125.00	$175.00	$600.00	
1911 (139)	915,139	115.00	125.00	140.00	225.00	$5,500
1911D	72,500	140.00	200.00	325.00	2,000	
1911S	1,416,000	115.00	125.00	175.00	350.00	
1912 (144)	790,144	115.00	125.00	140.00	225.00	5,500
1912S	392,000	115.00	125.00	175.00	800.00	
1913 (99)	916,000	115.00	125.00	140.00	225.00	5,500
1913S	408,000	115.00	125.00	250.00	800.00	
1914 (125)	247,125	115.00	125.00	140.00	225.00	5,500
1914D	247,000	115.00	125.00	140.00	225.00	
1914S	263,000	115.00	125.00	175.00	600.00	
1915 (75)	588,075	115.00	125.00	140.00	225.00	6,500
1915S	164,000	115.00	125.00	200.00	1,000	
1916S	240,000	115.00	125.00	175.00	350.00	
1929	662,000	1,400	2,000	2,750	3,750	

Values of common gold coins are based on the prevailing price of gold bullion, and will vary according to current market price. See Bullion Chart.

EAGLES ($10.00 Gold Pieces) — 1795-1933

Coinage authority including specified weights and fineness of the eagle conforms to that of the half eagle. The small eagle reverse was used until 1797 when the large, heraldic eagle replaced it.

CAPPED BUST TO RIGHT, SMALL EAGLE 1795-1797

F-12 FINE—*Details on turban and head obliterated.*
VF-20 VERY FINE—*Neck hairlines and details under turban and over forehead are worn but distinguishable.*
EF-40 EXTREMELY FINE—*Definite wear on hair to left of eye and strand of hair across and around turban, also on eagle's wing tips.*
MS-60 UNCIRCULATED—*No trace of wear. Light blemishes.*

	Quan. Minted	F-12	VF-20	EF-40	MS-60
1795	5,583	$3,500	$5,000	$8,000	$20,000
1796	4,146	3,500	5,000	9,000	27,500
1797 Small eagle	3,615	3,750	6,000	12,500	32,500

CAPPED BUST TO RIGHT, HERALDIC EAGLE 1797-1804

	Quan. Minted	F-12	VF-20	EF-40	MS-60
1797 Large eagle	10,940	1,100	1,800	3,000	8,000
1798, 8 over 7, 9 stars left, 4 right	900	2,500	5,000	8,750	25,000
1798, 8 over 7, 7 stars left, 6 right	842	6,000	12,000	—	—

EAGLES

	Quan. Minted	F-12	VF-20	EF-40	MS-60
1799	37,449	$1,000	$1,600	$2,750	$6,000
1800	5,999	1,000	1,600	3,000	7,000

	Quan. Minted	F-12	VF-20	EF-40	MS-60
1801	44,344	1,000	1,600	2,750	6,000
1803	15,017	1,000	1,600	2,750	6,000
1804	3,757	1,750	2,500	4,200	12,000

CORONET TYPE, No Motto Above Eagle 1838-1866

In 1838 the weight and diameter of the eagle were reduced and the obverse and reverse were redesigned. Liberty now faces left and the word liberty is placed on the coronet.

VF-20 VERY FINE—*Hairlines above coronet partly worn. Curls under ear worn but defined.*

EF-40 EXTREMELY FINE—*Small amount of wear on top of hair and below L in LIBERTY. Wear evident on wing tips and neck of eagle.*

AU-50 ABOUT UNCIRCULATED—*Trace of wear on tip of coronet and hair above eye.*

MS-60 UNCIRCULATED—*No trace of wear. Light blemishes.*

Mint mark location on reverse below eagle.

	Quan. Minted	VF-20	EF-40	AU-50	MS-60
1838	7,200	$400.00	$950.00	$2,600	$12,000
1839 Large letters	25,801	275.00	500.00	1,700	8,500
1839 Small letters	12,447	325.00	900.00	2,100	9,500
1840	47,338	190.00	225.00	450.00	3,400
1841	63,131	190.00	225.00	450.00	3,200
1841O	2,500	400.00	1,500	3,500	11,000
1842	81,507	190.00	225.00	400.00	3,000
1842O	27,400	190.00	250.00	800.00	4,500
1843	75,462	190.00	225.00	400.00	3,500
1843O	175,162	190.00	225.00	375.00	3,500
1844	6,361	250.00	800.00	1,300	4,500
1844O	118,700	190.00	225.00	350.00	4,000
1845	26,153	190.00	225.00	350.00	4,000
1845O	47,500	190.00	225.00	350.00	4,000
1846	20,095	200.00	400.00	800.00	4,500
1846O	81,780	200.00	250.00	700.00	5,000
1847	862,258	190.00	225.00	300.00	1,500
1847O	571,500	190.00	225.00	325.00	2,000
1848	145,484	190.00	225.00	300.00	1,750
1848O	35,850	210.00	400.00	1,000	4,500
1849	653,618	190.00	225.00	325.00	1,600

EAGLES

	Quan. Minted	*VF-20*	*EF-40*	*AU-50*	*MS-60*	*Proof-63*
1849O	23,900	$225.00	$450.00	$1,750	$5,500	
1850	291,451	190.00	225.00	300.00	1,500	
1850O	57,500	190.00	250.00	1,000	3,500	
1851	176,328	190.00	225.00	350.00	2,000	
1851O	263,000	190.00	225.00	350.00	2,500	
1852	263,106	190.00	225.00	300.00	1,800	
1852O	18,000	200.00	400.00	1,450	7,000	
1853, 3 over 2	201,253	225.00	400.00	750.00	3,500	
1853		190.00	225.00	300.00	1,500	
1853O	51,000	190.00	225.00	400.00	3,000	
1854	54,250	190.00	225.00	300.00	1,800	
1854O	52,500	190.00	225.00	350.00	2,750	
1854S	123,826	190.00	225.00	325.00	2,300	
1855	121,701	190.00	225.00	300.00	1,500	—
1855O	18,000	220.00	450.00	1,400	5,400	
1855S	9,000	350.00	900.00	2,700	8,000	—
1856	60,490	190.00	225.00	325.00	1,600	
1856O	14,500	200.00	650.00	1,500	4,500	
1856S	68,000	190.00	225.00	400.00	2,000	
1857	16,606	190.00	225.00	500.00	2,250	—
1857O	5,500	300.00	600.00	1,750	6,000	
1857S	26,000	190.00	225.00	450.00	2,500	
1858	2,521	2,200	4,000	7,000	16,000	—
1858O	20,000	190.00	250.00	500.00	2,500	
1858S	11,800	300.00	1,000	2,500	6,500	
1859	(80) 16,093	190.00	225.00	400.00	2,200	$16,000
1859O	2,300	1,000	2,800	5,500	14,000	
1859S	7,000	650.00	1,900	4,000	12,500	
1860	(50) 15,105	190.00	225.00	475.00	3,000	12,000
1860O	11,100	210.00	450.00	1,000	4,800	
1860S	5,000	900.00	2,400	4,500	13,000	
1861	(69) 113,233	190.00	225.00	300.00	1,600	12,000
1861S	15,500	375.00	750.00	2,200	7,500	
1862	(35) 10,995	210.00	350.00	650.00	3,000	12,000
1862S	12,500	400.00	950.00	2,200	15,000	
1863	(30) 1,248	1,500	3,500	7,000	—	13,500
1863S	10,000	450.00	1,000	1,800	6,000	
1864	(50) 3,580	500.00	950.00	1,600	4,500	12,000
1864S	2,500	2,100	4,800			
1865	(25) 4,005	450.00	1,000	1,500	6,500	12,000
1865S	16,700	450.00	1,200	1,800	6,500	
1866S	8,500	400.00	900.00	1,800	6,500	

Motto Above Eagle 1866-1907

Mint mark location on the reverse below eagle.

VF-20 VERY FINE—*Half of hairlines over coronet visible. Curls under ear worn but defined. IN GOD WE TRUST and its ribbon are sharp.*

EF-40 EXTREMELY FINE—*Small amount of wear on top of hair and below L in LIBERTY. Wear evident on wing tips and neck of eagle.*

AU-50 ABOUT UNCIRCULATED—*Trace of wear on hair above eye and on coronet.*

MS-60 UNCIRCULATED—*No trace of wear. Light blemishes.*

EAGLES

	Quan. Minted	VF-20	EF-40	AU-50	MS-60	Proof-63
1866	(30) 3,780	$235.00	$450.00	$1,200	$4,500	$8,500
1866S	11,500	375.00	700.00	1,500	5,500	
1867	(50) 3,140	375.00	600.00	1,300	6,000	7,500
1867S	9,000	550.00	1,500	2,500	10,000	
1868	(25) 10,655	250.00	350.00	650.00	3,500	7,500
1868S	13,500	350.00	700.00	1,200	6,000	
1869	(25) 1,855	350.00	850.00	1,300	6,200	7,500
1869S	6,430	350.00	700.00	1,300	6,000	
1870	(35) 4,025	250.00	350.00	800.00	2,800	7,500
1870CC	5,908	2,200	3,750	12,500		
1870S	8,000	250.00	600.00	1,500	6,500	
1871	(30) 1,820	350.00	600.00	1,000	3,500	8,000
1871CC	8,085	800.00	1,800	4,500		
1871S	16,500	300.00	400.00	1,200	4,000	
1872	(30) 1,650	700.00	1,200	3,000	7,500	7,500
1872CC	4,600	850.00	2,500	4,000		
1872S	17,300	225.00	300.00	1,000	3,500	
1873	(25) 825	1,500	3,000	7,000	14,000	15,000
1873CC	4,543	1,200	2,500	6,500		
1873S	12,000	225.00	550.00	1,200	3,800	
1874	(20) 53,160	150.00	160.00	190.00	450.00	10,000
1874CC	16,767	275.00	600.00	1,800	6,500	
1874S	10,000	275.00	600.00	1,800	6,500	
1875	(20) 120	16,000	—	—		—
1875CC	7,715	1,200	2,400	7,000	—	
1876	(45) 732	900.00	2,100	3,500	12,000	12,000
1876CC	4,696	900.00	2,200	4,200	9,500	
1876S	5,000	350.00	850.00	2,200	4,800	
1877	(20) 817	700.00	2,000	3,000	7,500	14,000
1877CC	3,332	650.00	1,800	3,500	8,000	
1877S	17,000	160.00	225.00	850.00	3,500	
1878	(20) 73,800	160.00	170.00	190.00	310.00	8,000
1878CC	3,244	950.00	2,100	4,500	8,500	
1878S	26,100	160.00	250.00	900.00	3,200	
1879	(30) 384,770	150.00	160.00	190.00	210.00	7,500
1879CC	1,762	1,500	3,000	8,000	13,000	
1879O	1,500	650.00	1,400	3,500	8,500	
1879S	224,000	150.00	160.00	190.00	300.00	
1880	1,644,876	150.00	160.00	180.00	200.00	7,500
1880CC	11,190	175.00	225.00	350.00	2,500	
1880O	9,200	160.00	200.00	325.00	2,200	
1880S	506,250	150.00	155.00	160.00	170.00	
1881	(40) 3,877,260	150.00	155.00	160.00	170.00	7,500
1881CC	24,015	160.00	200.00	400.00	1,400	
1881O	8,350	165.00	250.00	500.00	1,600	
1881S	970,000	150.00	160.00	170.00	180.00	
1882	(40) 2,324,480	150.00	160.00	170.00	180.00	7,500
1882CC	6,764	175.00	325.00	1,200	3,750	
1882O	10,820	160.00	170.00	400.00	1,900	
1882S	132,000	150.00	160.00	190.00	250.00	
1883	(40) 208,740	150.00	160.00	190.00	200.00	7,500
1883CC	12,000	160.00	250.00	900.00	3,000	
1883O	800	1,500	3,000	5,000	13,000	
1883S	38,000	150.00	160.00	190.00	275.00	
1884	(45) 76,905	150.00	160.00	190.00	350.00	12,000
1884CC	9,925	160.00	275.00	950.00	3,200	
1884S	124,250	150.00	160.00	190.00	250.00	
1885	(65) 253,527	150.00	155.00	160.00	170.00	7,000
1885S	228,000	150.00	155.00	160.00	170.00	

Values of common gold coins are based on the prevailing price of gold bullion, and will vary according to current market price. See Bullion Chart.

EAGLES

	Quan. Minted	VF-20	EF-40	AU-50	MS-60	Proof-63
1886	(60) 236,160	$150.00	$155.00	$170.00	$225.00	$7,000
1886S	826,000	150.00	155.00	160.00	170.00	
1887	(80) 53,680	150.00	160.00	200.00	250.00	7,000
1887S	817,000	150.00	155.00	160.00	170.00	
1888	(75) 132,996	150.00	155.00	170.00	225.00	7,000
1888O	21,335	150.00	155.00	180.00	300.00	
1888S	648,700	150.00	155.00	160.00	170.00	
1889	(45) 4,485	170.00	200.00	250.00	600.00	7,500
1889S	425,400	150.00	155.00	160.00	170.00	
1890	(63) 58,043	150.00	155.00	190.00	375.00	7,000
1890CC	17,500	150.00	155.00	200.00	500.00	
1891	(48) 91,868	150.00	155.00	160.00	170.00	7,000
1891CC	103,732	150.00	155.00	200.00	350.00	
1892	(72) 797,552	150.00	155.00	160.00	170.00	7,000
1892CC	40,000	155.00	160.00	225.00	900.00	
1892O	28,688	150.00	155.00	160.00	170.00	
1892S	115,500	150.00	155.00	160.00	170.00	
1893	(55) 1,840,895	150.00	155.00	160.00	170.00	6,500
1893CC	14,000	160.00	180.00	500.00	1,200	
1893O	17,000	150.00	165.00	250.00	350.00	
1893S	141,350	150.00	155.00	160.00	170.00	
1894	(43) 2,470,778	150.00	155.00	160.00	170.00	6,500
1894O	107,500	150.00	155.00	170.00	225.00	
1894S	25,000	150.00	155.00	250.00	900.00	
1895	(56) 567,826	150.00	155.00	160.00	170.00	6,500
1895O	98,000	150.00	155.00	160.00	170.00	
1895S	49,000	150.00	155.00	225.00	600.00	
1896	(78) 76,348	150.00	155.00	160.00	170.00	6,500
1896S	123,750	150.00	155.00	210.00	600.00	
1897	(69) 1,000,159	150.00	155.00	160.00	170.00	6,500
1897O	42,500	150.00	155.00	160.00	170.00	
1897S	234,750	150.00	155.00	190.00	350.00	
1898	(67) 812,197	150.00	155.00	160.00	170.00	6,500
1898S	473,600	150.00	155.00	160.00	170.00	
1899	(86) 1,262,305	150.00	155.00	160.00	170.00	6,500
1899O	37,047	150.00	155.00	190.00	250.00	
1899S	841,000	150.00	155.00	160.00	170.00	
1900	(120) 293,960	150.00	155.00	160.00	170.00	6,000
1900S	81,000	150.00	155.00	170.00	225.00	
1901	(85) 1,718,825	150.00	155.00	160.00	170.00	6,000
1901O	72,041	150.00	155.00	160.00	170.00	
1901S	2,812,750	150.00	155.00	160.00	170.00	
1902	(113) 82,513	150.00	155.00	160.00	170.00	6,000
1902S	469,500	150.00	155.00	160.00	170.00	
1903	(96) 125,926	150.00	155.00	160.00	170.00	6,000
1903O	112,771	150.00	155.00	160.00	170.00	
1903S	538,000	150.00	155.00	160.00	170.00	
1904	(108) 162,038	150.00	155.00	160.00	170.00	6,000
1904O	108,950	150.00	155.00	160.00	170.00	
1905	(86) 201,078	150.00	155.00	160.00	170.00	6,000
1905S	369,250	150.00	155.00	170.00	400.00	
1906	(77) 165,497	150.00	155.00	160.00	170.00	6,000
1906D	981,000	150.00	155.00	160.00	170.00	
1906O	86,895	150.00	155.00	160.00	170.00	
1906S	457,000	150.00	155.00	160.00	225.00	
1907	(74) 1,203,973	150.00	155.00	160.00	170.00	6,000
1907D	1,030,000	150.00	155.00	160.00	170.00	
1907S	210,500	150.00	155.00	160.00	170.00	

Values of common gold coins are based on the prevailing price of gold bullion, and will vary according to current market price. See Bullion Chart.

EAGLES
INDIAN HEAD TYPE 1907-1933

No Motto

With Motto
IN GOD WE TRUST

Mint mark location is above left tip of branch on 1908D no motto, and at left of arrow points thereafter.

VF-20 VERY FINE—*Bonnet feathers worn near band. Hair high points show wear.*
EF-40 EXTREMELY FINE—*Slight wear on cheekbone and headdress feathers. Eagle's eye and left wing will show slight wear.*
AU-50 ABOUT UNCIRCULATED—*Trace of wear on hair above eye and on forehead.*
MS-60 UNCIRCULATED—*No trace of wear. Light blemishes.*

Uncirculated (MS-65) coins are worth substantial premiums.

No Motto on Reverse 1907-1908

	Quan. Minted	*VF-20*	*EF-40*	*AU-50*	*MS-60*	*Proof-63*
1907 Wire rim, periods	500			$3,000	$5,000	
1907 Rounded rim, periods before and after •E•PLURIBUS•UNUM•	42					$16,000
1907 No periods	239,406	$250.00	$260.00	285.00	300.00	
1908 No motto	33,500	220.00	250.00	275.00	450.00	
1908D No motto	210,000	200.00	225.00	260.00	425.00	

Motto on Reverse 1908-1933

	Quan. Minted	*VF-20*	*EF-40*	*AU-50*	*MS-60*	*Matte Proof-63*
1908 (116)	341,486	200.00	225.00	250.00	275.00	7,500
1908D	836,500	200.00	250.00	300.00	425.00	
1908S	59,850	200.00	275.00	350.00	800.00	
1909 (74)	184,863	200.00	250.00	275.00	325.00	7,500
1909D	121,540	200.00	250.00	275.00	325.00	
1909S	292,350	200.00	250.00	275.00	325.00	
1910 (204)	318,704	200.00	225.00	250.00	275.00	7,500
1910D	2,356,640	200.00	225.00	250.00	275.00	
1910S	811,000	200.00	250.00	275.00	375.00	
1911 (95)	505,595	200.00	225.00	250.00	275.00	7,500
1911D	30,100	275.00	375.00	425.00	2,200	
1911S	51,000	200.00	250.00	350.00	600.00	
1912 (83)	405,083	200.00	225.00	250.00	275.00	7,500
1912S	300,000	200.00	225.00	250.00	400.00	
1913 (71)	442,071	200.00	225.00	250.00	275.00	7,500
1913S	66,000	200.00	300.00	400.00	2,200	
1914 (50)	151,050	200.00	225.00	250.00	275.00	8,500
1914D	343,500	200.00	225.00	250.00	275.00	
1914S	208,000	200.00	250.00	275.00	375.00	
1915 (75)	351,075	200.00	225.00	275.00	350.00	9,500
1915S	59,000	200.00	250.00	400.00	1,700	
1916S	138,500	200.00	250.00	300.00	450.00	
1920S	126,500	2,200	3,500	5,000	10,000	
1926	1,014,000	200.00	225.00	250.00	275.00	
1930S	96,000	1,500	1,950	4,000	5,750	
1932	4,463,000	200.00	225.00	250.00	275.00	
1933	312,500				35,000	

Values of common gold coins are based on the prevailing price of gold bullion, and will vary according to current market price. See Bullion Chart.

DOUBLE EAGLES ($20.00 Gold Pieces) — 1850-1933

This largest denomination of all regular United States issues was authorized to be coined by the Act of March 3, 1849. Its weight was 516 grains, .900 fine.

Mint mark location is below the eagle

VF-20 VERY FINE—*LIBERTY is bold. Prongs on crown defined. Lower half worn flat. Hair worn about ear.*
EF-40 EXTREMELY FINE—*Trace of wear on rounded prongs of crown and down hair curls. Minor bag marks.*
AU-50 ABOUT UNCIRCULATED—*Trace of wear on hair over eye and on coronet.*
MS-60 UNCIRCULATED—*No trace of wear. Light blemishes.*

Without Motto on Reverse 1850-1866

	Quan. Minted	*VF-20*	*EF-40*	*AU-50*	*MS-60*	*Proof-63*
1850	1,170,261	$375.00	$400.00	$500.00	$2,100	
1850O	141,000	375.00	450.00	1,600	11,000	
1851	2,087,155	350.00	375.00	400.00	1,500	
1851O	315,000	375.00	400.00	650.00	5,500	
1852	2,053,026	350.00	375.00	400.00	1,500	
1852O	190,000	375.00	400.00	700.00	5,500	
1853	1,261,326	350.00	375.00	400.00	1,800	
1853O	71,000	375.00	425.00	1,000	11,000	
1854	757,899	375.00	400.00	450.00	2,000	
1854O	3,250	16,500	26,000	37,000		
1854S	141,468	375.00	400.00	450.00	1,600	
1855	364,666	375.00	400.00	450.00	2,500	
1855O	8,000	1,200	2,200	5,500	—	
1855S	879,675	375.00	400.00	450.00	2,500	
1856	329,878	375.00	400.00	450.00	2,500	
1856O	2,250	16,000	26,000	52,000		
1856S	1,189,750	375.00	400.00	450.00	1,500	
1857	439,375	375.00	400.00	450.00	1,500	
1857O	30,000	400.00	450.00	12,500	6,500	
1857S	970,500	375.00	400.00	450.00	1,700	
1858	211,714	375.00	400.00	500.00	1,800	
1858O	35,250	400.00	500.00	1,200	7,000	
1858S	846,710	375.00	400.00	500.00	3,200	
1859 (80)	43,677	375.00	550.00	1,600	9,000	
1859O	9,100	1,200	2,200	5,500	13,500	
1859S	636,445	375.00	400.00	450.00	1,400	
1860 (59)	577,729	375.00	400.00	450.00	1,200	
1860O	6,600	1,250	2,600	6,200	22,000	
1860S	544,950	375.00	400.00	500.00	2,200	
1861 (66)	2,976,519	375.00	400.00	450.00	950.00	
1861O	17,741	600.00	1,500	2,750	13,000	
1861S	768,000	375.00	400.00	600.00	2,750	
1862 (35)	92,168	375.00	450.00	700.00	3,800	$18,000
1862S	854,173	375.00	400.00	500.00	3,800	

Values of common gold coins are based on the prevailing price of gold bullion, and will vary according to current market price. See Bullion Chart.

DOUBLE EAGLES

	Quan. Minted	VF-20	EF-40	AU-50	MS-60	Proof-63
1863 .....(30)	142,820	$375.00	$400.00	$500.00	$4,200	$17,000
1863S	966,570	375.00	400.00	450.00	2,200	
1864 .....(50)	204,285	375.00	400.00	500.00	2,500	17,000
1864S	793,660	375.00	400.00	450.00	2,000	
1865 .....(25)	351,200	375.00	400.00	450.00	1,900	18,500
1865S	1,042,500	375.00	400.00	450.00	1,800	
1866S .....est	*12,000*	600.00	1,250	3,400	12,000	

Motto Above Eagle, Value TWENTY D. 1866-1876

	Quan. Minted	VF-20	EF-40	AU-50	MS-60	Proof-63
1866 .....(30)	698,775	$320.00	$350.00	$425.00	$1,800	$14,500
1866S	842,250	320.00	350.00	600.00	4,200	
1867 .....(50)	251,065	320.00	350.00	385.00	650.00	14,500
1867S	920,750	320.00	350.00	500.00	3,500	
1868 .....(25)	98,600	320.00	350.00	425.00	2,000	14,500
1868S	837,500	320.00	350.00	385.00	2,000	
1869 .....(25)	175,155	320.00	350.00	385.00	1,300	14,500
1869S	686,750	320.00	350.00	385.00	1,200	
1870 .....(35)	155,185	320.00	350.00	400.00	2,200	14,500
1870CC	3,789	24,000	40,000	—	—	
1870S	982,000	320.00	350.00	385.00	1,500	
1871 .....(30)	80,150	320.00	350.00	425.00	900.00	14,500
1871CC	17,387	950.00	2,000	4,500		
1871S	928,000	320.00	350.00	425.00	1,100	
1872 .....(30)	251,880	320.00	350.00	385.00	800.00	14,500
1872CC	26,900	400.00	650.00	2,100	8,000	
1872S	780,000	320.00	350.00	385.00	700.00	
1873 .....(25)	1,709,825	320.00	350.00	385.00	400.00	14,500
1873CC	22,410	450.00	625.00	2,000	8,000	
1873S	1,040,600	320.00	350.00	385.00	600.00	
1874 .....(20)	366,800	320.00	350.00	375.00	400.00	15,000
1874CC	115,085	460.00	500.00	675.00	2,800	
1874S	1,214,000	320.00	350.00	385.00	550.00	
1875 .....(20)	295,740	320.00	350.00	375.00	400.00	—
1875CC	111,151	425.00	450.00	525.00	1,000	
1875S	1,230,000	320.00	350.00	375.00	425.00	
1876 .....(45)	583,905	320.00	350.00	375.00	400.00	14,500
1876CC	138,441	400.00	450.00	500.00	1,800	
1876S	1,597,000	320.00	350.00	375.00	400.00	

Values of common gold coins are based on the prevailing price of gold bullion, and will vary according to current market price. See Bullion Chart.

DOUBLE EAGLES
TWENTY DOLLARS 1877-1907

	Quan. Minted	VF-20	EF-40	AU-50	MS-60	Proof-63
1877 (20)	397,670	$290.00	$295.00	$300.00	$325.00	$13,000
1877CC	42,565	450.00	500.00	725.00	2,500	
1877S	1,735,000	290.00	295.00	300.00	325.00	
1878 (20)	543,645	290.00	295.00	300.00	325.00	12,000
1878CC	13,180	450.00	500.00	1,500	4,500	
1878S	1,739,000	290.00	295.00	300.00	325.00	
1879 (30)	207,630	290.00	295.00	300.00	325.00	12,000
1879CC	10,708	550.00	650.00	1,500	4,500	
1879O	2,325	1,100	1,650	3,600	9,500	
1879S	1,223,800	290.00	295.00	300.00	425.00	
1880 (36)	51,456	300.00	315.00	350.00	800.00	12,000
1880S	836,000	290.00	295.00	300.00	350.00	
1881 (61)	2,260	1,200	3,000	5,500	12,500	17,000
1881S	727,000	290.00	295.00	300.00	350.00	
1882 (59)	630	2,000	6,000	12,000	22,000	—
1882CC	39,140	425.00	450.00	600.00	1,800	
1882S	1,125,000	290.00	295.00	300.00	325.00	
1883 Proofs only (92)	92					—
1883CC	59,962	300.00	375.00	600.00	2,000	
1883S	1,189,000	290.00	295.00	300.00	325.00	
1884 Proofs only (71)	71					—
1884CC	81,139	300.00	350.00	550.00	1,100	
1884S	916,000	290.00	295.00	300.00	325.00	
1885 (77)	828	1,200	2,500	5,000	12,500	—
1885CC	9,450	500.00	700.00	1,250	4,200	
1885S	683,500	290.00	295.00	300.00	325.00	
1886 (106)	1,106	2,750	5,000	9,000	18,500	21,000
1887 Proofs only (121)	121					21,000
1887S	283,000	290.00	295.00	300.00	325.00	
1888 (105)	226,266	290.00	295.00	300.00	325.00	11,000
1888S	859,600	290.00	295.00	300.00	325.00	
1889 (41)	44,111	290.00	295.00	300.00	325.00	11,000
1889CC	30,945	320.00	350.00	600.00	1,500	
1889S	774,700	290.00	295.00	300.00	325.00	
1890 (55)	75,995	290.00	295.00	300.00	325.00	11,000
1890CC	91,209	320.00	350.00	600.00	1,250	
1890S	802,750	290.00	295.00	300.00	325.00	
1891 (52)	1,442	800.00	1,600	2,600	6,000	13,000
1891CC	5,000	600.00	1,100	1,600	4,500	
1891S	1,288,125	290.00	295.00	300.00	325.00	
1892 (93)	4,523	500.00	650.00	900.00	2,500	11,000
1892CC	27,265	320.00	425.00	600.00	1,400	
1892S	930,150	290.00	295.00	300.00	325.00	
1893 (59)	344,339	290.00	295.00	300.00	325.00	9,000
1893CC	18,402	320.00	350.00	550.00	1,000	

Values of common gold coins are based on the prevailing price of gold bullion, and will vary according to current market price. See Bullion Chart.

DOUBLE EAGLES

	Quan. Minted	VF-20	EF-40	AU-50	MS-60	Proof-63
1893S	996,175	$290.00	$295.00	$300.00	$325.00	
1894	(50) 1,368,990	290.00	295.00	300.00	325.00	$9,000
1894S	1,048,550	290.00	295.00	300.00	325.00	
1895	(51) 1,114,656	290.00	295.00	300.00	325.00	9,000
1895S	1,143,500	290.00	295.00	300.00	325.00	
1896	(128) 792,663	290.00	295.00	300.00	325.00	9,000
1896S	1,403,925	290.00	295.00	300.00	325.00	
1897	(86) 1,383,261	290.00	295.00	300.00	325.00	9,000
1897S	1,470,250	290.00	295.00	300.00	325.00	
1898	(75) 170,470	290.00	295.00	300.00	325.00	9,000
1898S	2,575,175	290.00	295.00	300.00	325.00	
1899	(84) 1,669,384	290.00	295.00	300.00	325.00	9,000
1899S	2,010,300	290.00	295.00	300.00	325.00	
1900	(124) 1,874,584	290.00	295.00	300.00	325.00	9,000
1900S	2,459,500	290.00	295.00	300.00	325.00	
1901	(96) 111,526	290.00	295.00	300.00	325.00	9,000
1901S	1,596,000	290.00	295.00	300.00	325.00	
1902	(114) 31,254	290.00	295.00	300.00	450.00	9,000
1902S	1,753,625	290.00	295.00	300.00	325.00	
1903	(158) 287,428	290.00	295.00	300.00	325.00	9,000
1903S	954,000	290.00	295.00	300.00	325.00	
1904	(98) 6,256,797	290.00	295.00	300.00	325.00	9,000
1904S	5,134,175	290.00	295.00	300.00	325.00	
1905	(92) 59,011	290.00	295.00	300.00	500.00	9,000
1905S	1,813,000	290.00	295.00	300.00	325.00	
1906	(94) 69,690	290.00	295.00	300.00	325.00	9,000
1906D	620,250	290.00	295.00	300.00	325.00	
1906S	2,065,750	290.00	295.00	300.00	325.00	
1907	(78) 1,451,864	290.00	295.00	300.00	325.00	9,000
1907D	842,250	290.00	295.00	300.00	325.00	
1907S	2,165,800	290.00	295.00	300.00	325.00	

SAINT-GAUDENS TYPE 1907-1933

The $20 gold piece designed by Augustus Saint-Gaudens is considered to be the most beautiful United States coin. The first coins issued were 11,250 high relief pieces struck for general circulation. The relief is much higher than later issues and the date 1907 is in Roman numerals. A few of the proof coins were made using the lettered edge collar from the extremely high relief version. These can be distinguished by a pronounced bottom left serif on the N in UNUM, and other minor differences. Flat-relief double eagles were issued later in 1907 with Arabic numerals, and continued through 1933.

The field of the rare extremely high relief experimental pieces is excessively concave and connects directly with the edge without any border, giving it a sharp knifelike appearance; Liberty's skirt shows two folds on the side of her right leg; the Capitol building in the background at left is very small; the sun, on the reverse side, has 14 rays, as opposed to the regular high relief coins that have only 13 rays extending from the sun. High relief proofs are trial or experimental pieces.

DOUBLE EAGLES

VF-20 VERY FINE—*Minor wear on legs and toes. Eagle's left wing and breast feathers worn.*
EF-40 EXTREMELY FINE—*Drapery lines on chest visible. Wear on left breast, knee and below. Eagle's feathers on breast and right wing are bold.*
AU-50 ABOUT UNCIRCULATED—*Trace of wear on nose, breast, and knee. Wear visible on eagle's wings.*
MS-60 UNCIRCULATED—*No trace of wear. Light marks or blemishes.*

	Proof
1907 Ex. high relief, plain edge (Unique)	—
1907 Ex. high relief, lettered edge	—

	Quan. Minted	*VF-20*	*EF-40*	*AU-50*	*MS-60*	*Proof*
1907 high relief, Roman numerals (MCMVII),	11,250	$1,800	$2,400	$3,300	$5,200	—

Arabic Numerals

No Motto **Motto** IN GOD WE TRUST. **1908-1933**

Mint mark location is on obverse above date.

	Quan. Minted	*VF-20*	*EF-40*	*AU-50*	*MS-60*	*Matte Proof-63*
1907 no motto	361,667	$300.00	$315.00	$340.00	$375.00	
1908 no motto	4,271,551	290.00	300.00	310.00	350.00	
1908D no motto	663,750	290.00	300.00	310.00	350.00	
1908 with motto (101)	156,359	300.00	315.00	340.00	375.00	$9,500
1908D with motto	349,500	290.00	300.00	310.00	330.00	
1908S with motto	22,000	370.00	500.00	700.00	2,100	

1909, 9 over 8

	Quan. Minted	*VF-20*	*EF-40*	*AU-50*	*MS-60*	*Matte Proof-63*
1909, 9 over 8	} 161,282	290.00	300.00	310.00	500.00	
1909 (67)		290.00	300.00	310.00	400.00	10,000
1909D	52,500	290.00	350.00	425.00	725.00	
1909S	2,774,925	290.00	300.00	310.00	330.00	
1910 (167)	482,167	290.00	300.00	310.00	330.00	10,000
1910D	429,000	290.00	300.00	310.00	330.00	
1910S	2,128,250	290.00	300.00	310.00	330.00	
1911 (100)	197,350	290.00	300.00	310.00	330.00	10,000
1911D	846,500	290.00	300.00	310.00	330.00	
1911S	775,750	290.00	300.00	310.00	330.00	
1912 (74)	149,824	290.00	300.00	310.00	375.00	10,000
1913 (58)	168,838	290.00	300.00	310.00	375.00	10,000
1913D	393,500	290.00	300.00	310.00	330.00	
1913S	34,000	290.00	300.00	400.00	600.00	
1914 (70)	95,320	290.00	300.00	310.00	375.00	10,000
1914D	453,000	290.00	300.00	310.00	330.00	
1914S	1,498,000	290.00	300.00	310.00	330.00	
1915 (50)	152,050	290.00	300.00	310.00	400.00	10,000

Values of common gold coins are based on the prevailing price of gold bullion, and will vary according to current market price. See Bullion Chart.

DOUBLE EAGLES

	Quan. Minted	*VF-20*	*EF-40*	*AU-50*	*MS-60*	*Matte Proof-63*
1915S	567,500	$290.00	$300.00	$310.00	$330.00	
1916S	796,000	290.00	300.00	310.00	330.00	
1920	228,250	290.00	300.00	310.00	330.00	
1920S	558,000	3,200	4,600	6,200	15,000	
1921	528,500	4,800	6,200	8,500	18,000	
1922	1,375,500	290.00	300.00	310.00	330.00	
1922S	2,658,000	310.00	350.00	400.00	425.00	
1923	566,000	290.00	300.00	310.00	330.00	
1923D	1,702,250	290.00	300.00	310.00	330.00	
1924	4,323,500	290.00	300.00	310.00	330.00	
1924D	3,049,500	450.00	475.00	550.00	1,000	
1924S	2,927,500	450.00	475.00	575.00	1,250	
1925	2,831,750	290.00	300.00	310.00	330.00	
1925D	2,938,500	400.00	500.00	800.00	1,600	
1925S	3,776,500	400.00	500.00	800.00	2,750	
1926	816,750	290.00	300.00	310.00	330.00	
1926D	481,000	500.00	800.00	1,200	3,000	
1926S	2,041,500	400.00	525.00	650.00	850.00	
1927	2,946,750	290.00	300.00	310.00	330.00	
1927D	180,000			55,000	150,000	
1927S	3,107,000	1,500	2,250	3,250	6,250	
1928	8,816,000	290.00	300.00	310.00	330.00	
1929	1,779,750	1,500	2,400	3,250	5,250	
1930S	74,000	3,000	5,500	7,000	12,000	
1931	2,938,250	2,500	4,500	5,500	9,000	
1931D	106,500	2,500	4,750	5,250	8,500	
1932	1,101,750	2,750	5,200	6,500	10,000	
1933	445,500	None placed in circulation				

COMMEMORATIVE SILVER COINS

Isabella Quarter

In 1892, to commemorate the World's Columbian Exposition in Chicago, Congress authorized the coinage of a special half dollar and quarter dollar, thus starting a long line of United States commemorative coins. Nearly all commemorative coins have been distributed by private individuals or commissions; they paid the mint the face value of the coins and in turn sold the pieces at a premium to collectors. There are a few instances in which some of the very large issues were later released to circulation at face value.

	Quan. Available	*AU-50*	*MS-60*
1893 Isabella Quarter (Columbian Exposition)	24,214	$220.00	$300.00

COMMEMORATIVE SILVER
(Half Dollars Listed alphabetically)
Alabama, Albany, Antietam, Arkansas

2x2 in Field

		Quan. Available	*AU-50*	*MS-60*
1921	Alabama, "2 x 2" in field	6,006	$110.00	$190.00
1921	Same, no "2 x 2"	59,038	70.00	125.00

1936	Albany, New York	17,671	115.00	130.00

1937	Battle of Antietam 1862-1937	18,028	260.00	290.00

1935	Arkansas Centennial	13,012	Set	125.00
1935D	Same	5,505		
1935S	Same	5,506		

COMMEMORATIVE SILVER
Arkansas, Bay Bridge, Boone

		Quan. Available		AU-50	MS-60
1936	Arkansas Centennial, same as 1935 — date 1936 on reverse	9,660	Set		$130.00
1936D	Same	9,660			
1936S	Same	9,662			
1937	Arkansas Centennial, same as 1935	5,505	Set		135.00
1937D	Same	5,505			
1937S	Same	5,506			
1938	Arkansas Centennial, same as 1935	3,156	Set		200.00
1938D	Same	3,155			
1938S	Same	3,156			
1939	Arkansas, same as 1935	2,104	Set		400.00
1939D	Same	2,104			
1939S	Same	2,105			
	Single type coin			$33.00	45.00

1936S	San Francisco-Oakland Bay Bridge	71,424		57.00	67.00

1934 added on reverse

1934	Daniel Boone Bicentennial	10,007		40.00	45.00
1935	Same	10,010	Set		135.00
1935D	Same	5,005			
1935S	Same	5,005			
1935	Daniel Boone Bicentennial, same as 1934 but small 1934 added on reverse	10,008	Set		400.00
1935D	Same	2,003			
1935S	Same	2,004			
1936	D. Boone Bicentennial, same as 1934	12,012	Set		130.00
1936D	Same	5,005			
1936S	Same	5,006			
1937	D. Boone Bicentennial, same as 1934	9,810	Set		370.00
1937D	Same	2,506			
1937S	Same	2,506			
1938	Daniel Boone, same as 1934	2,100	Set		500.00
1938D	Same	2,100			
1938S	Same	2,100			
	Single type coin			40.00	45.00

COMMEMORATIVE SILVER
Bridgeport, California, Carver-Washington, Cincinnati

		Quan. Available	AU-50	MS-60
1936	Bridgeport, Conn., Centennial	25,015	$60.00	$75.00

1925S	California Diamond Jubilee	86,394	60.00	75.00

1951 Carver-Washington

1951	110,018	Set	45.00
1951D	10,0044		
1951S	10,004		
1952	2,006,292	Set	42.00
1952D	8,006		
1952S	8,006		
1953	8,003	Set	42.00
1953D	8,003		
1953S	108,020		
1954	12,006	Set	42.00
1954D	12,006		
1954S	122,024		
Single type coin			8.00

1936	Cincinnati Music Center	5,005	Set	440.00
1936D	Same	5,005		
1936S	Same	5,006		
	Single type coin		125.00	140.00

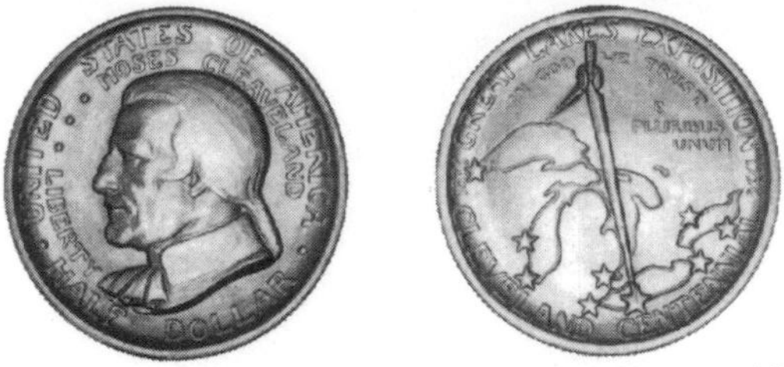

		Quan. Available	AU-50	MS-60
1936	Cleveland, Great Lakes Exposition	50,030	$34.00	$45.00

		Quan. Available	AU-50	MS-60
1936	Columbia, S.C., Sesquicentennial	9,007	Set	340.00
1936D	Same	8,009		
1936S	Same	8,007		
	Single type coin		100.00	110.00

		Quan. Available	AU-50	MS-60
1892	Columbian Exposition	950,000	8.00	14.00
1893	Same	1,550,405	7.00	14.00

		Quan. Available	AU-50	MS-60
1935	Connecticut Tercentenary	25,018	100.00	120.00

Delaware, Elgin, Gettysburg, Grant

		Quan. Available	AU-50	MS-60
1936	Delaware Tercentenary	20,993	$120.00	$130.00

1936	Elgin, Illinois, Centennial	20,015	100.00	115.00

1936	Battle of Gettysburg 1863-1938	26,928	155.00	175.00

1922	Grant Memorial, small star above word "Grant" in obv. field	4,256	425.00	650.00
	(Fake stars have flattened spot on reverse.)			
1922	Same, no star in obverse field	67,405	44.00	52.00

COMMEMORATIVE SILVER
Hawaiian, Hudson, Huguenot, Illinois

		Quan. Available	AU-50	MS-60
1928	Hawaiian Sesquicentennial	10,008	$700.00	$900.00

1935	Hudson N. Y. Sesquicentennial	10,008	275.00	300.00

1924	Huguenot-Walloon Tercentenary	142,080	55.00	70.00

1918	Illinois Centennial	100,058	46.00	60.00

		Quan. Available	AU-50	MS-60
1946	Iowa Centennial	100,057	$32.50	$40.00

1925	Lexington-Concord Sesquicentennial	162,013	30.00	40.00

1936	Long Island Tercentenary	81,826	32.50	40.00

1936	Lynchburg, Va., Sesquicentennial	20,013	90.00	110.00

COMMEMORATIVE SILVER
Maine, Maryland, Missouri, Monroe

		Quan. Available	*AU-50*	*MS-60*
1920	Maine Centennial	50,028	$50.00	$67.50

1934	Maryland Tercentenary	25,015	60.00	70.00

2 ★ 4 in field

1921	Missouri Centennial "2 ★ 4" above "1821"	5,000	225.00	300.00
1921	Same, no "2 ★ 4"	15,428	135.00	250.00

1923S	Monroe Doctrine Centennial	274,077	14.00	24.00

COMMEMORATIVE SILVER
New Rochelle, Norfolk, Oregon, Panama-Pacific

		Quan. Available	AU-50	MS-60
1938	New Rochelle, N. Y. 1688-1938	15,266	$165.00	$180.00

1936	Norfolk, Va., Bicentennial	16,936	250.00	265.00

		Quan. Avail.	AU-50	MS-60
1926	Oregon Trail	47,955	$50.00	$60.00
1926S	Same	83,055	50.00	60.00
1928	Same	6,028	85.00	100.00
1933D	Same	5,008	130.00	150.00
1934D	Same	7,006	70.00	85.00
1936	Same	10,006	60.00	75.00
1936S	Same	5,006	65.00	80.00
1937D	Same	12,008	70.00	80.00

		Quan. Avail.	AU-50	MS-60
1938	Same	6,006	Set	$340.00
1938D	Same	6,005		
1938S	Same	6,006		
1939	Same	3,004	Set	775.00
1939D	Same	3,004		
1939S	Same	3,005		
	Single type coin		50.00	60.00

1915S	Panama-Pacific Exposition	27,134	125.00	200.00

		Quan. Available	AU-50	MS-60
1920	Pilgrim Tercentenary	152,112	$30.00	$40.00
1921	Same, with 1921 date added in field	20,053	60.00	70.00

1936	Rhode Island Tercentenary	20,013	Set	125.00
1936D	Same	15,010		
1936S	Same	15,011		
	Single type coin		35.00	42.50

1937	Roanoke Island, N. C., 1587-1937	29,030	95.00	120.00

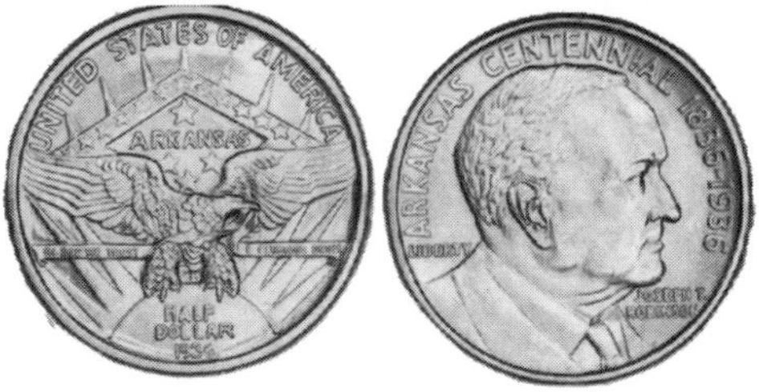

1936	Arkansas Centennial (Robinson)	25,265	50.00	65.00

COMMEMORATIVE SILVER
San Diego, Sesquicentennial, Spanish Trail, Stone Mountain

		Quan. Available	*AU-50*	*MS-60*
1935S	San Diego, California-Pacific Expo	70,132	$30.00	$35.00
1936D	Same	30,092	30.00	37.00

1926	Sesquicentennial of American Independence	141,120	30.00	45.00

1935	Old Spanish Trail 1535-1935	10,008	520.00	575.00

1925	Stone Mountain Memorial	1,314,709	18.00	24.00

Texas, Vancouver, Vermont

		Quan. Available		*AU-50*	*MS-60*
1934	Texas Centennial	61,463		$48.00	$55.00
1935	Texas Centennial, same as 1934	9,996			
1935D	Same	10,007	Set		165.00
1935S	Same	10,008			
1936	Texas Centennial, same as 1934	8,911			
1936D	Same	9,039	Set		165.00
1936S	Same	9,055			
1937	Texas Centennial, same as 1934	6,571			
1937D	Same	6,605	Set		165.00
1937S	Same	6,637			
1938	Texas Centennial, same as 1934	3,780			
1938D	Same	3,775	Set		375.00
1938S	Same	3,814			
	Single type coin			48.00	55.00

1925S	Fort Vancouver Centennial	14,994		138.00	175.00

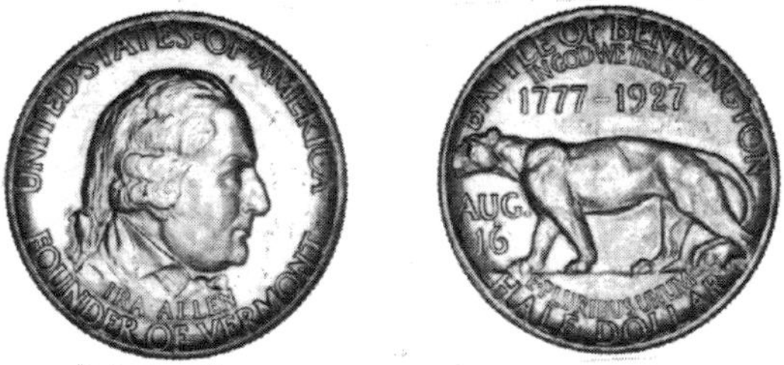

1927	Vermont Sesquicentennial (Bennington)	28,142		90.00	100.00

	Quan. Available		*MS-60*
1946 Booker T. Washington Memorial	1,000,546	Set	$23.00
1946D	200,113		
1946S	500,279		
1947	100,017	Set	38.00
1947D	100,017		
1947S	100,017		
1948	8,005	Set	83.00
1948D	8,005		
1948S	8,005		

	Quan. Available		*MS-60*
1949	6,004	Set	$130.00
1949D	6,004		
1949S	6,004		
1950	6,004	Set	65.00
1950D	6,004		
1950S	512,091		
1951	510,082	Set	60.00
1951D	7,004		
1951S	7,004		
Single type coin			7.50

		Quan. Available	*AU-50*	*MS-60*
1936	Wisconsin Centennial	25,015	$85.00	$100.00

1936	York County, Maine Tercentenary	25,015	85.00	95.00

COMMEMORATIVE SILVER
Lafayette

		Quan. Available	AU-50	MS-60
1900	Lafayette Dollar	36,026	$200.00	$375.00

COMMEMORATIVE GOLD
Grant, Lewis & Clark, Louisiana Purchase, McKinley, Panama-Pacific

		Quan. Available	AU-50	MS-60
1922	Grant Memorial Dollar, star above word "Grant"	5,016	$750.00	$890.00
1922	Same, without star	5,000	710.00	750.00
1904	Lewis and Clark Exposition Dollar	10,025	350.00	500.00
1905	Lewis and Clark Exposition Dollar	10,041	350.00	600.00

1903	Louisiana Purchase Jefferson Dollar	17,500	210.00	275.00
1903	Louisiana Purchase McKinley Dollar	17,500	200.00	250.00
1916	McKinley Memorial Dollar	*15,000*	160.00	235.00
1917	McKinley Memorial Dollar	*5,000*	220.00	350.00

1915S	Panama-Pacific Exposition Dollar	15,000	190.00	235.00
1915S	Panama-Pacific Exposition $2.50	6,749	750.00	935.00

COMMEMORATIVE GOLD
Panama-Pacific, U.S. Sesquicentennial

		Quan. Available	*AU-50*	*MS-60*
1915S	Panama-Pacific $50 Round	483	$16,000	$18,000
1915S	Panama-Pacific $50 Octagonal	645	15,000	16,000

1926	United States Sequicentennial $2.50	46,019	160.00	190.00

MODERN COMMEMORATIVES
Washington, Los Angeles Olympiad

		Quan. Issued	MS-63	Proof-63
1982D	Geo. Washington-250th Anniversary	2,210,458	$4.00	
1982S	Same, proof	(4,894,044)		$4.00

		Quan. Issued	MS-63	Proof-63
1983P	Discus Thrower Silver Dollar	294,543	7.00	
1983D	Same type D mint	174,014	7.50	
1983S	Same type S mint (1,577,025)	174,014	7.50	7.00

		Quan. Issued	MS-63	Proof-63
1984P	Olympic Coliseum Silver Dollar	217,954	8.00	
1984D	Same type D mint	116,675	12.00	
1984S	Same type S mint (1,801,210)	116,675	13.00	7.50

MODERN COMMEMORATIVES
Los Angeles Olympiad, Statue of Liberty

		Quan. Issued	*MS-63*	*Proof-63*
1984P	Olympic Gold Eagle ....(33,309)			$170.00
1984D	Olympic Gold Eagle ....(34,533)			170.00
1984S	Olympic Gold Eagle ....(48,551)			150.00
1984W	Olympic Gold Eagle ....(381,085)	75,886	$150.00	150.00

1986D	Statue of Liberty	928,008	3.50	
1986S	Same type S mint, proof	(6,925,627)		3.50

1986P	Statue of Liberty Dollar	723,635	8.00	
1986S	Same type S mint, proof	(6,414,638)		8.00

1986W	Statue of Liberty Gold $5.00............(404,013)	95,248	70.00	70.00

Constitution, Olympiad 1988

	Quan. Issued	MS-63	Proof-63
1987P Constitution Dollar	451,629	$7.50	
1987S Same type S mint, proof	(2,747,116)		$7.50

	Quan. Issued	MS-63	Proof-63
1987W U.S. Constitution Gold $5.00 ....(651,659)	214,225	70.00	70.00

	Quan. Issued	MS-63	Proof-63
1988D Olympic Silver Dollar	191,368	7.50	
1988S Same type S mint, proof	(1,359,366)		7.50

	Quan. Issued	MS-63	Proof-63
1988W Olympic Gold $5.00..................................(281,465)	62,913	70.00	70.00

MODERN COMMEMORATIVES
Congress, Eisenhower

	Quan. Issued	MS-63	Proof-63
1989D Congress Bicentennial Half Dollar	163,753	$4.00	
1989S Congress Bicentennial Half Dollar.........................	(767,897)		$3.00

1989D Congress Silver Dollar..	135,203	10.00	
1989S Congress Silver Dollar...	(762,198)		9.00

1989W Congress Bicentennial Gold $5.00 (164,690)...........	46,899	68.00	75.00

1990W Eisenhower Silver Dollar	241,669	10.00	
1990P Same type P mint, proof	(1,144,461)		10.00

MODERN COMMEMORATIVES
Mt. Rushmore, Korean War

	Quan. Issued	*MS-63*	*Proof-63*
1991D Mount Rushmore Half Dollar....................................	172,754	$6.00	
1991S Same type S mint, proof..	(753,257)		$6.00

1991P Mount Rushmore Silver Dollar.................................	133,139	19.00	
1991S Same type S mint, proof..	(738,419)		21.00

1991W Mount Rushmore Gold $5.00 ....(111,991)	31,959	90.00	90.00

1991D Korean War Silver Dollar...	213,049	9.50	
1991P Same type P mint, proof..	(618,488)		9.50

MODERN COMMEMORATIVES
U.S.O., Olympiad 1992

	Quan. Issued	MS-65	Proof-65
1991D U.S.O. Silver Dollar	124,958	$10.00	
1991S Same type S mint proof	(321,275)		$9.00

1992P Olympic Clad Half Dollar	161,619	3.00	
1992S Same type S mint proof	(519,699)		4.00

1992D Olympic Silver Dollar	187,562	14.00	
1992S Same type S mint proof	(504,544)		16.50

1992W Olympic Gold $5.00	(77,313) 27,732	90.00	90.00

MODERN COMMEMORATIVES
White House, Columbus

	Quan. Issued	*MS-65*	*Proof-65*
1992D White House Silver Dollar	123,803	$22.00	
1992W Same type W mint proof	(375,849)		$18.00

1992D Columbus Half Dollar	135,718	7.00	
1992S Same type S mint proof	(390,255)		7.50

1992D Columbus Silver Dollar	106,962	17.00	
1992P Same type P mint proof	(385,290)		22.00

MODERN COMMEMORATIVES
Columbus, Bill of Rights

	Quan. Issued	MS-65	Proof-65
1992W Columbus Gold $5.00	(79,734) 24,331	$90.00	$90.00

1993W Bill of Rights Silver Half Dollar	173,224	7.50	
1993S Same type S mint proof	(559,758)		7.50

1993D Bill of Rights Silver Dollar	92,415	12.00	
1993S Same type S mint proof	(515,038)		12.00

1993W Bill of Rights Gold $5.00	(79,422) 22,897	80.00	85.00

MODERN COMMEMORATIVES

World War II, World Cup Soccer

	Quan. Issued	MS-65	Proof-65
(1993) 1991-1995P World War II Clad Half Dollar	(290,343) 192,968	$8.00	$8.00

	Quan. Issued	MS-65	Proof-65
(1993) 1991-1995D World War II Silver Dollar	94,700	17.00	
(1993) Same type W mint proof	(322,422)		22.00

	Quan. Issued	MS-65	Proof-65
(1993) 1991-1995W World War II Gold $5	(65,461) 23,089	100.00	90.00

	Quan. Issued	MS-65	Proof-65
1994D World Cup Tournament Clad Half Dollar	52,836	6.00	
1994P Same type P mint proof	(122,412)		6.00

World Cup Soccer, Thomas Jefferson

	Quan. Issued	MS-65	Proof-65
1994D World Cup Tournament Silver Dollar	81,698	$17.00	
1994S Same type S mint proof	(576,978)		$19.00

	Quan. Issued	MS-65	Proof-65
1994W World Cup Tournament Gold $5	(89,619) 22,464	80.00	80.00

	Quan. Issued	MS-65	Proof-65
1993 (1994) P Thomas Jefferson Silver Dollar	266,927	17.00	
1993 (1994) S Same type S mint proof	(332,891)		19.00

Vietnam War Memorial, POWs, Women Veterans

	Quan. Issued	MS-65	Proof-65
1994W Vietnam War Memorial Silver Dollar	57,317	$30.00	
1994P Same type P mint proof	(226,262)		$34.00

1994W U.S. POW Silver Dollar	54,790	32.00	
1994P Same type P mint proof	(220,100)		20.00

1994W Women Veterans Silver Dollar	53,054	15.00	
1994P Same type P mint proof	(213,201)		14.00

U.S. Capital, Civil War Battlefields

	Quan. Issued	MS-65	Proof-65
1994D U.S. Capitol Silver Dollar	68,352	$13.00	
1994S Same type S mint proof	(279,416)		$13.00

	Quan. Issued	MS-65	Proof-65
1995S Civil War Battlefield Clad Half Dollar	119,510	14.00	
1995S Same type S mint proof	(330,099)		13.00

	Quan. Issued	MS-65	Proof-65
1995P Civil War Battlefield Silver Dollar	45,866	20.00	
1995S Same type S mint proof	(55,246)		27.00

Civil War Battlefields, Olympic Games

	Quan. Issued	MS-65	Proof-65
1995W Civil War Battlefield Gold $5	12,735	$210.00	
1995W Same type W mint proof	(55,246)		$160.00

	Quan. Issued	MS-65	Proof-65
1995D Basketball Clad Half Dollar	171,001	13.00	
1995S Same type S mint proof	(169,655)		12.00
1995D Baseball Clad Half Dollar	164,605	12.00	
1995S Same type S mint proof	(118,087)		7.00
1996D Swimming Clad Half Dollar	49,533	30.00	
1996S Same type S mint proof	(114,315)		7.00
1996D Soccer Clad Half Dollar	52,836	22.00	
1996S Same type S mint proof	(122,412)		38.00

	Quan. Issued	MS-65	Proof-65
1995D Gymnastics Silver Dollar	42,497	35.00	
1995P Same type P mint proof	(182,676)		18.00
1995D Paralympics Silver Dollar	28,649	45.00	
1995P Same type P mint proof	(138,337)		19.00
1995D Track and Field Silver Dollar	24,796	32.00	
1995P Same type P mint proof	(136,935)		15.00
1995D Cycling Silver Dollar	19,662	40.00	
1995P Same type P mint proof	(118,795)		18.00

MODERN COMMEMORATIVES
Olympic Games, Special Olympics, Community Service

	Quan. Issued	*MS-65*	*Proof-65*
1996D Tennis Silver Dollar	15,983	$80.00	
1996P Same type P mint proof	(92,016)		$30.00
1996D Paralympics Silver Dollar	14,497	100.00	
1996P Same type P mint proof	(84,280)		30.00
1996D Rowing Silver Dollar	16,258	90.00	
1996P Same type P mint proof	(151,890)		22.00
1996D High Jump Silver Dollar	15,697	100.00	
1996P Same type P mint proof	(124,502)		20.00

	Quan. Issued	*MS-65*	*Proof-65*
1995W Torch Runner Gold $5	14,675	130.00	
1995W Same type W mint proof	(57,442)		100.00
1995W Stadium Gold $5	10,579	200.00	
1995W Same type W mint proof	(43,124)		110.00
1996W Flag Bearer Gold $5	9,174	170.00	
1996W Same type W mint proof	(32,886)		140.00
1996W Cauldron Gold $5	9,210	170.00	
1996W Same type W mint proof	(38,555)		140.00

	Quan. Issued	*MS-65*	*Proof-65*
1995W Special Olympics Silver Dollar	89,301	13.00	
1995P Same type P mint proof	(351,764)		11.00

	Quan. Issued	*MS-65*	*Proof-65*
1996S Community Service Silver Dollar	23,468	135.00	
1996S Same type S mint proof	(100,787)		22.00

SMITHSONIAN INSTITUTION

	Quan. Issued	*MS-65*	*Proof-65*
1996D Smithsonian Silver Dollar	30,593	$50.00	
1996P Same type P mint proof	(126,616)		$22.00
1996W Smithsonian Gold $5	21,840	210.00	
1996W Same type W mint proof	(8,948)		130.00

BOTANIC GARDENS

1997P Botanic Gardens Silver Dollar	57,272	23.00	
1997P Same type P mint proof	(264,528)		25.00

JACKIE ROBINSON

1997S Jackie Robinson Silver Dollar	30,180	32.00	
1997S Same type S mint proof	(110,002)		22.00
1997W Jackie Robinson Gold $5	5,174	650.00	
1997W Same type W mint proof	(24,072)		185.00

FRANKLIN D. ROOSEVELT

1997W Roosevelt Gold $5	11,805	140.00	
1997W Same type W mint proof	(29,233)		130.00

NATIONAL LAW ENFORCEMENT OFFICERS MEMORIAL

1997P Law Enforcement Silver Dollar	28,575	55.00	
1997P Same type P mint proof	(110,428)		50.00

ROBERT F. KENNEDY

1998S Robert F. Kennedy Silver Dollar	106,422	18.00	
1998S Same type S mint proof	(99,020)		22.00

BLACK REVOLUTIONARY WAR PATRIOTS

1998S Black Patriots Silver Dollar	37,210	50.00	
1998S Same type S mint proof	(75,070)		45.00

DOLLEY MADISON COMMEMORATIVE

1999P Dolley Madison Silver Dollar	89,100	24.00	
1999P Same type P mint proof	(224,400)		25.00

GEORGE WASHINGTON COMMEMORATIVE GOLD

1999W George Washington Gold $5	22,511	145.00	
1999W Same type W mint proof	(41,693)		155.00

YELLOWSTONE NATIONAL PARK

1999P Yellowstone Silver Dollar	*62,000*	22.00	
1999P Same type P mint proof	*(144,900)*		23.00

MODERN COMMEMORATIVES

LIBRARY OF CONGRESS BICENTENNIAL

	Quan. Issued	MS-65	Proof-65
2000P Library of Congress Silver Dollar		$20.00	
2000P Same type P mint proof			$22.00
2000W Library of Congress bimetallic $10		450.00	
2000W Same type W mint proof			300.00

LEIF ERICSON MILLENNIUM

	Quan. Issued	MS-65	Proof-65
2000P Leif Ericson Silver Dollar	28,100	24.00	
2000P Same type P mint proof	(142,900)		24.00

AMERICAN BUFFALO COMMEMORATIVE

	Quan. Issued	MS-65	Proof-65
2001D Buffalo/Indian Silver Dollar		75.00	
2001P Same Type P mint proof			75.00

CAPITOL VISITORS CENTER

	Quan. Issued	MS-65	Proof-65
2001P Capitol Clad Half Dollar		5.50	
2001P Same type P mint proof			5.50
2001P Capitol Silver Dollar		16.50	
2001P Same type P mint proof			16.50
2001P Capitol Gold $5		110.00	
2001P Same type P mint proof			110.00

SALT LAKE OLYMPIC GAMES

	Quan. Issued	MS-65	Proof-65
2002P Salt Lake Olympic Silver Dollar		17.00	
2002P Same type P mint proof			18.00
2002W Salt Lake Olympic $5		95.00	
2002W Same type W mint proof			100.00

UNITED STATES MILITARY ACADEMY

	Quan. Issued	MS-65	Proof-65
2002W West Point Silver Dollar		18.00	
2002W Same type W mint proof			19.00

MODERN COMMEMORATIVES
Government Sets–In Original Holders

1983-84 OLYMPICS

Date	*Price*
1983 and 1984 proof dollars	$14.00
1983 and 1984 6 coin set. One 1983 and one 1984 uncirculated and proof dollar. One uncirculated and one proof gold $10	260.00
1983 Collector set. 1983 PDS uncirculated dollars	17.00
1984 Collector set. 1984 PDS uncirculated dollars	28.00
1983 and 1984 gold and silver uncirculated set. One 1983 and one 1984 uncirculated dollar and one 1984 uncirculated gold $10	130.00
1983 and 1984 gold and silver proof set. One 1983 and one 1984 proof dollar and one 1984 proof $10.*	130.00

1986 STATUE OF LIBERTY

1986 2 coin set: proof silver dollar and clad half dollar	10.00
1986 3 coin set: proof silver dollar, clad half dollar and gold $5	78.00
1986 2 coin set: uncirculated silver dollar and clad half dollar	10.00
1986 3 coin set: uncirculated silver dollar, clad half dollar and gold $5	78.00
1986 6 coin set: 1 each of proof and uncirculated*	160.00

1987 CONSTITUTION

1988 2 coin set: uncirculated silver dollar and gold $5	75.00
1988 2 coin set: proof silver dollar and gold $5	75.00
1988 4 coin set: 1 each of proof and uncirculated	150.00

1988 OLYMPIAD

1988 2 coin set: uncirculated silver dollar and gold $5	75.00
1988 2 coin set: proof silver dollar and gold $5	75.00
1988 4 coin set: 1 each of proof and uncirculated*	155.00

1989 CONGRESS

1989 2 coin set: proof silver dollar and clad half dollar	11.00
1989 3 coin set: proof silver dollar, clad half dollar and gold $5	75.00
1989 2 coin set: uncirculated silver dollar and clad half dollar	12.00
1989 3 coin set: uncirculated silver dollar, clad half dollar and gold $5	80.00
1989 6 coin set: 1 each of proof and uncirculated*	150.00

MODERN COMMEMORATIVES
Government Sets–In Original Holders

1991 MOUNT RUSHMORE

Date	Price
1991 2 coin set: uncirculated half dollar and dollar	$21.00
1991 2 coin set: proof half dollar and silver dollar	21.00
1991 3 coin set: uncirculated half dollar, silver dollar and gold $5	100.00
1991 3 coin set: proof half dollar, silver dollar and gold $5	100.00
1991 6 coin set: 1 each of proof and uncirculated*	200.00

1992 XXV OLYMPIAD

1992 2 coin set: uncirculated half dollar and dollar	15.00
1992 2 coin set: proof half dollar and dollar	19.00
1992 3 coin set: uncirculated half dollar, dollar and gold $5	100.00
1992 3 coin set: proof half dollar, dollar and gold $5	100.00
1992 6 coin set: 1 each proof and uncirculated*	200.00

1992 COLUMBUS

1992 2 coin set: uncirculated half dollar and dollar	20.00
1992 2 coin set: proof half dollar and silver dollar	22.00
1992 3 coin set: uncirculated half dollar, silver dollar and gold $5	110.00
1992 3 coin set: proof half dollar, silver dollar and gold $5	100.00
1992 6 coin set: 1 each of proof and uncirculated*	220.00

1993 BILL OF RIGHTS

1993 2 coin set: uncirculated half dollar and dollar	16.00
1993 2 coin set: proof half dollar and silver dollar	17.00
1993 3 coin set: uncirculated half dollar, silver dollar and gold $5	110.00
1993 3 coin set: proof half dollar, silver dollar and gold $5	90.00
1993 6 coin set: 1 each of proof and uncirculated*	200.00
1993 "Young Collector" set: silver half dollar	10.00
1993 "Educational" set: silver half dollar and Madison medal	8.00

1993 THOMAS JEFFERSON

1993 3 piece set: Jefferson dollar, nickel and $2 note	60.00

1993 WORLD WAR II

1993 2 coin set: uncirculated half dollar and dollar	17.00
1993 2 coin set: proof half dollar and silver dollar	22.00
1993 3 coin set: uncirculated half dollar, silver dollar and gold $5	110.00
1993 3 coin set: proof half dollar, silver dollar and gold $5	110.00
1993 6 coin set: 1 each of proof and uncirculated*	230.00
1993 "Young Collector" set: silver half dollar	9.00
1993 "Victory" set: silver dollar, French franc	8.00

1994 WORLD SOCCER CUP

1994 2 coin set: uncirculated half dollar and dollar	18.00
1994 2 coin set: proof half dollar and silver dollar	19.00
1994 3 coin set: uncirculated half dollar, silver dollar and gold $5	110.00
1994 3 coin set: proof half dollar, silver dollar and gold $5	105.00
1994 6 coin set: 1 each of proof and uncirculated*	185.00
1994 "Young Collector" set: uncirculated silver half dollar	8.00
1994 "Special Edition" set: proof clad half dollar and silver dollar	17.00

1994 U.S. VETERANS

1994 3 coin set: Unc. POW, Vietnam and Women dollar	65.00
1994 3 coin set: proof POW, Vietnam and Women dollar	60.00

1995 SPECIAL OLYMPICS

1995 2 coin set: proof Schriver Dol., 1995S Kennedy Half Dol.	42.00

**Packaged in cherrywood box.*

MODERN COMMEMORATIVES
Government Sets

1995 CIVIL WAR BATTLEFIELD PRESERVATION

Date	*Price*
1995 2 coin set: uncirculated half dollar and dollar	$32.00
1995 2 coin set: proof half dollar and silver dollar	42.00
1995 3 coin set: uncirculated half dollar, dollar and gold $5	240.00
1995 3 coin set: proof half dollar, dollar and gold $5	210.00
1995 6 coin set: 1 each of proof and uncirculated.*	450.00
1995 "Young Collector" set: uncirculated half dollar	10.00
1995 2 coin "Union Set": half dollar and dollar	20.00
1995 3 coin "Union Set": half dollar, dollar and $5	185.00

1995–96 CENTENNIAL OLYMPIC GAMES

1995 4 coin set #1: uncirculated 50¢ Basketball, $1 Gymnast, $1 Blind, $5 Torch	170.00
1995 4 coin set #1: proof 50¢ Basketball, $1 Gymnast, $1 Blind, $5 Torch	130.00
1995 2 coin set #1: proof $1 Gymnast, $1 Blind	40.00
1995 "Young Collector" set: uncirculated Basketball half dollar	8.00
1995-96 16 coin set: 1 each all uncirculated coins*	600.00
1995-96 16 coin set: 1 each all proof coins*	500.00
1995-96 32 coin set: 1 each all uncirculated and proof coins*	1,800

1996 NATIONAL COMMUNITY SERVICE

1996 proof silver dollar and Saint-Gaudens stamp	35.00

1996 SMITHSONIAN INSTITUTION 150TH ANNIVERSARY

1996 2 coin set: proof dollar and gold $5	140.00
1996 4 coin set: 1 each of proof and uncirculated. *	500.00
1996 "Young Collector" set: proof silver dollar	20.00

1997 BOTANIC GARDENS

1997 Dollar, Jefferson nickel and $1 note	160.00

1997 JACKIE ROBINSON

1997 2 coin set: proof dollar and $5 gold	160.00
1997 4 coin set: 1 each of proof and uncirculated	800.00
1997 3 piece legacy set: Baseball card, pin and $5 gold	175.00

1997 NATIONAL LAW ENFORCEMENT OFFICERS MEMORIAL

1997 Insignia set: dollar, lapel pin and patch	60.00

1998 ROBERT F. KENNEDY

1998 2 coin set: RFK dollar and JFK silver half dollar	240.00
1998 2 coin set: RFK dollar, proof and uncirculated	50.00

1998 BLACK REVOLUTIONARY WAR PATRIOTS

1998 2 coin set: uncirculated and proof dollar	60.00
1998 "Young Collector" set: uncirculated dollar	32.00
1998 Coin and 4 stamps set	32.00

1999 DOLLEY MADISON COMMEMORATIVE

1999 2 coin set: proof and uncirculated dollars	37.50

1999 GEORGE WASHINGTON

1999 2 coin set: 1 each proof and uncirculated $5 gold	300.00

1999 YELLOWSTONE NATIONAL PARK

1999 2 coin set: 1 each proof and uncirculated dollars	45.00

** Packaged in cherrywood box.*

MODERN COMMEMORATIVES
Government Sets

2000 LEIF ERICSON MILLENNIUM

Date	*Price*
2000 2 coin set: proof $1 and Islandic 1,000 kronur	$45.00

2001 AMERICAN BUFFALO

2001 2 coin set: proof and uncirculated dollars	150.00
2001 coinage and currency set	70.00

2001 CAPITOL VISITORS CENTER

2001 3 coin proof set: 50¢, $1, $5	170.00

2002 SALT LAKE OLYMPIC GAMES

2002 2 coin proof set: $1 and $5	150.00
2002 4 coin proof and uncirculated set	310.00

PRIVATE OR TERRITORIAL GOLD COINS

Private coins were circulated in most instances because of a shortage of regular coinage. The words "Private Gold," used with reference to coins struck outside of the United States Mint, are a general term. In the sense that no state or territory had authority to coin money, private gold simply refers to those interesting necessity pieces of various shapes, denominations and degrees of intrinsic worth which were circulated in isolated areas of our country by individuals, assayers, bankers, etc. Some will use the words "Territorial" and "State" to cover certain issues because they were coined and circulated in a territory or state. While the state of California properly sanctioned the ingots stamped by F. D. Kohler as state assayer, in no instance were any of the gold pieces struck by authority of any of the territorial governments.

The stamped ingots put out by Augustus Humbert, the United States assayer of gold, were not recognized at the United States Mint as an official issue of coins, but simply as ingots, though Humbert placed the value and fineness on the pieces as an official agent of the federal government.

TEMPLETON REID
Georgia 1830

The first private gold coinage under the Constitution was struck by Templeton Reid, a jeweler and gunsmith, in Milledgeville, Georgia in July, 1830. To be closer to the mines, he moved to Gainesville where most of his coins were made. Although weights were accurate, Reid's assays were not and his coins were slightly short of claimed value. Accordingly, he was severely attacked in the newspapers and soon lost the public's confidence.

	V. Fine
1830 $2.50	$22,500
1830 $5.00	52,500

	V. Good
1830 TEN DOLLARS	$45,000
(No date) TEN DOLLARS	40,000

TEMPLETON REID
"California Gold 1849"

1849 TEN DOLLAR CALIFORNIA GOLD (Smithsonian Collection) .... Unique

THE BECHTLERS
Rutherford County, N. C. 1830-1852

Two skilled German metallurgists, Christopher Bechtler and his son August, and later Christopher Bechtler, Junior, a nephew of Christopher the elder, operated a "private" mint at Rutherfordton, North Carolina. Rutherford county in which Rutherfordton is located was the principal source of the nation's gold supply from 1790 to 1840.

CHRISTOPHER BECHTLER

	V. Fine	E. Fine	Unc.
ONE DOLLAR CAROLINA, 28 gr. N reversed	$750.00	$1,100	$2,400
ONE DOLLAR N. CAROLINA, 28 gr. no star	1,300	2,500	5,500

ONE DOLLAR N. CAROLINA, 30 gr.	850.00	1,500	3,800
$2.50 CAROLINA, 67 gr. 21 carats	1,800	2,700	6,000

$2.50 CAROLINA, 70 gr. 20 carats	1,700	2,800	5,500
$2.50 GEORGIA, 64 gr. 22 carats	1,800	3,000	5,800

THE BECHTLERS

	V. Fine	*E. Fine*	*Unc.*
$2.50 NORTH CAROLINA, 75 gr. 20 carats.			
RUTHERFORD in a circle. Border of lg. beads	$3,200	$5,500	$10,000
$2.50 NORTH CAROLINA, without 75 G	3,000	5,000	9,000

5 DOLLARS CAROLINA, RUTHERFORD,			
140 gr. 20 carats. AUGUST 1, 1834.			
Plain edge	2,000	3,300	6,700
Reeded edge	2,400	3,700	7,500
BECHTLER without star and C	—		
5 DOLLARS CAROLINA, 134 gr. 21 carats, with star	1,700	3,000	6,250

5 DOLLARS GEORGIA, RUTHERF.			
128 GR. 22 CARATS	2,000	3,300	7,100
5 DOLLARS GEORGIA, RTHERF. 128 gr. 22 carats	2,000	3,300	7,100
5 DOLLARS CAROLINA, RUTHERF.			
140 gr. 20 carats. AUGUST 1, 1834 (illustrated)	2,500	3,800	—
Similar. 20 distant from carats	3,500	5,000	—

Without 150 G

5 DOLLARS NORTH CAROLINA, 150 gr. 20 carats	3,250	4,800	12,000
5 DOLLARS. Same as last variety without 150 G	3,750	5,500	13,500

THE BECHTLERS
AUGUST BECHTLER
1842-1852

	V. Fine	E. Fine	Unc.
1 DOLLAR CAROLINA, 27 gr. 21 carats	$500.00	$750.00	$1,800
5 DOLLARS CAROLINA, 134 gr. 21 carats	1,700	3,000	6,250

5 DOLLARS CAROLINA, 128 gr. 22 carats	3,250	4,000	8,500
5 DOLLARS CAROLINA, 141 gr. 20 carats	3,000	3,800	7,800

NORRIS, GREGG & NORRIS
San Francisco 1849

These pieces are considered the first of the California private gold coins. A newspaper account dated May 31, 1849, described a five-dollar gold coin, struck at Benicia City, though with the imprint San Francisco, and the private stamp of Norris, Gregg and Norris.

	Fine	V. Fine	E. Fine	Unc.
1849 HALF EAGLE — Plain edge	$1,600	$2,200	$4,000	$11,000
1849 HALF EAGLE — Reeded edge	1,600	2,200	4,000	11,000
1850 HALF EAGLE with STOCKTON beneath date				(Unique)

MOFFAT & CO.

San Francisco 1849-1853

The firm of Moffat and Company was perhaps the most important of the California private coiners. The assay office they conducted was semi-official in character, and successors to this firm later established the United States branch mint of San Francisco.

In June or July, 1849, Moffat & Co. began to issue small rectangular pieces of gold in values from $9.43 to $264. The $9.43, $14.25 and $16.00 varieties are the only types known today.

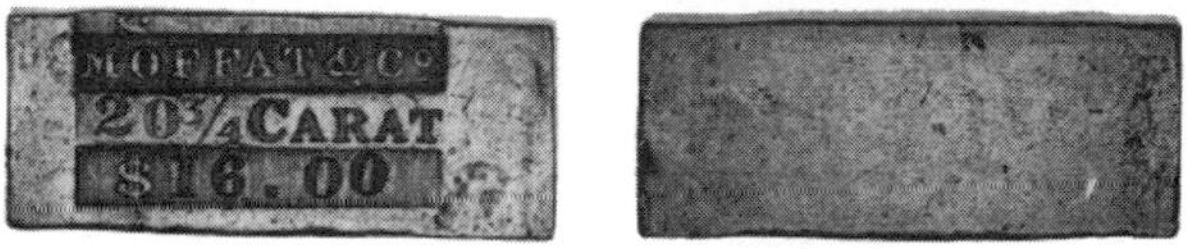

$9.43 Ingot (Unique)		—
$14.25 Ingot (Unique)		—
$16.00 Ingot	E.F.	$15,000

The dies for the $10 piece were cut by Albert Kuner. The words MOFFAT & CO. appear on the coronet of Liberty instead of the word LIBERTY as in regular United States issues.

	Fine	V. Fine	E. Fine	A. Unc.	Unc.
1849 FIVE DOL.	$600.00	$850.00	$1,400	$2,500	$4,500
1850 FIVE DOL.	600.00	850.00	1,400	2,500	4,500
1849 TEN DOL.	1,000	1,500	3,000	4,800	7,750
1849 TEN D.	1,100	1,600	3,200	5,000	7,900

United States Assay Office

AUGUSTUS HUMBERT

U. S. Assayer 1851

When Augustus Humbert was appointed United States Assayer, he placed his name and the government stamp on the ingots of gold issued by Moffat & Co. The assay office, a Provisional Government Mint, was a temporary expedient to accommodate the Californians until the establishment of a permanent branch mint.

The fifty-dollar gold piece was accepted as legal tender on a par with standard U.S. gold coins.

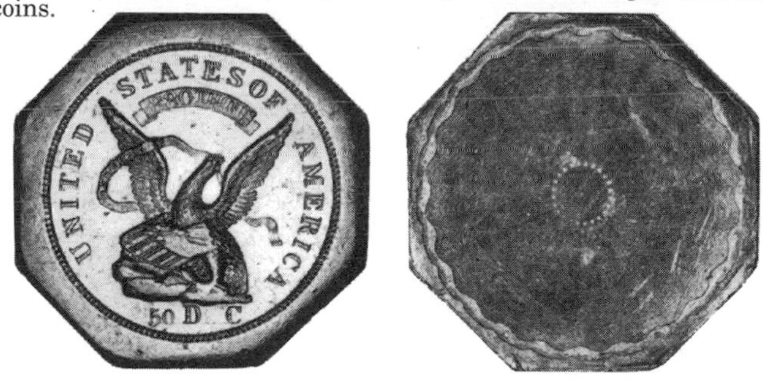

MOFFAT — HUMBERT
LETTERED EDGE VARIETIES

50 on reverse

		Fine	V. Fine	E. Fine	A. Unc.	Unc.
1851	50 D C 880 THOUS., no 50 on Reverse. Sunk in edge: AUGUSTUS HUMBERT UNITED STATES ASSAYER OF GOLD CALIFORNIA 1851	$4,000	$5,000	$8,000	$10,000	—
1851	50 D C Similar to last variety, but 50 on Reverse	4,300	5,500	10,000	13,000	—
1851	Similar to last variety, but 887 THOUS	4,300	5,500	9,500	12,000	—

REEDED EDGE VARIETIES

1851	FIFTY DOLLS 880 THOUS. "Target" Reverse	3,000	3,800	5,500	8,000	13,000
1851	FIFTY DOLLS 887 THOUS. "Target" Reverse	3,000	3,800	5,500	8,000	13,000
1852	FIFTY DOLLS 887 THOUS.	3,000	3,800	5,750	9,500	15,000

Moffat & Co. proceeded in January, 1852 to issue a new ten-dollar piece bearing the stamp MOFFAT & CO.

1852	TEN D. MOFFAT & CO.	900.00	1,650	2,800	6,500	—

		Fine	V. Fine	E. Fine	A. Unc.	Unc.
1852	TWENTY DOLS. 1852, 2 over 1	$1,600	$2,200	$3,800	$7,500	—

		Fine	V. Fine	E. Fine	A. Unc.	Unc.
1852	TEN DOLS. 1852, 2 over 1	650.00	1,100	2,000	3,500	—
1852	TEN DOLS.	600.00	900.00	1,500	2,750	$5,000

UNITED STATES ASSAY OFFICE OF GOLD

1852

The firm of Moffat & Co. dissolved and a new reorganized company known as the United States Assay Office of Gold, composed of Curtis, Perry and Ward took over the contract.

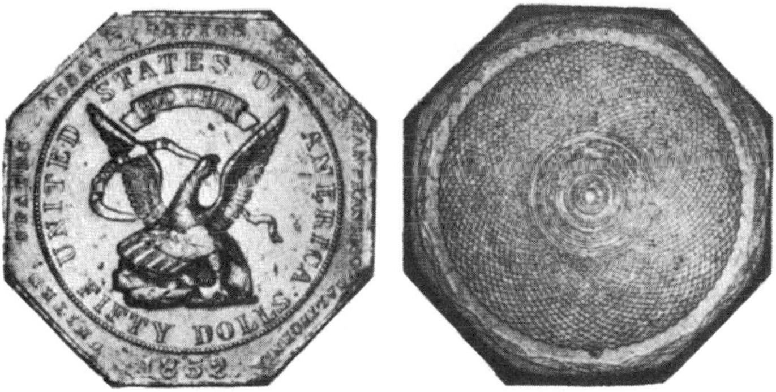

		Fine	V. Fine	E. Fine	A. Unc.	Unc.
1852	FIFTY DOLLS. 887 THOUS.	3,000	3,800	5,500	8,000	15,000
1852	FIFTY DOLLS. 900 THOUS.	3,000	3,800	5,750	8,500	18,000

UNITED STATES ASSAY OFFICE

	Fine	V. Fine	E. Fine	A. Unc.	Unc.
1852 TEN DOLS 884 THOUS.	$600.00	$1,000	$1,400	$2,500	$5,000
1853 TEN D. 884 THOUS.	1,600	2,500	5,750	8,500	—
1853 TEN D. 900 THOUS.	1,300	1,900	3,200	4,400	—
1853 TWENTY D. 884 THOUS.	2,000	4,000	6,000	9,000	—
1853 TWENTY D. 900 THOUS.	700.00	1,000	1,400	2,200	3,500

The last Moffat issue was the 1853 twenty dollar piece which is very similar to the U.S. double eagle of that period. It was struck after the retirement of Mr. Moffat from the Assay Office.

1853 TWENTY D.	1,200	1,400	2,200	3,000	5,500

CINCINNATI MINING & TRADING CO.

The origin and location of this company are unknown.

	E. Fine	Unc.
1849 FIVE DOLLARS	—	—
1849 TEN DOLLARS	—	—

MASSACHUSETTS AND CALIFORNIA COMPANY

San Fransisco 1849

This company was believed to have been organized in Northampton, Mass. in May, 1849.

	V. Fine
1849 FIVE D.	$35,000

MINERS' BANK

San Francisco 1849

The institution of Wright & Co., exchange brokers located in Portsmouth Square, San Francisco, was known as the Miners' Bank.

A ten dollar piece was issued in the autumn of 1849, but the coins were not readily accepted because they were worth less than face value.

	V. Fine	E. Fine	A. Unc.	Unc.
(1849) TEN. D.	$3,500	$6,500	$9,500	$20,000

J.S. ORMSBY

Sacramento 1849

The initials J. S. O. which appear on certain issues of California privately coined gold pieces represent the firm of J. S. Ormsby & Co. They struck both five and ten dollar denominations, all undated.

	V. Fine
(1849) 5 DOLLS. (Unique)	—
(1849) 10 DOLLS	—

PACIFIC COMPANY

San Francisco 1849

The origin of the Pacific Co. is very uncertain. All data regarding the firm is based on conjecture.

Edgar H. Adams wrote that he believed that the coins bearing the stamp of the Pacific Company were produced by the coining firm of Broderick and Kohler.

	E. Fine
1849 1 DOLLAR	—
1849 5 DOLLARS	$55,000
1849 10 DOLLARS	75,000

F. D. KOHLER

California State Assayer 1850

The State Assay Office was authorized April 12, 1850. Governor Burnett appointed F. D. Kohler that year who thereupon sold his assaying business to Baldwin & Co. He served at both San Francisco and Sacramento Offices. The State Assay Offices were discontinued at the time the U. S. Assay Office was established Feb. 1, 1851.

$36.55 Sacramento	—
$37.31 San Francisco	—
$40.07 San Francisco	—
$45.34 San Francisco	—
$50.00 San Francisco	—
$54.09 San Francisco	—

DUBOSQ & COMPANY

San Francisco 1850

Theodore Dubosq, a Philadelphia jeweler who took melting and coining machinery to San Francisco in 1849, produced the following pieces.

	V. Fine
1850 FIVE D.	$22,000
1850 TEN D.	25,000

BALDWIN & COMPANY
San Francisco 1850

George C. Baldwin and Thomas S. Holman were in the jewelry business in San Francisco and were known as Baldwin & Co. They were the successors to F. D. Kohler & Co., taking over their machinery and other equipment in May, 1850.

	Fine	V. Fine	E. Fine	Unc.
1850 FIVE DOL.	$2,000	$3,000	$6,000	$9,500
1850 TEN DOLLARS — Horseman type	9,500	18,000	25,000	—

	Fine	V. Fine	E. Fine	Unc.
1851 TEN D.	3,000	5,000	9,500	—

1851 TWENTY D.	40,000	—

SHULTZ & COMPANY
San Francisco 1851

The firm located in back of Baldwin's establishment operated a brass foundry beginning in 1851. Judge G. W. Shultz and William T. Garratt were partners in the enterprise.

	Fine	V. Fine
1851 FIVE D.	$8,500	$16,000

DUNBAR & COMPANY
San Francisco 1851

Edward E. Dunbar operated the California Bank in San Francisco. He later returned to New York and organized the famous Continental Bank Note Co.

	E. Fine
1851 FIVE D	$45,000

WASS, MOLITOR & COMPANY
San Francisco 1852-1855

The gold smelting and assaying plant of Wass, Molitor & Co. was operated by Count S. C. Wass and A. P. Molitor. They maintained an excellent laboratory and complete apparatus for analysis and coinage of gold.

	Fine	*V. Fine*	*E. Fine*	*Unc.*
1852 FIVE DOLLARS	$1,350	$2,100	$4,000	$12,000

Large Head

Small Head

1852 TEN D. Large head	800.00	1,300	2,300	—
1852 TEN D. Small head	1,500	2,500	5,000	—
1855 TEN D.	4,400	7,000	8,500	—

Large Head

Small Head

1855 TWENTY DOL. Large head	—	—	—	—
1855 TWENTY DOL. Small head	3,500	6,500	11,500	—

WASS, MOLITOR & COMPANY

	Fine	V. Fine	E. Fine	Unc.
1855 50 DOLLARS	$6,750	$9,000	$14,000	—

KELLOGG & COMPANY
San Francisco 1854-1855

When the U.S. Assay Office ceased operations a period ensued during which no private firm was striking gold. The new San Francisco branch mint did not produce coins for some months after Curtis & Perry took the contract for the government. The lack of coin was again keenly felt by businessmen who petitioned Kellogg & Richter to "supply the vacuum" by issuing private coin. Their plea was answered on Feb. 9, 1854, when Kellogg & Co. placed their first twenty-dollar piece in circulation.

	Fine	V. Fine	E. Fine	Unc.
1854 TWENTY D.	$750.00	$1,000	$1,600	$4,500
1855 TWENTY D.	750.00	1,000	1,600	4,500

	Proof
1855 FIFTY DOLLS.	—

OREGON EXCHANGE COMPANY
Oregon City, 1849
THE BEAVER COINS OF OREGON

On February 16, 1849, the legislature passed an act providing for a mint and specified five and ten dollar gold coins without alloy. Oregon City, the largest city in the territory with a population of about 1,000, was designated as the location for the mint. At the time this act was passed Oregon had been brought into the United States as a territory by act of Congress. When the new governor arrived March 2, he declared the coinage act unconstitutional.

	Fine	V. Fine	E. Fine	Unc.
1849 5 D	$5,500	$8,500	$15,000	—
1849 TEN D	12,500	25,000	37,500	—

MORMON GOLD PIECES
Salt Lake City, Utah 1849-1860

Brigham Young was the instigator of this coinage system and personally supervised the mint which was housed in a little adobe building in Salt Lake City. The mint was inaugurated late in 1849 as a public convenience.

	Fine	V. Fine	E. Fine	Unc.
1849 TWO AND HALF DO	$2,400	$4,250	$6,000	—
1849 FIVE DOLLARS	2,250	3,500	4,750	$12,500

	Fine	V. Fine
1849 TEN DOLLARS	$40,000	$60,000
1849 TWENTY DOLLARS	18,000	33,000

MORMON GOLD PIECES

		Fine	V. Fine	E. Fine	Unc.
1850	FIVE DOLLARS	$2,400	$3,750	$5,200	$13,000
1860	5D	4,000	6,000	10,000	22,000

COLORADO GOLD PIECES

Clark, Gruber & Co. — Denver 1860-1861

Clark, Gruber and Co. was a well known private minting firm in Denver, Colo. in the early sixties.

		Fine	V. Fine	E. Fine	Unc.
1860	$2\frac{1}{2}$ D	$500.00	$800.00	$1,300	$4,500
1860	FIVE D	575.00	950.00	1,400	4,750

1860	TEN D	2,000	3,000	5,000	13,000
1860	TWENTY D	12,000	24,000	40,000	—

1861	$2\frac{1}{2}$ D	500.00	800.00	1,300	5,000
1861	FIVE D	700.00	1,000	1,900	8,500
1861	TEN D	800.00	1,100	2,100	7,000

COLORADO GOLD PIECES

	Fine	V. Fine	E. Fine	Unc.
1861 TWENTY D	$2,500	$4,500	$10,000	—

JOHN PARSONS & COMPANY

Tarryall Mines — Colorado 1861

Very little is known about the mint of John Parsons and Co. It probably operated in Colorado, near (the original) Tarryall, in the summer of 1861.

PIKES PEAK GOLD

	V. Fine
(1861) Undated $2^1/_2$ D	$40,000
(1861) Undated FIVE D	50,000

J. J. CONWAY & COMPANY

Georgia Gulch, Colorado, 1861

The value of gold dust caused disagreement among the merchants and the miners in all gold mining areas. The firm of J. J. Conway & Co. solved this difficulty by bringing out its gold pieces in August, 1861.

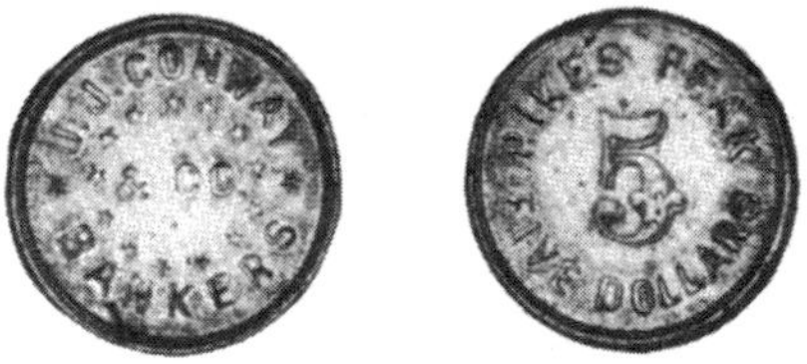

	V. Fine
(1861) Undated 2 1/2 DOLL'S	$30,000
(1861) Undated FIVE DOLLARS	50,000
(1861) Undated FIVE DOLLARS, Similar. Variety without numeral 5 on reverse	—

J. J. CONWAY & COMPANY

	V. Fine
(1861) Undated TEN DOLLARS	—

CALIFORNIA SMALL DENOMINATION GOLD

There was a scarcity of small coins during the California gold rush and starting in 1852, quarter, half and dollar pieces were privately minted from native gold to alleviate the shortage. The need and acceptability of these pieces declined after 1856 and they then became popular as souvenirs. Authentic pieces all have CENTS, DOLLAR, or an abbreviation thereof on the reverse. The tokens are much less valuable. Modern restrikes and replicas have no numismatic value.

Values are only for genuine coins with the denomination on the reverse expressed as: CENTS, DOL., DOLL. or DOLLAR.

		EF-40	*AU-50*	*MS-60*
25c Octagonal:	Liberty head	$37.50	$50.00	$100.00
	Indian head	45.00	60.00	100.00
	Washington head	200.00	265.00	425.00
25c Round:	Liberty head	37.50	50.00	100.00
	Indian head	50.00	80.00	120.00
	Washington head	225.00	325.00	475.00
50c Octagonal:	Liberty head	50.00	70.00	110.00
	Liberty head/Eagle	310.00	425.00	685.00
	Indian head	90.00	115.00	160.00
50c Round:	Liberty head	47.50	80.00	110.00
	Indian head	75.00	95.00	130.00
$1.00 Octagonal:	Liberty head	120.00	165.00	235.00
	Liberty head/Eagle	550.00	850.00	1,400
	Indian head	235.00	325.00	500.00
$1.00 Round:	Liberty head	525.00	700.00	1,100
	Indian head	575.00	600.00	1,300

ARE YOUR COINS GENUINE?

Coin authentication and certification service is available at a fee through the following associations. Coins must not be submitted without first requesting mailing instructions and a schedule of fees charged for this service. Inquiries about coin authentication should be accompanied by a self-addressed stamped envelope and send to:

American Numismatic Association
Certification Service
818 N. Cascade Avenue
Colorado Springs, CO 80903

International Numismatic Society
Authentication Bureau
P.O. Box 2091
Aston, PA 19014

CIVIL WAR TOKENS — 1861-1864

Civil War Tokens are generally divided into two groups: tradesmen's tokens, and anonymously issued pieces with political or patriotic themes. They came into existence only because of the scarcity of government coins and disappeared as soon as the bronze coins of 1864 met the public demand for small copper change.

These tokens are of great variety in composition and design. A number were more or less faithful imitations of the copper-nickel cent. A few of this type have the word "not" in very small letters above the words "ONE CENT."

	Fine	V. Fine	Unc.
Copper or Brass Tokens	$3.75	$4.75	$16.00
Nickel or German Silver Tokens	11.00	18.00	42.00
White Metal Tokens	14.00	23.00	47.00
Copper-Nickel Tokens	20.00	30.00	65.00
Silver Tokens	50.00	80.00	185.00

BULLION VALUE OF COINS

Common date silver coins are valued according to the price of silver bullion. In recent years the price of silver bullion has been subject to extreme fluctuation. Therefore, when you read this it is highly probable that the current bullion price may differ from the prevailing market price used in tabulating valuations of many 19th and 20th century silver coins (priced in italics) listed in this edition. The following chart will help to determine the approximate bullion value of these coins at various price levels. Or, the approximate value may be calculated by multiplying the current spot price of silver times the content for each coin as indicated below. Dealers generally purchase common silver coins at 15% below bullion value, and sell them at 15% above bullion value.

Silver Price Per Ounce	*Wartime Nickel .05626 oz.*	*Dime .07234 oz.*	*Quarter .18084 oz.*	*Half Dollar .36169 oz.*	*Silver Clad Half Dollar .14792 oz.*	*Silver Dollar .77344 oz.*
$4.00	$.23	$.29	$.72	$1.45	$.59	$3.09
4.50	.25	.33	.81	1.63	.67	3.48
5.00	.28	.36	.90	1.81	.74	3.87
5.50	.31	.40	1.00	1.99	.81	4.25
6.00	.34	.44	1.09	2.17	.89	4.64
6.50	.36	.47	1.18	2.35	.96	5.03

The value of common date gold coins listed in this book may be affected by the rise or fall in the price of gold bullion. Nearly all U.S. gold coins have an additional premium value beyond their bullion content, and thus are not subject to the minor variations described for silver coins. The premium amount is not necessarily tied to the bullion price of gold, but is usually determined by supply and demand levels for actual gold coins occurring in the numismatic marketplace. Because these factors can vary significantly, there is no reliable formula for calculating "percentage above bullion" prices that would remain accurate over time. For this reason the chart below lists bullion values based on gold content only. Consult your nearest coin dealer to ascertain current premium prices.

Gold Price Per Ounce	*$5.00 Liberty Head 1839-1908 Indian Head 1908-1929*	*$10.00 Liberty Head 1838-1907 Indian Head 1907-1933*	*$20.00 1849-1933*
$250.00	$60.47	$120.94	$241.88
275.00	66.50	133.03	266.07
300.00	72.56	145.13	290.25
325.00	78.60	157.22	314.44
350.00	84.65	169.31	338.63
375.00	90.70	181.40	362.81
400.00	96.75	193.50	387.00
425.00	102.80	205.60	411.19

UNITED STATES BULLION COINS

Silver

Designers: Adolph A. Weinman (obverse), John Mercanti (reverse); composition 99.93% silver, .07% copper; weight 31.101 grams; diameter 40.6mm; net weight one oz. fine silver; reeded edge; mints: Philadelphia, San Francisco and West Point.

	Quan. Issued	*Unc.*	*Proof*
$1 1986	5,393,005	$7.50	
$1 1986S	(1,446,778)		$14.00
$1 1987	11,442,335	5.75	
$1 1987S	(904,732)		14.00
$1 1988	5,004,500	5.75	
$1 1988S	(557,370)		40.00
$1 1989	5,203,327	5.75	
$1 1989S	(617,694)		14.00
$1 1990	5,840,210	5.75	
$1 1990S	(695,510)		14.00
$1 1991	7,191,066	5.75	
$1 1991S	(511,925)		24.00
$1 1992	5,540,068	5.75	
$1 1992S	(498,654)		15.00
$1 1993	6,763,762	5.75	
$1 1993P	(403,025)		50.00
$1 1994	4,227,319	6.00	
$1 1994P	(372,168)		45.00
$1 1995	4,672,051	$5.75	
$1 1995P	(395,400)		$40.00
$1 1995W	(30,125)		1,000
$1 1996	3,603,386	11.00	
$1 1996P	(473,021)		20.00
$1 1997	4,295,004	5.75	
$1 1997P	(429,682)		40.00
$1 1998	4,847,549	5.75	
$1 1998P	(422,319)		20.00
$1 1999	9,133,000	5.75	
$1 1999P	(549,769)		30.00
$1 2000(W)		5.50	
$1 2000P			15.00
$1 2001(W)		5.50	
$1 2001P			15.00
$1 2002(W)		5.50	
$1 2002W			15.00

UNITED STATES BULLION COINS
Gold

Designers: Augustus Saint-Gaudens (obverse), Miley Busiek (reverse); composition, 91.67% gold, 3% silver, 5.33% copper; reeded edge; mints: Philadelphia, West Point.
$50 diameter 32.7mm; weight 33.931 grams; net weight one oz. fine gold.
$25 diameter 27mm; weight 16.966 grams; net weight 1/2 oz. fine gold.
$10 diameter 22mm; weight 8.483 grams; net weight 1/4 oz. fine gold.
$5 diameter 16.5mm; weight 3.393 grams; net weight 1/10 oz. fine gold.

	Quan. Issued	*Unc.*	*Proof*
$5 (1986)	912,609	$30.00	
$5 (1987)	580,266	30.00	
$5 (1988)	159,500	50.00	
$5 (1988)P	(143,881)		$35.00
$5 (1989)	264,790	32.00	
$5 (1989)P	(84,924)		35.00
$5 (1990)	210,210	32.00	
$5 (1990)P	(99,349)		36.00
$5 (1991)	165,200	40.00	
$5 (1991)P	(70,334)		36.00
$5 1992	209,300	30.00	
$5 1992 P	(64,902)		38.00
$5 1993	210,709	30.00	
$5 1993P	(58,649)		40.00
$5 1994	206,380	30.00	
$5 1994W	(62,100)		35.00
$5 1995	223,025	30.00	

	Quan. Issued	*Unc.*	*Proof*
$5 1995W	(48,675)		$35.00
$5 1996	401,964	$30.00	
$5 1996W	(57,449)		45.00
$5 1997	528,266	30.00	
$5 1997W	(35,164)		50.00
$5 1998	1,344,520	30.00	
$5 1998W	(39,706)		35.00
$5 1999	2,750,338	30.00	
$5 1999W	(19,919)		35.00
$5 2000	569,153	30.00	
$5 2000W			45.00
$5 2001	269,147	30.00	
$5 2001W			45.00
$5 2002		30.00	
$5 2002W			35.00

UNITED STATES BULLION COINS

		Quan. Issued	Unc.	Proof
$10	(1986)	726,031	$75.00	
$10	(1987)	269,255	75.00	
$10	(1988)	49,000	75.00	
$10	(1988)P	(98,028)		$100.00
$10	(1989)	81,789	75.00	
$10	(1989)P	(53,593)		85.00
$10	(1990)	41,000	75.00	
$10	(1990)P	(62,674)		85.00
$10	(1991)	36,100	90.00	
$10	(1991)P	(50,840)		85.00
$10	1992	59,546	75.00	
$10	1992 P	(42,290)		85.00
$10	1993	71,864	75.00	
$10	1993P	(46,271)		85.00
$10	1994	72,650	75.00	
$10	1994W	(47,600)		85.00
$10	1995	83,752	75.00	
$10	1995W	(46,825)		85.00
$10	1996	60,318	75.00	
$10	1996W	(37,755)		85.00
$10	1997	108,805	75.00	
$10	1997W	(29,984)		85.00
$10	1998	309,829	75.00	
$10	1998W	(29,731)		85.00
$10	1999	564,232	75.00	
$10	1999W	(34,410)		85.00
$10	2000	128,964	75.00	
$10	2000W			95.00
$10	2001	71,280	75.00	
$10	2001W			95.00
$10	2002		75.00	
$10	2002W			85.00

		Quan. Issued	Unc.	Proof
$25	(1986)	599,566	150.00	
$25	(1987)	131,255	150.00	
$25	(1987)P	(143,398)		170.00
$25	(1988)	45,000	150.00	
$25	(1988)P	(76,528)		170.00
$25	(1989)	44,829	200.00	
$25	(1989)P	(44,264)		170.00
$25	(1990)	31,000	200.00	
$25	(1990)P	(51,636)		170.00
$25	(1991)	24,100	210.00	
$25	(1991)P	(53,125)		170.00
$25	1992	54,404	150.00	
$25	1992P	(40,982)		170.00
$25	1993	73,324	150.00	
$25	1993P	(43,319)		170.00
$25	1994	62,400	$150.00	
$25	1994W	(44,100)		$170.00
$25	1995	53,474	150.00	
$25	1995W	(46,200)		170.00
$25	1996	39,287	150.00	
$25	1996W	(34,769)		170.00
$25	1997	79,605	150.00	
$25	1997W	(26,801)		170.00
$25	1998	169,029	150.00	
$25	1998W	(25,550)		170.00
$25	1999	263,013	150.00	
$25	1999W	(30,452)		170.00
$25	2000	79,287	150.00	
$25	2000W			180.00
$25	2001	48,047	150.00	
$25	2001W			180.00
$25	2002		150.00	
$25	2002W			170.00

		Quan. Issued	Unc.	Proof
$50	(1986)	1,362,650	300.00	
$50	(1986)W	(446,290)		350.00
$50	(1987)	1,045,500	300.00	
$50	(1987)W	(147,498)		350.00
$50	(1988)	465,000	300.00	
$50	(1988)W	(87,133)		350.00
$50	(1989)	415,790	300.00	
$50	(1989)W	(53,960)		350.00
$50	(1990)	373,210	300.00	
$50	(1990)W	(62,401)		350.00
$50	(1991)	243,100	300.00	
$50	(1991)W	(50,411)		350.00
$50	1992	275,000	300.00	
$50	1992W	(44,835)		350.00
$50	1993	480,192	300.00	
$50	1993W	(34,389)		350.00
$50	1994	221,633	300.00	
$50	1994W	(46,300)		350.00
$50	1995	200,636	300.00	
$50	1995W	(48,075)		350.00
$50	1996	189,148	300.00	
$50	1996W	(36,086)		350.00
$50	1997	664,508	300.00	
$50	1997W	(27,803)		350.00
$50	1998	1,468,530	300.00	
$50	1998W	(26,047)		350.00
$50	1999	1,505,026	300.00	
$50	1999W	(31,446)		350.00
$50	2000	433,319	300.00	
$50	2000W			400.00
$50	2001	143,605	300.00	
$50	2001W			375.00
$50	2002		300.00	
$50	2002W			350.00

UNITED STATES BULLION PLATINUM COINS

American Eagle platinum coins are made in four denominations and sizes that are different from the similar gold coins. The one ounce coin is designated $100.00 and contains one ounce of pure platinum. Fractional denominations containing 1/2 ounce, 1/4 ounce or 1/10 ounce, are called $50, $25 and $10 respectively.

Designers: John M. Mercanti (obverse) and Thomas D. Rogers, Sr. (reverse). Composition, .9995 fine platinum. Mints: Philadelphia, West Point.

ONE OUNCE PLATINUM $100.00

	Quan. Issued	*Unc.*	*Proof*
1997	56,000	$550.00	
1997W	(16,000)		$560.00
1998	133,002	550.00	
1998W	(26,047)		560.00
1999	56,701	550.00	
1999W	(12,351)		560.00
2000	10,003	550.00	
2000W			560.00
2001	14,070	550.00	
2001W			560.00
2002		550.00	
2002W			560.00

HALF-OUNCE PLATINUM $50.00

1997	20,500	275.00	
1997W	(14,637)		280.00
1998	32,415	275.00	
1998W	(13,913)		280.00
1999	32,309	275.00	
1999W	(11,098)		280.00
2000	18,892	275.00	
2000W			280.00
2001	12,815	285.00	
2001W			280.00
2002		275.00	
2002W			280.00

QUARTER-OUNCE PLATINUM $25.00

	Quan. Issued	*Unc.*	*Proof*
1997	27,100	$140.00	
1997W	(18,726)		$145.00
1998	38,887	140.00	
1998W	(14,203)		145.00
1999	39,734	140.00	
1999W	(13,524)		145.00
2000	20,054	160.00	
2000W			145.00
2001	21,815	140.00	
2001W			145.00
2002		140.00	
2002W			145.00

TENTH-OUNCE PLATINUM $10.00

1997	70,250	52.00	
1997W	(37,260)		57.00
1998	39,525	52.00	
1998W	(19,919)		57.00
1999	55,955	52.00	
1999W	(19,123)		57.00
2000	34,027	52.00	
2000W			57.00
2001	52,017	52.00	
2001W			62.00
2002		52.00	
2002W			57.00

PROOF GOLD SETS

		Proof
1987	Gold Set $50.00, 25.00	$500.00
1988	Gold Set $50.00, 25.00, 10.00, 5.00	600.00
1989	Gold Set $50.00, 25.00, 10.00, 5.00	600.00
1990	Gold Set $50.00, 25.00, 10.00, 5.00	600.00
1991	Gold Set $50.00, 25.00, 10.00, 5.00	600.00
1992	Gold Set $50.00, 25.00, 10.00, 5.00	600.00
1993	Gold Set $50.00, 25.00, 10.00, 5.00	600.00
1993	Bicentennial Gold Set $25.00, 10.00, 5.00, $1 Silver Eagle and medal	275.00
1994	Gold Set $50.00, 25.00, 10.00, 5.00	600.00
1995	Gold Set $50.00, 25.00, 10.00, 5.00	600.00
1995	Anniversary Gold Set $50.00, 25.00, 10.00, 5.00, and $1 silver Eagle	1,800
1996	Gold Set $50.00, 25.00, 10.00, 5.00	600.00
1997	Gold Set $50.00, 25.00, 10.00, 5.00	600.00
1997	Impressions of Liberty Set, $100 platinum, $50 gold, $1 silver	850.00
1998	Gold Set $50.00, 25.00, 10.00, 5.00	600.00
1999	Gold Set $50.00, 25.00, 10.00, 5.00	600.00
2000	Gold Set $50.00, 25.00, 10.00, 5.00	700.00
2001	Gold Set $50.00, 25.00, 10.00, 5.00	600.00
2002	Gold Set $50.00, 25.00, 10.00, 5.00	600.00

Bullion values are based on spot gold at $300.00 per ounce, and silver at $4.75 per ounce.

UNITED STATES BULLION COIN SETS
PLATINUM

	Quan. Issued	*Proof*
1997 Platinum Set, $100.00, 50.00, 25.00, 10.00		$1,100
1998 Platinum Set, $100.00, 50.00, 25.00, 10.00		1,000
1999 Platinum Set, $100.00, 50.00, 25.00, 10.00		1,000
2000 Platinum Set, $100.00, 50.00, 25.00, 10.00		1,100
2001 Platinum Set, $100.00, 50.00, 25.00, 10.00		1,100
2002 Platinum Set, $100.00, 50.00, 25.00, 10.00		1,000

INDEX